World Food

INDIA

Martin Hughes
with
Sheema Mookherjee
Richard Delacy

WORLD FOOD India
1st edition – August 2001

Published by Lonely Planet Publications Pty Ltd ABN 36 005 607 983

Lonely Planet Offices
Australia Locked Bag 1, Footscray, Victoria 3011
USA 150 Linden Street, Oakland CA 94607
UK 10a Spring Place, London NW5 3BH
France 1 rue du Dahomey, 75011 Paris

Publishing manager Peter D'Onghia
Series editor Lyndal Hall
Series design & layout Brendan Dempsey
Editor Patrick Witton
Mapping Natasha Velleley
Photography Greg Elms

Photography
Many images in this guide are available for licensing from
Lonely Planet Images. email: lpi@lonelyplanet.com.au

Front cover – Unloading white pumpkins in the Koyambatu market in Chennai, Tamil Nadu
Back cover – Strolling back to the kitchen in Barada near Udaipur, Rajasthan

ISBN 1 86450 328 9

text & maps © Lonely Planet Publications Pty Ltd, 2001
photos © photographers as indicated 2001

Printed by
The Bookmaker International Ltd
Printed in China

MAP KEY

○ Place to Eat & Drink	State Border	🛕 Buddhist Temple
Market	Primary Road	Hindu Temple
Building	Secondary Road	Sikh Temple
Campus	Tertiary Road	Mosque
Park, Garden	Steps	Church
Sports Ground	Railway, Station	Ghat
International Border	National Capital	Fort
Disputed Border	State Capital	Monument
	Town	Stately Home
	Museum	Gate

Acknowledgements

About the Authors

Martin Hughes was born and bred in Dublin where, as an adult, he dithered for five years between journalism and public relations. Feeling at home in neither estate, he fled the country with a backpack and an appetite for pastures new. After three years of grazing in foreign fields, including an extended period in India, he settled in Melbourne, Australia. He worked for Lonely Planet for almost four years where, as series editor, he helped set up the World Food series before jumping the fence to become a full-time writer. He also wrote World Food Ireland.

Martin wishes to thank co-author Sheema for her diligence and hospitality; Jhampan for laughs and most of the drinks chapter; Malini Jayaganesh for firing my enthusiasm; Jayaram in Bangalore for taking care of me when I got sick; Sririvisan, Swarthi and Rani in Srinrangapatnam for welcoming me to their home; Steve Waugh for providing two words that opened every door; everyone at Palolem's Cosy Nook for providing the cosy nook; Masood Shrieff for his patience and advice; Jyothi; Paras Gadiya for showing me that it's okay to hold another man's hand; Rahat Mishat and family; Robin Borthakur of ABITA for nothing; Pramod Krishna of the Indian Alcoholic Beverages Manufacturers Association, Marybong Tea Gardens for a most enchanting afternoon; everyone at Ganpathi Guest House in Varanasi; all at Haritha Farms in Kerala; Kartika for the wedding invitation; Bhichoo J. Manekshaw for Parsi info; Dusty Menon; Dibakar Chatterjee; most Indian tourist info offices; Nilan Singh; LP author Joyce Connolly for being a bunny (at pool); Pankaj, head chef at the Oberoi, Delhi; Kalpana Sharma; Jagdeep Syan for Shimla guidance; Ravi Chouthoy; Pheroza Godraj and friends for their hospitality and a wonderful Parsi meal in Mumbai; Gita Mitra; all at Lonely Planet; Mum for unwavering love and support; Kirsti for being adventurous and providing me with a better half; and every person I have ever met in India for giving me perspective.

Sheema Mookherjee was brought up on the no-nonsense diet of a working mother and never imagined food would become her mainstay – until she married into a family of unabashed foodies and got sucked in. Putting a journalistic career on hold to feed her ever-hungry family, she took to part-time food writing and has never stopped mixing masalas even though she is now back to a full-time book publishing career in Delhi. Sheema wrote the regional chapter as well as some other sections for this book and provided most of the recipes.

About the Linguists

Richard Delacy has been a student of Hindi and Urdu for over ten years, travelling to the subcontinent throughout this period. He has also taught Hindi at various tertiary institutions in Melbourne, Australia and produced Lonely Planet Hindi-Urdu phrasebook (2nd edition) in 1998.

Richard wishes to thank Mrs Sudha Joshi, Rashid Sultan, Dr Dinesh Srivastava, Mrs Sunita Joshi and Ms Shalini Joshi. Thanks also goes to the following people for their assistance, advice and translations: Poonam Arora, Chhandashi Bandopadhayay, Sheema Mookherjee, Anupama Pande, Sutanu Panigrahi, Deena Pathy, Sheela Sharma, Shashi Srikumar, Vijay Susarla, Manjeet Thethi, Chander Wanchoo and Pravin Vaghani.

About the Photographer

Playing with knives and fire in the kitchen of his father's hotel led Greg Elms to a lukewarm vocation in catering. His life changed when he saw a black & white photograph of a pepper – now others cook while he eats the props. He is a fine art graduate (VCA), has a Bachelor of Arts and works out of a disused church in Melbourne where he produces blasphemous Christmas cards – when he's not freelancing for various Australian and international magazines.

Greg wishes to thank his partner Jacquelyn for helping lug camera gear, keep track of 200 rolls of film, make eating the props so enjoyable, and help cut, mount and edit over 7000 shots. Also thanks to Malini Jayaganesh for her invaluable assistance with captioning; Sameena our Bombay guide; chef Pankaj Mehra in New Delhi for preparing a huge array of dishes and providing his restaurant; and to the helpful and informative staff at the Hotel Asma Tower in Kozhikode.

From the Publisher

This first edition of World Food India was edited by Patrick Witton and designed by Brendan Dempsey of Lonely Planet's Melbourne office. Natasha Velleley mapped, Carolyn Papworth proofed, Lyndal Hall coordinated production and Bridget Blair indexed. The language section was compiled by Richard Delacy, and was edited by Vicki Webb and Emma Koch and proofed by Malini Jayaganesh and Lara Morcombe. Lyndal Hall oversaw the language section's production. Valerie Tellini, of Lonely Planet Images, coordinated the supply of photographs. Shelley Preston captioned and catalogued and Julie Young assisted. Brett Pascoe managed the pre-press work with Gerard Walker and Ryan Evans. Sally Steward, publisher, developed the series and Martin Hughes, former series editor, assisted with pre-production.

Warning & Request

Things change; markets give way to supermarkets, prices go up, good places go bad and not much stays the same. Please tell us if you've discovered changes and help make the next edition even more useful. We value all your feedback, and strive to improve our books accordingly. We have a well-travelled, well-fed team that reads and acknowledges every letter, postcard and email and ensures that every morsel of information finds its way to the appropriate people.

Each correspondent will receive the latest issue of Planet Talk, our quarterly printed newsletter, or Comet, our monthly email newsletter. Subscriptions to both are free. The newsletters might even feature your letter so let us know if you don't want it published.

If you have an interesting anecdote or story to do with your culinary travels, we'd love to hear it. If we publish it in the next edition, we'll send you a free Lonely Planet book of your choice.

Send your correspondence to the nearest Lonely Planet office:

Australia Locked Bag 1, Footscray, Victoria 3011
UK 10a Spring Place, London NW5 3BH
USA 150 Linden St, Oakland CA 94607
France 1 rue du Dahomey, Paris 75011

Or email us at: talk2us@lonelyplanet.com

Contents

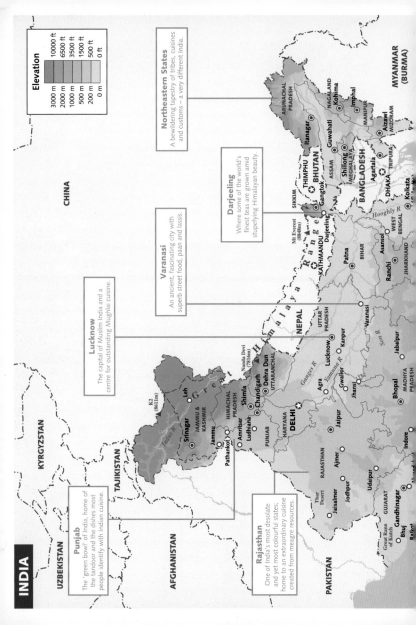

INDIA

Elevation

3000 m	10000 ft
2000 m	6500 ft
1000 m	3500 ft
500 m	1500 ft
200 m	500 ft
0 m	0 ft

Punjab
The 'green bowl' of India, home of the tandoor and the dishes most people identify with Indian cuisine.

Lucknow
The capital of Muslim India and a centre for outstanding Mughlai cuisine.

Varanasi
An ancient, fascinating city with superb street food, paan and lassis.

Northeastern States
A bewildering tapestry of tribes, cuisines and customs – a very diverse India.

Darjeeling
Where some of the world's finest teas are grown amid stupefying Himalayan beauty.

Rajasthan
One of India's most desolate and yet most colourful states; home to an extraordinary cuisine created from meagre resources.

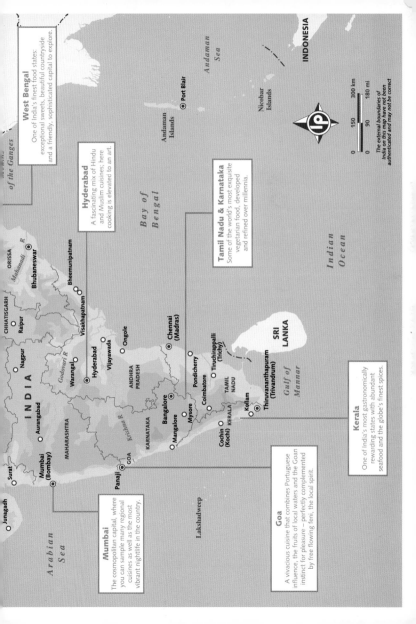

West Bengal
One of India's finest food states: exceptional sweets, beautiful countryside and a friendly, sophisticated capital to explore.

Hyderabad
A fascinating mix of Hindu and Muslim cuisines; here cooking is elevated to an art.

Tamil Nadu & Karnataka
Some of the world's most exquisite vegetarian food, developed over millennia.

Mumbai
The cosmopolitan capital, where you can sample many regional cuisines as well as the most vibrant nightlife in the country.

Goa
A vivacious cuisine that combines Portuguese influence, the fruits of local waters and the Goan instinct for pleasure – perfectly complemented by free flowing feni, the local spirit.

Kerala
One of India's most gastronomically rewarding states with abundant seafood and the globe's finest spices.

Mouths of the Ganges

INDONESIA

Andaman Sea

● Port Blair

Andaman Islands

Nicobar Islands

Bay of Bengal

SRI LANKA

Gulf of Mannar

Indian Ocean

The external boundaries of India on this map have not been authenticated and may not be correct

0   150   300 km
0   90   180 mi

CHHATTISGARH
Raipur ●

ORISSA
Mahanadi R
Bhubaneswar ●

Bheemunipatnam ○

Visakhapatnam ○

Warangal ○
Godavari R

Hyderabad ◉
ANDHRA PRADESH
Vijayawada ○
Ongole ○

KARNATAKA
Krishna R
Bangalore ◉

Chennai (Madras) ◉

Mysore ○
Pondicherry ○
Tiruchirappalli (Trichy) ○
Coimbatore ○
TAMIL NADU

Mangalore ○
KERALA
Cochin (Kochi) ○
Kollam ○
Thiruvananthapuram (Trivandrum) ◉

Nagpur ○
Aurangabad ○

MAHARASHTRA
Surat ○
Mumbai (Bombay) ◉

Junagadh ○

I N D I A

GOA
Panaji ◉

Lakshadweep

Arabian Sea

India is a vast and varied land, a bewildering tapestry of contrasts that every year lures millions of visitors, each pursuing the traveller's holy grail, 'the real India'. By far the best way of cutting to the heart of this astonishing culture is by exploring its deliciously protean gastronomy.

If cooking were painting, India would have one of the world's most colourful palettes. When you consider the palm-fringed beaches of Kerala, the snow-capped peaks of the Himalaya, and Rajasthan's shimmering Thar Desert, you can't help but lick your lips with the prospect of such regional diversity. But India's geographical range is both a blessing and a curse. While it brings bounty to some, it wreaks misery on others.

Most profoundly, Indian cuisine is shaped by myriad religious influences. What Indians eat, why, how and when, is integral to their identity, and you must eat here to appreciate that food and drink are as important for nourishing the spirit as sustaining the body. Through its food, you'll discover that India is a banquet expressed in colours, smells, flavours and personalities. It is the ancient vegetarian fare of the south, the meaty traditions of the Mughals, the glowing tandoor of Punjab and the Euro-Indian fusions of former colonies. It is the heavenly aroma of cooking spices, the juice of exotic fruits running down your chin, and rich, fiery curries that will make your taste-buds stand to attention. It is the theatre of the street food, the verve of the markets, and the energising smiles as you're welcomed across each threshold.

This book is an exploration of what fuels this vibrant culture and these spirited people, who frustrate and infuriate before charming you into giddy submission. And it is a platform for you to make your own culinary discoveries about food, drink and India itself.

In all the languages of India there is no equivalent word for 'goodbye'. Indians don't like the finality of the expression and prefer to say 'go and return'. Sink your teeth into the food and customs of this mad, manic and magical civilisation and you'll happily oblige.

the **culture** of
indian cuisine

Dining in Indian restaurants abroad cannot prepare you for the experience of eating here, as Indian cuisine is inextricably linked to place and not easily exported. It reflects the multi-layered culture of a billion people who practise five major faiths, speak 15 major languages (along with thousands of dialects) and live in 29 states, each as ethnically distinct as the countries of Europe.

Indian cuisine is certainly an elusive thing to define or grasp, but despite its mind-boggling variety of techniques and ingredients there are enough fundamentals to help us identify it. One is the masterful use of spices shared by every Indian cook. There is a wealth of items in the Indian spice box with which cooks create a spectrum of tantalising flavours, from the sweetest to the most sour and everything in between. They achieve this by treating each spice individually, and by combining them in various **masalas** (spice blends).

Indians are very adventurous when it comes to spices, and few dishes leave the kitchen without being pepped up by them in some way. This doesn't mean that Indian food is always hot. Chilli is used selectively; in the searing south it's valued for its cooling effect on the body through perspiration. In the north, food is rarely too fiery for western tastes, and hot pickles are available if you have a penchant for a little fire.

The basis of every Indian meal is grain: rice in the south, and wheat in the form of **roti** (generic term for bread) in the north. Each is generally eaten with **daal** (generic term for lentils or pulses; dishes made with these), **sabzi** (vegetables) and pickles. Depending on circumstances, fish and meat may be added. Beyond these staples, the diversity of Indian food is limited only by any cook's circumstances and imagination.

Most profoundly, food in India is integral to spiritual advancement. Regardless of creed, Indians share the belief that food is just as important for fine-tuning the spirit as it is for sustaining the body. Modern culinary practises have their roots in the **Ayurveda,** the ancient science of life, health and longevity. The Ayurveda classifies foods according to their positive or negative energies as well as their medicinal qualities. Many people say they only turn to Ayurveda in times of illness but its principles are ingrained in daily life and cooks seem to have an instinct for the science (see the boxed text Ayurveda – Spiritual Sustenance later in this chapter).

The strong association between spiritual purity and vegetarianism ensures the majority of Indians are vegetarian, even though meat (with the exception of beef) is not strictly taboo in Hinduism. Buddhists and Jains adhere to **ahimsa** (the philosophy of non-injury), but the Hindu view tends to equate vegetarianism with personal spiritual advancement, not the welfare of animals. Even those who eat meat hold vegetarianism in high esteem.

Religion is the most important aspect of Indian life, and food its most precious resource. Certain foods are deemed pure or sacred and may feature prominently in temple ritual. In the Hindu pantheon each deity has its own favourite dish. Krishna, for example, has an insatiable penchant for dairy products. Ganesh, the elephant-headed god so popular with us tourists, is rarely depicted without a bowl of **modak** (sweet rice-flour dumplings). Any food which is first offered to the gods then shared among devotees is known as **prasad.**

Figurines of Ganesh, the elephant-headed god and
Laxshmi (wife of Vishnu), Varanasi, Uttar Pradesh

INDIAN FOOD FALLACIES

National Cuisine
The classic dishes that most of us know as Indian cuisine – think daal, tandoori chicken, naan, aloo gobi, lassi, chicken tikka, etc – almost all come from Punjab, just one of India's 29 states. Following the partition of India in 1947, millions of Punjabis were displaced and sought new homes in other parts of India or abroad. Many opened restaurants that popularised their favourite foods and so Punjabi cooking came to represent Indian cuisine the world over. So if you fear you may tire of Indian food, remember that there are 29 states in India, each one a distinct cultural entity with its own language, customs and food.

Curry & Curry Powder
Believe it or not, there's hardly such a thing as 'curry' in Indian cuisine, and if you see it on a menu, you can bet you're in a tourist restaurant.

The word 'curry' is an anglicisation of the Tamil word *kari*, meaning black pepper. By the 17th century, the gentlemen of the British Empire were using the word 'curry' as an all-encompassing term to describe any broth, stew or even dry preparation that included spices. In this book we do use the term curry to describe dishes with spicy gravies, even though Indians themselves do not.

No self-respecting Indian cook would dream of using the same blend of spices for multiple dishes. Curry powder was invented purely for export to Britain and those chaps nostalgic for a taste of the Raj.

Balti Cuisine
According to Indian foodies, the genre popularised in Britain's Balti Houses was created as a marketing gimmick by entrepreneurial restaurateurs. Balti is a northwestern name for the common Indian wok used all over the country and better known as a **kadhai** so, in one sense, every Indian curry is a balti.

While food is revered and used in worship in India, this is not an austere food culture. On the contrary, food is joy and celebration. You can hardly make it through a week here without getting caught up in the excitement of some looming festival, which will be marked with special feasts and dishes (see the Celebrating with Food chapter).

Amazingly, many travellers 'do' India *despite* the food, regarding it as something suspect, to be tolerated or even avoided. We presume that you have different plans. If you don't, you'll be like a pebble skimming across the cultural surface. You might get splashed every now and then but you'll never

Spices and puja supplies, Bangalore City market, Karnataka

be immersed in India's cultural riches. Yes, you stand a chance of getting a dose of the runs but – with equal measures of good sense and adventure – a few desperate dashes to the toilet will seem trifling inconveniences compared to the culinary rewards and cultural insight you will glean.

India's finest food is concealed in its millions of homes. Fortunately for the traveller, Indians are inherently hospitable and keen to strike up friendships. If you show interest in the food and curiosity in the customs, you'll be a most welcome guest. Sample as many regional specialities as you can. They will please your palate and nourish your soul.

History

One of the most amazing things about Indian cuisine – and India in general – is how little the fundamentals have changed over time. Successive invaders brought new foods and customs, which were integrated with the deep-rooted traditions of the indigenous populations. Nothing, not even okra, was rejected; it was just Indianised.

From around 5000 BC, the people of the Indus Valley Civilisation (also known as the Harappan Civilisation) developed a diet largely based on rice, wheat, barley, pulses, game, fruits, coconuts and vegetables. The world's earliest ploughed field, believed to date back to before 2800 BC, was found in Rajasthan. Elaborate arrangements for storing grain have also been unearthed, suggesting that theirs was a sophisticated food culture. The discovery of querns hint that spices and grains were ground the same way they are today, and clay plates similar to the modern **tawa** (hotplate used for making roti) suggest that people of this time may have enjoyed roti just as Indians do today.

Just as the Harappan Civilisation was taking off, a group of tribes known as the Aryans (from a Sanskrit word meaning 'superior') entered North India from Central Asia. They transformed the ethos into one where the inner, contemplative life was exalted. Around 1200 BC the Aryans wrote the sacred Hindu scriptures, the *Vedas*, and this era is known as the Vedic Civilisation.

AYURVEDA – Spiritual Sustenance

Ayurveda (from the Sanskrit for 'life knowledge') is the ancient science of diet, healing and health, which was developed by the Aryans in the second millennium BC. It continues to influence virtually all aspects of Indian life and cuisine, among all creeds and classes. It is still the most widely practised form of medicine in India, although it's getting stiff competition from the trend to pop-a-pill western medicine sweeping through the middle class.

In many cases, ingredients are added to a dish as much for their medicinal qualities as their flavour. Every plant has its medicinal function (eg turmeric is antiseptic, cardamom relieves heartburn, coriander seeds are good for urinary complaints) and Indians seem to be subconsciously aware of each of them. Ayurvedic principles are seemingly ingrained in the national psyche and cooks appear to have an instinct for the right Ayurvedic ingredients. Ayurveda is a very complex science but its fundamental principle is simple: you cannot maintain a healthy body with unsuitable food.

India's very particular food ethos is inspired at every level by Aryan beliefs (see the boxed text Ayurveda later in this chapter).

The caste system, which still dominates today, was formalised to distinguish the Aryans from the indigenous Indians. The original inhabitants, the Dravidians, were pushed down south, where their culture still dominates. It was during this period that regional variations were established. Wheat could be grown all year round in the north and therefore became a staple. In the balmy south, rice was the most practical crop.

The Aryans introduced cattle-raising and established many agricultural practises still used today: oxen for ploughs, organised irrigation, cultivated rice, rotated crops and identified the benefits of land fallowing. They enjoyed cereals and pulses and dairy products, and sweetened their foods with honey. They also ate a variety of fruit and vegetables, including dates, mango, cucumber, gourds, ginger, coconut, banana, jackfruit, grapes and spinach. The Aryans were slow to embrace spices although mustard, turmeric, black pepper and asafoetida were used.

Before the Vedic Civilisation, meat-eating and ritual animal slaughter were common. However, the Aryans' prime focus was on personal purification and they began to question the taking of life for food, particularly the bounteous cow. The diet at the time – as now – relied heavily on dairy products and demand probably outstripped supply. It made economic

---

In Ayurveda, everything in the universe is comprised of the five elements of earth, wind, fire, ether and water. The combination of these, inherent to each individual determines their constitution. Ayurveda recognises three main constitutions: **Vata** (which has air and ether for dominant elements), **Pitta** (fire and water) and **Kapha** (earth and water).

One purpose of Ayurveda is to maintain balance in each constitution. Because each item of food is dominated by one or two elements, it can influence each constitution in different ways. What could be good for one person might imbalance the constitution of another, affecting physical, mental or spiritual health. Rice, for example, is said to cure Pitta and stimulate Vata, while onions promote Kapha and cure Vata but not Pitta. Still with us?

The idea is to identify your constitution and eat according to its needs. The good news, for those who don't have time to explore the complexities, is that you crave the taste that you are missing in yourself. But it's not as simple as sweet tooths eating candy to stay healthy, because even foods of the same flavour can have vastly different properties. For more on Ayurveda see the Recommended Reading chapter.

Whizzing through the streets of Lucknow, Uttar Pradesh

sense to protect the cow as it provided milk and both ploughed and fertilised the fields. Religions like Buddhism and Jainism emerged with strong philosophies against killing for food. One after another, animals found protection under religious law and the cow gained sacred status. Vegetarianism became widespread under the Buddhist Emperor Ashoka, who ruled most of India during the 3rd century BC.

The next culinary shake-up came with Muslim raids. By the 16th century, the Mughal Empire had power over most of the country. The Muslims brought their favourite dishes and cooking methods that, combined with Indian staples, led to the evolution of Mughlai cuisine. They brought a taste for lamb and goat, infused local foods with nuts, raisins and spices, combined rice and meat in **pulaos** (or pilafs; aromatic fried rice) and **biryanis** (fragrant rice casseroles), and transformed meat into rich, tasty **kababs** (meats cooked on skewers) and **kormas** (see Some Indian Ways of Cooking Meat in the Staples & Specialities chapter). The Muslims also introduced desserts like **kulfi** (ice cream) and **jalebis** (orange-coloured whorls of fried batter dipped in syrup).

The wealth and refinement of Mughlai cuisine, together with the extravagance of the Mughlai courts, made the existing Hindu diet and cus-

THE INDIAN MUTINY

The Indian Mutiny (1857-8) was sparked by the introduction of the Enfield rifle. To load this weapon, soldiers had to bite off the end of cartridges lubricated with pig and cow lard. This was sacrilegious to both Hindus and Muslims, and when some soldiers were sent to jail for refusing the cartridges, their comrades rose up in rebellion.

toms seem terribly austere. In combination a very Indian version of Muslim cuisine was created, and may be savoured today in the cities of Delhi, Lucknow and Hyderabad.

The Mughal influence didn't extend to the isolated south, and the diet there continued to be shaped by spiritual advancement and vegetarianism. However, with its wealth of spices, the south had long been a magnet for traders from around the world, and this foreign contact brought new foods, including new spices, that were adopted into the local cuisine.

With the arrival of Vasco da Gama in 1498, India was exposed to the best and worst aspects of European culture and ambition. In culinary terms, it was generally for the better. It's hard to believe that it was only at this time that the Portuguese introduced India to the now indispensable chilli. The Portuguese also brought capsicum (peppers), tomatoes, pineapple and cashews in their basket, while the British offered cabbage and broad beans and the Dutch brought the potato.

The Europeans fought among themselves and with India's regional rulers for control of the lucrative spice trade. The British, French, Dutch and Portuguese all held colonies scattered around India and their lasting influence in these areas – the Portuguese in Goa and the French in Pondicherry for example – contributes to the kaleidoscopic nature of India's regional cuisines. The British East India Company eventually wrested control of the whole region and by the early 19th century India was effectively part of the British Empire.

Britain set about making India an efficient business, and large-scale spice, fruit, vegetable and grain estates were established. A new class of **sahibs** (sirs) and **memsahibs** (female sirs) was foisted upon India and led to the evolution of a hybrid Anglo-Indian cuisine. Tea plants were brought from China and by the middle of the 19th century tea was the national beverage.

Over time, Muslim, Hindu and European foods and influences have been thrown together, skewed, embraced and experimented with across the subcontinent. The resulting mix – albeit widely diverse – is Indian cuisine as we know it today.

Food, Religion, Castes & Culture

Myriad creeds, communities and castes exist to create a fascinating and multifarious Indian table. More than 80% of Indians are Hindu while Muslims make up a sizeable minority of about 12%. The rest of the population comprises significant numbers of Jains, Sikhs, Christians, Buddhists and Parsis, all with vastly different perspectives on food.

Morning puja on the banks of the Ganges river, old city of Varanasi

Hinduism

While many of India's foods and practises have been introduced, the food ethos is predominantly influenced by the *Vedas*, which provides the frame for what we know as Hindu culture.

The Aryans introduced the caste system, into which all Hindus are divided by rank or status. The five main castes, in order of prescribed superiority, are: **Brahmins** (temple priests), **Kshatriyas** (warriors), **Vaishyas** (merchants), **Shudras** (serfs) and **Dalits** (formerly known as untouchables; technically outside the caste system). Within these major distinctions are thousands of sub-castes, so varied and complex that they are impossible to describe here. Each has different rituals and customs to do with food, and in Hinduism the old adage 'you are what you eat' can just as easily be inverted to 'you eat according to what you are.'

All Hindus avoid foods that are thought to inhibit physical and spiritual development, although there are few hard and fast rules. The taboo on eating beef is the most rigid restriction yet some Hindus – especially middle class Hindus – eat it in restaurants and in non-Hindu homes. The pure vegetarian diet of the Brahmins should be another clear-cut distinction, yet the Brahmins of Kashmir eat whatever meat comes their way, while their brethren in Goa and West Bengal have no qualms about eating fish. At official functions and on festive occasions all Hindus stick to vegetarian meals.

The Ayurveda also heavily influences food customs (see the boxed text Ayurveda – Spiritual Sustenance earlier in this chapter). Devout Hindus avoid alcohol and foods such as garlic and onions, which are thought to heat the blood and arouse passions. These items are universally banned from ashrams and temples and during most religious feasts. Some foods, such as dairy products, are considered innately pure and are eaten to cleanse the body, mind and spirit.

There are more than 20 major religious feast days in the Hindu calendar, and there are many regional events and personal celebrations such as weddings and funerals (see the Celebrating with Food chapter). Fasting is just about as common as feasting. Many people fast – or curtail their diets – before feasts, during religious festivals and certain lunar phases, and on personal anniversaries. Many also fast on specific days of the week associated with their favourite gods. Tuesday, for example, is often meat free at the behest of Hanuman, the monkey god.

Islam

Muslims have had a disproportionate, and are responsible for most Indian meat dishes. Perhaps it's to distinguish themselves from the Hindu majority, but boy do they like a lot of meat, and no occasion organised by a Muslim can pass without a feast that stars flesh.

We were told many times that there's no such thing as a 'traditional' Muslim, there's just Muslim. Most of the rules governing protocol are in the *Quran* (the Muslim holy book). **Halal** is the term for all permitted foods, and **haram** for those prohibited. Pork and alcohol are forbidden, but many Muslims bend the rules on booze. Stimulants such as coffee and tea are avoided by the most devout. For meat to be halal, the animal's jugular vein is severed while the butcher recites the name of Allah, as in the *Quran*.

Overindulgence is discouraged and no food should be wasted. Leftovers are rarely discarded and during religious festivals surplus food is shared among the community's poor. Fasting is considered an opportunity to earn the approval of Allah, to wipe the sin-slate clean and to understand the suffering of the poor.

Beside these rules there is very little restrictive etiquette and dining with Muslims is generally a relaxed affair. Islam stresses the necessity to share food with others and mealtimes are rarely spent alone. Before Muslims eat they say the prayer **bismillah** (praise be to God).

Hyderabadi Biryani (Rice with Meat, Saffron & Spices)

Biryani can be had as a one-dish meal. It has become quite a pan-Indian favourite. People with a busy lifestyle just order this from speciality biryani makers and serve it along with a raita at parties.

Ingredients

1kg (32oz)	lamb shoulder with the bone kept on, cut in 5cm pieces
1kg (32oz)	basmati rice
100g (3¹/₂oz)	ghee
3	large onions halved and finely sliced lengthways
1 tsp	saffron
1 cup	milk
1 tbs	raw papaya paste (or any branded tenderiser)
1 cup	plain yoghurt or curds
1 tsp	red chilli powder (or paprika if you want it less hot)
2 tsp	ginger paste
1 tsp	garlic paste
1 tsp	garam masala
1 tsp	caraway seeds, ground
4	seeds of 4 cardamom pods, ground
6	cloves
2	cinnamon sticks
2 tsp	salt
¹/₂ cup	coriander, chopped
¹/₂ cup	mint, chopped
6	green chillies
4	limes, juiced

Heat the ghee and fry the onions until golden brown. Drain and set aside half the onions. Dissolve the saffron in the milk and set aside. Rub the papaya into the lamb and then marinate it with the curds, chilli powder, ginger, garlic, garam masala, caraway seeds and the drained portion of the onions for 1 hour.

Soak the rice in cold water for 20 minutes. Add the cardamom, cloves, cinnamon and 1 tsp salt to 10 cups of water and boil in a pan. Cook the rice in this boiling water, until half done. Drain the rice but reserve 1½ cups of the water.

Spread the marinated lamb at the bottom of a deep pan. On it pour half the saffron-milk mix, the reserved rice water, the onions with the ghee, coriander, mint and chillies.

Spread the rice over this, and on it sprinkle the remaining saffron-milk mix, lime juice and 1 tsp salt. Cover the pan with a tight-fitting lid and seal the edges with foil, so that no steam can escape. (Traditionally the lid is sealed with dough – sticklers can feel free to do it.)

Place the pan over medium heat. Once you can hear the water sputtering, place a thick skillet or frying pan on the flame and put the pan on this. Continue cooking the biryani for 30 minutes. Keep covered until serving. If you find water at the bottom of the biryani, cook it a while longer until the liquid is absorbed.

Serves 8

CULTURE

Sikhism

There are more than 15 million Sikhs in India, mainly in Punjab, Haryana and Delhi. The Sikh religion was created in the 15th century as a bridge between Hinduism and Islam, and draws on elements from both creeds. The *Guru Granth Sahib* is the Sikh holy book, and was written by the guru Arjan. Alcohol, tobacco and narcotics are strictly forbidden although the Sikhs have a reputation for letting their uncut hair down with a drink every now and then. 'Whiskey de peg (measure), chicken de leg' is a popular idiom, meaning they like one as much as the other. Apart from these restrictions, Sikhism seems to be pretty easy-going; there are no rituals or sacrifices, no prohibited foods (apart from animals killed 'the Muslim way') and it is actually a sin for a **Khalsa** ('pure', member of the Sikh religion) to fast.

Food's most important function in Sikh philosophy is to unite. In **gudwaras** (Sikh temples), visitors are first asked to visit the **langar** (communal dining hall) before practising their religion, whatever religion that may be. Food is the great leveller; people of different creeds and class eat the same food and are therefore equal (see the boxed text All You Can Eat at the Golden Temple in the Where to Eat & Drink chapter).

To this end, the making and giving of **karhah prasad** (sacred pudding consisting of wheat flour, sugar and ghee) is enshrined in the *Guru Granth Sahib*. This pudding is made while reciting the scriptures, and is offered to anybody who attends the temple.

Christianity

Christianity came to India in two phases. What is known as the Syrian Christian community came to India soon after the time of Christ. The second wave was the brutal proselytising that came with Portuguese colonialism from the 16th century. It impacted on Kerala and Goa, where the majority of India's 300 million Christians live. There are virtually no food taboos among the Christians, although those converted by the Portuguese generally abstain from eating meat (not fish) on Fridays and won't eat or drink less than one hour before receiving Holy Communion. Devout Christians may also curtail their diets during Lent.

Jainism

The Jains must be among the world's most finicky eaters. Jainism emerged around the 6th century and was quite closely allied to Buddhism. The central tenet of this religion is ultra-vegetarianism, and rigid restrictions are in place to avoid even potential injury to any living creature. Meat and fish are obvious no-nos, but Jains also abstain from eating vegetables that grow underground (onions, garlic, potatoes, carrots, etc) because of the potential to harm insects during cultivation. Other items avoided by orthodox

Industrious Sikhs clear away dirty dishes at the Golden Temple, Amristar, Punjab

Jains are the greens of any plant, pulses that divide themselves into two parts (like the chickpea), pickles more than a few days old and small fruits. Nor do Jains eat honey; its removal harms bees. In fact the non-injury philosophy is adhered to, to such an extent that Jains don't eat after dark, and drink only filtered water (not such a peculiarity in India) in case they inadvertently consume insects. There are over 7 million Jains in India, mainly in Mumbai, Bangalore, Gujarat, Punjab and Delhi.

Buddhism

Buddhism emerged in India partly as a reaction to the discriminatory caste system. Because they subscribe to the concept of ahimsa, most Indian Buddhists are vegetarians, but to varying degrees: some eat fish, some abstain only from beef. Buddhist monks fast completely on the days of the new moon and full moon; they also avoid eating any solid food after noon.

Parsis

This small community – concentrated around Mumbai and Gujarat – has a fascinating history and culture. Parsis believe in the existence of one invisible God and the constant battle between good and evil. The community fled Iran in the 7th century due to religious persecution. According to legend, boatloads of Parsis waited off the coast of Gujarat for permission to land. The Hindu king didn't want a new religion diluting the local culture and sent a glass of milk to symbolise that India was already full. The Parsis added sugar to the milk and returned it to the king, saying that their community would be like the sugar in the glass; they would enhance the culture without changing its complexion. They pledged not to promote their religion or marry into the existing population.

Since then, the Parsis have contributed to all facets of Indian culture including commerce, the arts and cuisine. However, because of their pledge not to integrate with the locals, the Parsi community faces extinction and after centuries of inbreeding their numbers are rapidly dwindling. There are currently fewer than 100,000 of them in India.

Parsis have very few food taboos. They abstain from meat for four days a month and during the 11th month of the year (lambing season). Meat is not eaten for three days after the death of a close relative and the fast ends with the Parsi signature dish **dhansak** (meat in a spiced puree of different lentils). Most Parsis abstain from beef out of respect for the Hindu community.

Parsi food is a mix of Iranian, Gujarati and Maharashtran. There is no meat, fish or vegetable isn't cooked. They also have a passion for eggs and these are used to enliven dishes such as **bheeda per eeda** (egg over okra). Another favourite, **patra ni machhi**, is fish marinated in Maharashtran coconut-coriander chutney, wrapped in banana leaves and grilled.

CULTURE

How Indians Eat

Provided the means, Indians eat with gusto. Three main meals a day is the norm with as many **tiffin** (snacks) as they can fit in without sabotaging their appetite. A meal in the south is something that involves rice. In the north, a meal is not a meal unless it comes with bread. Everything else is just tiffin.

Hobson Jobson, the venerable dictionary of Anglo-Indian words, defines tiffin as 'eating or drinking out of meal time'. It comes from the archaic English word 'tif', to sip. In South India, tiffin encompasses the enormous variety of snack items such as **dosas** (crepes of fermented rice-flour and daal) and **idlis** (steamed cakes of fermented rice-flour and daal). A **dabba** is a metal box with numerous sealed compartments and anything carried in it is called tiffin. You will see these all over India but they are particularly famous in Mumbai where millions of them are used in an elaborate delivery system which brings home-cooked lunches to busy office workers each day.

Workers take a break at a chaat stand, Kolkata, West Bengal

Breakfast is a light affair, maybe idlis and **sambar** (vegetable and daal stew) in the south, **parathas** (flaky flat bread) in the north, or cornflakes among the hurried middle class. Many grab a bite on the run, perhaps pulling their scooters over to the side of the street to enjoy a **kachori** (corn or daal savoury puff) washed down with steaming hot **chai** (tea; see Chai in the Drinks chapter).

CULTURE

SUPERSTITIONS & CUSTOMS

If someone asks for a specific food at night-time, especially if a child asks a mother or the guest asks a host, the request must be fulfilled. Throughout pregnancy, women are also given this kind of special treatment. But considering pregnant women are advised to avoid certain foods anyway (the exact types change according to caste, creed and community) she can put the family in a delicate situation with her cravings. Also, Indians believe that if they envy somebody whilst eating, the other person will end up with a tummy ache.

Lunch is a substantial meal and, whether you're in a home or restaurant, it will usually be the local version of the **thali** (plate meal). The thali is named after the dish in which it's traditionally served (usually a metal platter with small, fitted bowls known as **katori**) and features dry and wet vegetable dishes, roti, **pappadams** (daal wafers), rice, pickle, curd, a sweet and meat, if that's what you're looking for. Often you'll get the dry preparations served on a rimmed plate and the liquid ones in little bowls. Our favourite thali is served on a banana leaf with the various dishes strategically dobbed around it – you'll find these in most South Indian restaurants and at many communal feasts.

A Kerala-style thali from the Mezban Restaurant, Kozhikode, Kerala

A late-night feast of chicken tikka masala with roti at Surjit Chicken House, Amritsar, Punjab

Although a thali provides a great opportunity to explore regional variations, don't leave India until you've sampled the original Gujarati one. Even if you can't make it to Gandhi's original stomping ground, you'll find Gujarati thalis in neighbouring states and major towns (see the boxed text Tantalising Thalis).

Those who can take a post-lunch siesta on whatever flat surface they can find. Cycle-rickshaw wallahs happily nap with their bums perched on saddles and their feet balancing on handlebars. Nobody can wait until dinner before eating again so a substantial tiffin is had around 5pm. Women who keep home often visit friends at this time and catch up on the news over fried snacks and chai. Workers drift off to street stalls and do the same.

Dinner might not be until 10 or 11pm, depending on the region and the season. Whatever the circumstances, Indians eat their evening meal very late, so restaurants are deserted before 9pm. If you're invited to someone's home for dinner, you may find that you've lost your appetite by the time food is served and are ready for nigh-nighs. Dinner will usually have fewer dishes than a thali lunch, but they will often be bigger serves. Whatever the mealtime, dishes are rarely served in courses; rather they're served hot and together.

Desserts as we know them don't feature much in everyday home meals and, while sweet treats are a national passion, they are eaten more as tiffin or to celebrate a special occasion than a sweet end-of-meal treat. If there is a last course, it will usually be a piece of fresh fruit. Feasts will be finished off with **paan** (betel nut mix; see Paan in the Staples & Specialities chapter).

TANTALISING THALIS

Thali is the ubiquitous Indian lunch, and every traveller's dream. Not only is it a cheap all-you-can-eat affair, it is a perfectly balanced meal and gives you the opportunity to taste many Indian dishes at the one sitting. But if you're on your own, the first thali can be a daunting experience.

Walk into a restaurant during a busy afternoon and you'll be told that there's no menu, just meals. Hold your disappointment, save yourself the embarrassment, and presume he means there are vegetarian or non-vegetarian thalis.

Find the basin, wash your hands and take a seat. You'll notice that everyone in the restaurant is looking at you, and you may feel self-conscious because you don't know what's going to happen next. Within moments the plate will be laid in front of you with curds, pickles, **raita** (yoghurt or curds combined with any number of vegetables or fruit, served chilled) and dessert. The waiter will be excited to see a foreigner and will smile and nod a lot. He'll bring a steel tumbler and fill it with the house water. Responding to the anxious look on your face, he'll chirp "mineral?" Another waiter will come from your blind side and start piling your plate with various dishes, deftly scooping them from one of four small containers hanging from a rotating tray. By the time you've managed to break the seal on your mineral water – the thirstier you are, the more difficult the seal, it's just the way it is – another waiter will enter the scene with a bucket full of rice. Catch his eye and he, seeing that your thali is incomplete, will dash over to shovel rice onto the middle of your plate. You've got everything. What now?

The other diners are watching to see what you do next. Maybe the foreigner is waiting for a fork. Tee hee, they can hardly contain themselves. The waiter stands over your shoulder, primed to pounce to your aid in case you confuse your dessert with your raita (ahem, it's been done). He likes nothing more than explaining thali etiquette to foreigners. The other diners are egging you on silently; they'll be pleased if you have learned their ways, and pleased if you provide lunchtime entertainment and make an arse of yourself. They can't lose.

What do you do? Pause for dramatic effect ... and get stuck in.

Flatten the rice and add the other dishes. Grab pinches of the dry ones, pours of the wet ones. Add a little pickle if you dare. Mix it all up with extravagant gestures, making a sumptuous gluggy mess and appearing as disinterested as the man on the cash desk. Meanwhile, the different textures and aromas enveloping your senses are whipping your appetite into frenzy. The little voice in your head lets out a little yelp as your hunger pushes it aside and roars, "I AM MAN. WATCH ME EAT!!"

Take a ball of food and scoop it into your mouth with your thumb. A bit too hot? Add a little curd and adjust the temperature. Take strips of bread by pushing it against the thali with your thumb while ripping the edges off with your fingers. Use it to pinch up mouthfuls of food. Nothing can stop you now. By the time you break the pappadam over the mound of food, you'll have gained the respect of everyone in the restaurant. You've passed the cultural test and are half expecting congratulatory pats on the back.

Once you've eaten even a nibble from any of the dishes, the waiter will race over to supply more. He won't ask and you've usually got your mouth full. Maybe the first time you'll let him get away with it but soon you'll get used to pointing to the dishes you want more of, and covering the ones you don't. You can even try it with your eyebrows. Eyebrows raised: I want more. Eyebrows tensed: no more. In time you will get more demanding. "Oi! I don't have much roti over here. Don't make me wait." "Hey! Rice! What am I going to do without rice?" "I need more green stuff, don't make me come looking for you". No dilly-dallying. That's the thali way.

Assamese thali from Guwahati, anti-clockwise starting from the bottom is steamed rice, khar daal, papaya, potato & eggplant, dry vegetables, chicken, tenga (sweet & sour fish), bamboo shoots, chana powder and dahi (curds)

Etiquette

Most Indians – apart from 'modern' ones in the north – eat with their right hand. In the south, they use as much of the hand as is necessary while elsewhere they use the tips of the fingers. How much of the hand is used is sometimes seen as social distinction but we'll not perpetuate such nonsense. Never eat with your left hand, which is reserved for toilet duties and therefore not to be trusted. You can use your left for holding drinks and serving yourself from a communal bowl, but never use it to bring grub to your mouth. If you're hardy and sensitive enough not to clog up Indian sewers with toilet paper you'll eat with only your right hand by instinct. Otherwise, practise sandwiching the left between your body and the table and you'll soon get by without it.

*A thali luncheon at Nataraj, a popular
Gujarati-style restaurant, Udaipur, Rajasthan*

CULTURE

Before a meal in any home, or as soon as you walk into a restaurant, ask for the basin and wash your hands thoroughly. Immediately after your meal, go and wash again, splashing your mouth with water.

Once your meal is served, mix your food up until it is thick and sticky. If you are having daal and sabzi, only mix the daal into your rice and have the sabzi in small scoops with each mouthful. If you are having fish or mutton curry, mix the gravy into your rice and take the flesh off the bones from the side of your plate. Scoop up lumps of the mix and, with your knuckles facing the dish, use your thumb to shovel the food into your mouth.

In theory, fingers should never go into mouths. It's uncouth to make any contact, and regarded by sticklers as overwhelmingly uncool to lick your fingers. The trickiest bit is suppressing the impulse to clean your hand

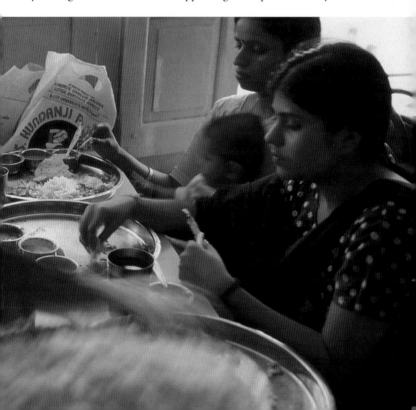

Serving up a thali in the Bhopathy Restaurant in Chennai, Tamil Nadu

once it becomes sticky, and not being self-conscious about daal and rice making unusual design motifs on your knuckles (it happens). Sure, people are watching but they do anyway. They are curious and pleased that you are adopting their customs. If you can, wait until you've finished eating before washing but if the mess is putting you off your meal, discreetly wipe your hand on the bread.

Indians are fastidious about hygiene, especially when it comes to food, and they are very sensitive about food becoming **jhoota** (contaminated). Because saliva can be polluting, it is unthinkable for a cook to taste a dish during preparation, which makes it all the more amazing how they blend their spices so exquisitely.

Similarly, drinks are never sipped from shared glasses or bottles. Stop, tilt your head back, and pour the water into your mouth. You don't have to follow the local example when drinking from your own water bottle but it is more hygienic. You're bound to dribble a bit at first but take small sips and you'll soon get into the hang of it.

These rules apply all over India. Whether you're dining in someone's home, in a restaurant or out on the street, observe them and you'll avoid any major faux pas. People are happy to explain their ways and playfully rib you as you bumble from one little mistake to another. Be sensitive, curious, adventurous and attentive but don't be inhibited; you'll quickly discover that braving the 'perils' of India's culinary culture is much more rewarding than restricting.

staples
& specialities

No matter how simple or complicated the expression, Indian food stands or falls on the quality of its ingredients. The astonishing variety of Indian food is shaped by geography, climate and the cook's insistence to use the freshest, seasonal produce available: still-shimmering fish, freshly picked vegetables, meat sold within moments of the animal's wince, spices ground for each meal and dairy products made within earshot of the cow's moo.

Spices

If it weren't for spices you probably wouldn't have bought a book on Indian cuisine, for without the potent alchemy of these culinary gems, Indian cuisine might still be just a cuisine for India, rather than a favourite the world over. Without them, Europe might not have been propelled into the Age of Exploration and Christopher Columbus wouldn't have accidentally found America.

Walk into an Indian home at mealtime and you'll be enveloped in a waft of exotic aromas that will make your taste-buds stand to attention. On a busy Indian street, just when you think you should stop breathing through your nose because of the stench, the smell of cooking spices will lure you into a restaurant, and the spice stall is always the most eye-catching and photogenic spectacle at the market.

STAPLES

Spices include mace, cardamom, turmeric, star anise and garlic at the Crawford market, Mumbai

Spices have been important in Indian life for over three millennia, as food and as medicines in Ayurvedic cures. India supplies almost half of the world's spices and the US$420 million it receives in exports adds much colour to the cheeks of its lacklustre economy.

India's pantheon of spices includes dried seeds, berries, rhizomes, flowers, leaves, bark, bulbs and stigmas. This realm also covers what we would normally call herbs. Whether they are used whole or ground; for flavour, aroma or colouring; for vegetables, fish, meat or dessert, each spice has its own culinary and medicinal use and is nearly always used in combinations called **masalas** (spice blends).

Curry leaf carrier at the Palayam market, Kozhikode, Kerala

CHILLIES

Indian food without chillies would be like a rickshaw driver without gumption: hardly conceivable. Even so, the Portuguese introduced chillies here less than 500 years ago. India is now the world's largest producer, exporter and consumer of these smarting little suckers.

Gujarati chillies

You can buy chillies fresh, dried, flaked, powdered, pickled, bottled, on your head, over the Internet or any other way you can think of. However, only the green ones are used fresh.

The most commonly used chilli is the **guntur** (hot, red; grown in Guntur) although there are over 20 varieties, including the exotic **pili tej mirch** (yellow, sharp) from North India. Other distinctive chillies to try are the **kashmiri**, **bedgi**, **reshampatti** and **nellore**, all named after their place of origin. The **tezpur** chilli has taken on mythical connotations. In 2000 Reuters reported the discovery of a 'Tezpur chilli' that had such a high capsaicin rating it made it the spiciest chilli in the world, bumping Mexico's habanero chilli from top spot. Even so, no one we spoke to knew anything about it and it seems that you have as much chance of a candlelit dinner with a yeti as you do of finding the tezpur chilli.

Goan chillies

While chilli is a common ingredient, don't think your taste-buds will be incinerated at every meal. Chillies are used more

Kashmiri chillies

for flavour and colour than heat, although their heat is very good for cooling the body down in hot weather. If you want to decrease the heat without compromising the flavour, remove the seeds before cooking.

If you do come off second best in a chilli encounter, avoid the temptation to guzzle water as this only spreads the heat around your mouth without extinguishing the fire (capsaicin is insoluble in water). It's much better to reach for a dairy product like milk, **lassi** (curds drink) or **dahi** (curds), which will neutralise the capsaicin and allow you to regain your composure. If you don't have a dairy extinguisher at hand, a few mouthfuls of plain rice should, at least, stop you banging the table.

Allspice

So called because it combines the flavours of black pepper, cloves, nutmeg and cinnamon. This brown-red berry is mainly added to kababs. It's a Caribbean import that has found its place on the subcontinental spice rack.

Amchur

Also called mango powder, amchur is made from green mangoes that are peeled, dried in the sun and powdered. The tart, fruity powder adds bite to a wide range of dishes.

Green mangoes

Asafoetida

Known as hing in Hindi, this fetid, ugly gum tastes lousy on its own but changes character when cooked, imparting a pleasant, earthy zing to many dishes. Most importantly though, asafoetida is a miraculous digestive and you should source it if you're having problems in the tummy department. While it's only grown in Kashmir you'll have no problems finding it in markets throughout the country. Buy the powdered form in airtight containers (because it really does stink).

Bay Leaves

Added whole to food to give it a rich, sweet scent; they are also ground and added to some masalas.

Black cardamom

Green cardamom

Cardamom

The queen of Indian spices. You'll find the small, green variety in savoury dishes, desserts and in winter **chai** (tea). It's also used as a mouth-refreshing digestive, as it has been since the Mughal Empire. The pods grown on the slopes of the Western Ghats are regarded as the best in the world. Once crushed, cardamom loses much of its flavour. The larger, black cardamom, grown in the northeast, is stronger in flavour and commonly added to meat dishes.

Kashmiri brides traditionally wear a silver locket filled with cardamom that they present to the groom during the wedding ceremony. As cardamom is believed to *cool* the blood, perhaps it's also a clever measure taken for self-preservation.

STAPLES

Cinnamon

The inner bark of a tropical evergreen tree native to Sri Lanka that is harvested during the rainy season when the bark is pliable. There are very few dishes that cinnamon will not enhance and it is integral to India's most popular spice blend, **garam masala**. Along with cardamom and saffron, cinnamon is a spice you'll also find in desserts. Cinnamon and **cassia** are commonly confused due to their similar shape and appearance. In Hindi, cinnamon is **dalchini**, cassia is **jungli dalchini**. The word 'dalchini' comes from the Arabian term 'wood of China' as China is traditionally the major supplier.

Cassia bark

Coriander

Both the seeds and leaves are used in cooking. The seeds lend flavour and body to just about every savoury dish. Believed to be the world's most popular herb, the leaf (cilantro or Chinese parsley) is the most commonly used garnish and its pleasantly sweet scent can cut through the worst of India's street smells.

Coriander seeds

Cloves

Although introduced, these have been cultivated in India now for centuries and are widely used in both medicine and food. The buds of the clove tree are picked when green and dried in the sun until they turn brown. They have a very powerful flavour, used the world over to provide distraction from toothache. If you find whole cloves in your dish – a biryani for example – consider moving them to the side of your plate, as the taste, although pleasant, is sharp and numbing. The word 'clove' is derivative of the Latin word *clavus* (nail); cloves are commonly used to fasten packets of **paan** (betel nut mix; see Paan later in this chapter).

Cloves

Cumin seeds

Cumin

This ancient spice is used throughout India to give dishes a bitter edge. Most curries begin with the crackle of cumin seeds in hot oil.

Curry Leaves

These flavour enhancers got their name because somebody decided they smelled like curry – which curry, we'll never know. Used mainly in the south, the leaves are freshly picked off the stem because the dried variety has only a fraction of the bitter flavour. The leaves add flavour but are not eaten; a person who is used for one task and then discarded is likened to a curry leaf.

Fennel

These seeds are as important in the medicine chest as the spice box. In cooking they are used to flavour stocks and sauces, to sweeten desserts and as an effective digestive. They are also used as a breath freshener after every restaurant meal, aid indigestion and promote menstruation. Babies are given a daily drink of fennel water to protect them from colic. **Aniseed** and fennel are both called **saunf** because of their similarity in flavour and appearance.

Fennel seeds

Fenugreek

These seeds are one of the strongest spices – although their flavour mellows with cooking – and are used in many popular spice blends. They are also closely associated with childbirth, as they are believed to promote lactation. New mothers are often fed fenugreek-flavoured sweets for a month after childbirth. The seeds are also crushed and fed to cattle to increase their supply of milk.

Garlic

Used widely in cooking and medicine. It is pounded, pureed and chopped before use in countless dishes, and employed for a plethora of ailments from the relieving the common cold to repelling evil demons.

Ginger

Ginger

Ginger is thought to have originated in South-East Asia and has been cultivated in India since ancient times. It was the first Indian spice known in Europe, and among the most highly prized of the eastern imports. You'll find ginger used both fresh and dried in a plethora of dishes, as well as in chai. Its name comes from the Sanskrit *gingabara*, meaning 'shaped like a horn'.

Holy Basil

This is the most sacred plant in Hinduism (known as **tulsi** in Hindi) and you'll find one outside the entrance of most Hindu homes. The god Vishnu wore a garland of holy basil leaves, and they are used extensively in temple worship and auspicious occasions such as weddings. In and around Vishnu temples, you will be blessed with an offering of water infused with holy basil leaves, which you are expected to drink. While the source of the water may cause some panic, have faith and Vishnu – the Preserver and Restorer – will protect you. Holy basil is never used in cooking although it is sometimes made into a tea that is good for relieving colds and flu.

Kokum

The deep-purple fruit of the kokum tree gives a purplish hue to any dish to which it is added. Along parts of the west coast, kokum is used to add a sour edge to vegetable dishes and coconut-based curries.

Lemongrass

This perennial grass grows in gardens across India and is used in tea, soft drinks and soups.

Mace

The bright-red lacy membrane that grows around the nutmeg seed. Although both from the same plant, nutmeg and mace are not inter-changeable. Mace turns orange after it has been dried, and is usually bought ground to be used in savoury dishes.

Mint

Used in the ubiquitous **chatni** (chutney) that graces North Indian tables at all times of the day. It is also commonly used in various street snacks, as an accompanying chatni or in raw form as a garnish. Mint is also used to add a refreshing zing in various street stall drinks, such as tea and **jal jeera** (see Jal Jeera in the Drinks chapter).

Mint

Mustard

Used widely in both auspicious and everyday fare. In the south, mustard oil is commonly used to temper spices and its distinctive baked-earth taste is the strongest flavour in many dishes (see Cooking Mediums later in this chapter). Besides adding flavour, mustard is reputedly good for the head: not only does it clear the mind, it promotes hair growth.

Nutmeg
Nutmeg's warm flavour is used to enhance many Indian meat dishes and desserts; it's also an essential ingredient of garam masala. The powdered form quickly loses its flavour so buy the whole kernels when possible.

Pomegranate
The flesh of this bulbous fruit is used as well as the sun-dried seeds, known as **anardana**. Primarily used in North India in powdered form, pomegranate seeds add a sour tang to curries, chatnis and daal.

Ripe pomegranates split-open to reveal vibrant flesh

STAPLES

Poppy Seeds
Both opium and poppy seeds come from the poppy plant but, no, you won't get a buzz from eating the seeds. Instead, your savoury dishes, pastries and sweets will acquire a nice nutty flavour and crunchy texture. Poppy seeds can also be used as a thickener.

Salt
Used copiously in Indian cuisine. Common sea salt is used for cooking while rock salt flavours most tangy drinks, **raita** (yoghurt or curds combined with any number of vegetables or fruit, served chilled) and **chaat** (any snack seasoned with chaat masala; see Chaat Masala later in this chapter). It is mined from the Gangetic Plains in Central India, and comes in a variety of colours from orange to grey. On its own, rock salt has an unpleasant odour but is metamorphosed when added to uncooked cold foods and drinks, and is an extremely handy antidote to dehydration, perhaps the traveller's single biggest problem.

Salt

PEPPER – The King of Spices

Christopher Columbus was actually looking for the black pepper of Kerala's Malabar Coast, when he stumbled upon America. Thank heavens De Gama eventually found it as the region still grows the finest quality of the world's favourite spice. You'll scarcely taste a savoury dish in India that hasn't been pepped up with it.

Pepper is the fruit of the *piper nigrum* vine that grows up to 10m in height, takes five years to yield and then bears clumps of berries annually for up to 35 years. India is the world's largest producer and exporter of black pepper, providing over 40,000 tonnes of the stuff for those of us who can't grow our own. The consumption of pepper is always growing and there's a fear that soon there might not be enough pepper to sustain the lucrative market.

Black, white and green pepper come from the same plant – the difference between them occurs at the processing stage. To make black pepper, the green berries are plucked, trampled on barefoot to separate the berries from the stalk, blanched in hot water and laid out to dry and turn black in the sun. Lighter and creamier white pepper is made when the ripe berries are softened in water, hulled and dried. Green pepper is produced when unripe berries are pickled in brine. The stalks of the pepper vine are traditionally slung out on the street to attract possible buyers, and superstitious farmers still do this to ensure harvest success.

Peppercorns near Quilandy, Kerala

Peppercorns for sale in Chandni Chowk, New Delhi, Haryana

SAFFRON – The Dashing Prince

Saffron evokes images of wealth and rarity unparalleled in the culinary lexicon. Spain and India are the only major producers of this flavoursome, fragile spice. Saffron is actually the dried stigmas of the crocus bulb, grown in Jammu & Kashmir. The plant flowers for a couple of weeks in October, when the blossoms are plucked at dawn before the heat can wilt them, and then the delicate stigmas are dried.

It takes more than 1500 hand-plucked stigmas to yield just one gram of saffron. Fortunately, a little saffron goes a long way and you should use it very sparingly. It loses much of it pizzazz when kept for too long so, if you're not going to use it all, share it around. Saffron is widely used in savoury and sweet dishes, and just a few strands soaked in warm water or milk will infuse your dish with colour and a rich, fragrant flavour.

Saffron is also closely associated with worship and you'll see temple deities anointed with a saffron paste, which is also used in Hindu weddings and by Buddhist priests. If you're still not convinced of saffron's worth, consider that it has long been regarded as a powerful aphrodisiac.

Saffron makes for a wonderful gift although, because of the prices it can fetch, it is frequently adulterated. The usual culprit is safflower, also rather appropriately known – no doubt by many disgruntled tourists – as 'bastard saffron'.

Sesame

Regarded in Ayurveda as a 'warming' food, sesame is popularly eaten in the chill of winter. The beige-coloured seeds are often added to sweets and breads to provide a sweet, nutty texture.

Tamarind

Tamarind

Sometimes known as the 'Indian date', tamarind is used predominately in the south. The brown pods used in cooking grow up to 15cm long and are the fruit of a tall evergreen tree indigenous to India. When dried, the pulp of the pod will keep indefinitely and its sour, fruity flavour is used to enhance a range of dishes including chatnis, **rasam** (spiced daal broth), daals and curries. It is also one of the essential ingredients of Worcestershire sauce. At the market you'll usually find tamarind in dried slabs or as a paste, which is broken up and used as required.

TURMERIC

Turmeric plant

Turmeric root

Turmeric powder, Mir Alam Market, Hyderabad

India is the world's largest producer, exporter and consumer of turmeric. It adds colour and flavour to a wide range of dishes including meats, lentils and vegetables (although not green ones, which it will turn grey). Turmeric is also used as a preservative, and is the essence of just about every Indian curry.

The ginger-like rhizome looks deceptively dull when picked but, inside the brown skin, languishes a vibrant yellow-orange root that will impart its rich colour to just about anything, including you, so be careful when handling it. Turmeric also helps to enhance and balance other spices in the pot.

Even Indians usually buy the powdered form because grinding it is too much work. At the market, its brilliant colour will catch your eye and have you reaching for a camera.

Considering its many uses, turmeric is probably India's most important spice. You'll find it in every home as a handy antiseptic as well as a natural cure for a host of ailments including a sore throat. Indian women frequently use turmeric as a skin-polisher and to discourage hair growth so you'll often see them with yellow ankles, necks and faces (we also thought this was a religious practice). It is also held sacred by Hindus and used as a religious mark on foreheads, as well as a mark of respect between friends. And a single line of turmeric across the threshold of a house is said to keep ants at bay.

Masalas (Spice Blends)

Just about every Indian dish is flavoured with a distinct blend of spices, whether it's simply nutmeg and cardamom in a **halwa** (sweet made with vegetables, cereals, lentils, nuts or fruit) or more than a dozen different ingredients in a southern **sambar** (vegetable and daal stew). Sometimes spices are added during cooking but, for more elaborate blends, the spices are usually premixed to produce signature flavours in the same way we use curry powder. There are as many masala recipes as rickshaws in Rajasthan, but these are some of the most common.

Garam Masala

This familiar and oft-used combo is an blend of up to 15 spices and is used in a multitude of ways – cooked with meat, sprinkled on **chatni** (chutney) – the possibilities are endless. The hot blend generally features black pepper, cumin seeds, cinnamon, cardamom, cloves, coriander seeds, bay leaves, nutmeg and mace, although each household or producer will have a different recipe. Garam means 'hot' and this masala is particularly popular in cooler areas where it is favoured over chilli.

These days we can get a commercial brand of garam masala in just about every western supermarket but it's a poor substitute for the freshly ground stuff. Visiting expats always seek out a reliable producer and bring supplies back to friends and family in their adopted countries.

Panch Phoron

Panch Phoron is the combination of whole spices that provides the distinct flavour, colour and aroma of Bengali cuisine. This aromatic mix is a blend of cumin seeds, fennel seeds, fenugreek seeds, black mustard seeds and **kalonji** (tear-shaped black seed, also called onion seed).

Panch phoron, Chowk Bazaar, Darjeeling

Sambar Powder

This is the distinctive blend of the predominantly vegetarian south, used to flavour sambar. It usually comprises mustard seeds, fenugreek seeds, cumin, chillies, black pepper, asafoetida, turmeric, curry leaves and coriander seeds. With so many ingredients flavours balance is paramount, and your best bet is to befriend a domestic producer to acquire the right mix.

Tandoori Masala

The unique taste of Punjabi food comes from the charcoal used in a **tandoor** (clay oven) and from the blend of spices in a tandoori masala that features cumin, coriander seeds, chilli, ginger, turmeric and a harmless, flavourless red colouring that gives the food its characteristic tinge. Tandoori cooks usually combine these ingredients while making the marinade. You can also buy ready-to-use tandoori masalas, which will add a tandoor touch to foods not cooked in a clay oven.

Masala used for making biryani, Mi Alam Market, Hyderabad

STAPLES

Kala Masala

Sometimes known as **goda masala**, this blend is the taste of Maharashtran fare. As well as the old reliables of cinnamon, cardamom, cloves, black pepper and coriander seeds, this masala may include poppy and sesame seeds along with star anise and allspice.

Chaat Masala

Chaat loosely means 'finger-licking good' and is the name generally applied to any snack foods seasoned with this masala. The two main ingredients are black salt and amchur, supported by cumin, sea salt, coriander powder, chilli powder, black pepper and ginger. Common chaat items are **golgappa** (tiny deep-fried puffs of dough), **aloo chaat** (boiled potatoes with chaat masala) and **bhelpuri** (see Maharashtra in the Regional Variations chapter).

Fennel seeds, green & black cardamom pods, sesame, peppercorn, cumin and mustard seeds, Karnataka

Rice

Rice is the most important staple, but in a place where food and spirituality are inseparable, it is much more than simply a nutritious grain. India has more land dedicated to rice cultivation than any other country, and the sight of sweeping, lush paddies will stay with you long after you've returned home. India's yield of 90 million tonnes of rice accounts for more than half of the country's total grain production, so you can imagine how important it is to the country's economy. But beyond the balance sheet, rice is integral to just about every Hindu ceremony: it's used to symbolise purity and fertility in wedding ceremonies and is often offered as **puja** (literally, respect; offering or prayers) in Hindu temples. As rice's function has barely altered since it was first cultivated over 3000 years ago, one single grain is also a powerful symbol of the continuity of Indian civilisation through millennia of change and upheaval.

In culinary terms, North and South India are often broadly divided by their most important staple; rice in the south and bread in the north. Although people in North India do eat plenty of rice, it is fundamental to the southern diet (and eastern and western, just to confuse matters). In the south, rice turns up in every course; be it **dosa** (crepe of fermented rice flour and daal) for breakfast, **thali** (plate meal) for lunch, perhaps a biryani for dinner capped off with **payasam** (rice pudding) for a special dessert. On average, Indians eat almost 2kg of rice a week.

Rice sack carriers, Panaji market, Goa

Long-grain white rice varieties are the most common, served piping hot with just about any 'wet' cooked dish. For special occasions, rice is often coloured with turmeric – saffron if it's really auspicious. Rice is cooked up in a **pulao** (or pilaf; aromatic rice casserole) or biryani in Muslim cuisine or as masala rice in the south. Between Assam's sticky rice in the far north-east to Kerala's red grains in the extreme south, you'll find countless regional varieties, which locals will claim to be the best in India. Many of these are indistinguishable to the visiting palate, although one stands out above all.

Basmati gets its name from the Hindi 'queen of fragrance', and its scent is well known around the world. The grains are white, long and silky, and its aroma is reminiscent of the uncluttered freshness of the Himalayan foothills, from where the best basmati comes. The most flavoursome basmati grows in the Dehra Dun valley, which also gives its name to the best commercial brand available internationally. Demand outside India helps to keep prices beyond the reach of most Indians, so it's mainly used for special occasions.

Patna rice is named after the capital of Bihar, around which this long-grain rice grows. You'll see people buying great big sacks of the stuff at markets because it's cheap, tasty and can be stored for several months. It is also versatile, lending itself well to a batter that can be

Aval, or 'flattened' rice

used for making crepes, fitters and pancakes. Red rice is more rustic and you'll only see it outside cities. The short, thick grains provide a slightly nutty taste, ideal for accompanying spicy dishes. Coarser than most long-grain varieties, what red rice lacks in sophistication it more than makes up for in valuable minerals, vitamins and carbohydrates. Rural folk often carry a stash of cooked red rice with them for when they need an instant lift.

Puffed rice is the closest thing to Indian popcorn and is a ubiquitous street snack. The rice grain is dried in its husk until all the moisture is gone. The grains are dropped into hot sand in a wok, where they puff up and are then removed with a slotted spoon, ready to munch. When roasted, the puffed rice is aromatic and tasty. It is used in the popular Mumbai street snack, **bhelpuri** (see Maharashtra in the Regional Variations chapter).

Cheap varieties of rice are often processed into rice flour and then made into batter, dough or crepes, or used as a thickening agent. Throughout the south (and the north during religious festivals) the outside of most homes will be adorned with intricately designed Hindu motifs that symbolise good fortune. Called **kolam** in the south, **rangoli** in the north, these motifs are traditionally made with rice flour (although philistine ants frequently eat the designs so some people use dust from white stone instead).

AUSPICIOUS GRAINS

Rice in all its forms is revered in India as a symbol of plenty, purity and fertility. When a Hindu bride steps over the threshold of her new home, she kicks a measure of rice into the house in an attempt to make as big a mess as possible. The bigger the spray, the more auspicious, as the rice is symbolic of the good fortune she brings to her new home.

When stacked closely together, hessian bags filled with rice reveal subtle differences

Breads & Cereals

While rice is paramount in the south, wheat is the mainstay in the north, where a variety of wheat breads are served with virtually every meal. **Roti**, the generic term for bread, is also a name used interchangeably with **chappati** to describe the most common variety, the irresistible unleavened bread made with fine whole-wheat flour and cooked on a **tawa** (hotplate). Making roti is time consuming and most middle-class women have hired help to assist them with their daily chores, like laundry, child minding and making roti.

There are countless variations of bread and even staples like chappati are made according to different recipes depending on the region, neighbourhood or household. Most breads are unleavened and made with **atta** (whole-wheat flour) although **makki** (corn meal), **bajri** (millet), and **jawar** (barley) are also used. Bread is made fresh for every meal.

However it is made or served, bread is always eaten with the fingertips of the right hand only (and some dexterity is required to remain composed while breaking bread with one hand). Small pieces of bread are broken off and wrapped around morsels of food, and eaten. At the end of a meal, most people use the leftover bread to mop up the remains.

Apart from bread making, wheat is also processed into fine grains to make semolina, which is regarded by Hindus as a pure ingredient and therefore associated with religious ceremonies. You're most likely to sample semolina in sweet **prasad** (blessed food) where it is cooked with other pure ingredients like milk, sugar and ghee. **Dalia** (cracked wheat) is used in porridge, cereals and snacks.

While it doesn't strictly belong in this section, **besan** (gram or chickpea flour) is widely used in myriad preparations including doughs, as a crunchy batter and a thickening agent. It's high in protein but not for the faint-bellied as it can be difficult to digest.

Jawar and bajri were very important crops of the Indus Valley Civilisation but are minor cereals these days, occasionally used in bread making but more frequently pounded with spice to make **pappadams** (daal wafers). Cornmeal is used for making thick roti in various parts of North India, particularly in Punjab where **makki ki roti** (cornmeal roti) is a firm rural favourite.

Pasta would be the last thing you'd expect to find on an Indian menu but **vermicelli** – Italian for 'little worms' – is an essential ingredient in **sevai**, a milk pudding that's one of the country's most popular sweets. Although eaten as a standard sweet anytime of the year, it reaches its peak of popularity during Ramadan (the Muslim month of fasting) when it's the first thing eaten to break fast after sunset.

STAPLES

DAILY BREADS

Roti/Chappati
Whatever you call it, this is the simplest and most common Indian bread. Roti is made with whole-wheat flour and water, and although always round, roti sizes can vary dramatically.

Poori
This delicious North Indian snack is a disc of dough that puffs up when deep fried. The disc is skilfully spun into a wok; after a few seconds of deep-frying it puffs up like soft, crispy balloon, and is eaten with various stewed meats and vegetables. The softer and more puffed up the better, and the street vendors of Varanasi are justly famous for their perfect pooris.

Kachori
This is like poori only the dough has been pepped up with corn or daal, which also makes it thicker. Popular in North India, kachori makes for a substantial snack at any time of the day.

Phulka
Literally 'puff', this is a mini poori, made with whole-wheat flour, and cooked on a naked flame.

Rumali
Rumali (literally, handkerchief) is a large superfine whole-wheat bread that is thrown like a pizza base. You're most likely to find rumali in the Muslim communities, where they are popularly eaten with kababs.

Bhatura
This Punjabi speciality is a deep-fried version of the naan, and is popularly eaten with spiced chickpeas.

Paratha
Unleavened, fried, flaky paratha, when combined with any North Indian sauce, makes for a delicious morning snack. Paratha is often jazzed up with a stuffing of **paneer** (fresh cheese) or grated vegetables for a substantial on-the-spot snack.

STAPLES

Kulcha

This soft, round leavened bread is native to Hyderabad, and is a mainstay of Indian restaurants around the world. It's delicious when filled with onion, spices, vegetables or meat.

Shirmal

Versions of this flaky unleavened bread can be found throughout Muslim India. Shirmal's main ingredients are plain flour, lots of **ghee** (clarified butter), salt, sugar, milk and a little more ghee. It is cooked inside the walls of tandoor-like ovens. Traditionally the baked bread is drizzled with saffron-infused milk to add fragrance and keep it moist, but with saffron being so expensive, bakers are more likely to use food colouring instead. In Lucknow, you can have shirmal at any time of the day, but you can't leave the old town without enjoying a breakfast of shirmal dunked in **nahari** (a tender meat stew which is cooked all night on embers).

A kulcha wallah with shirmals

Naan

This tear-shaped favourite originated in the Middle East, but Punjabis opened their hearths to naan and subsequently introduced them to the world. True naan has to be cooked along the walls of a tandoor. You can cook naan in a normal oven, but the results will inevitably disappoint; even Indians generally wait to savour them in restaurants, as very few homes are equipped with a tandoor. Laced with garlic, naan is difficult to resist; filled with paneer, impossible.

Daal Makhani with naan, from the Oberoi Hotel, New Delhi

STAPLES

Poori (Deep Fried Bread)

This is the basic poori recipe common to the whole of India, except Bengal where they use refined flour.

Ingredients

3 cups	whole-wheat flour
2 tsp	ghee
¼ tsp	salt
	vegetable or sunflower oil for deep-frying

Warm ½ - ¾ cups of water to lukewarm. Put the flour in a large bowl and mix in the salt and ghee. Slowly pour in enough of the water to make a firm but malleable dough with your hands. Knead the dough well (unlike pastry, this needs a lot of kneading). You should form a stiff dough, but pliable enough to roll out easily.

Form flattened 3cm balls. Dust each ball with flour and roll out into circles of 4cm. Arrange the pooris on a newspaper or paper towel, ready for frying.

Heat the oil in a small wok (if you use a large wok, you will need large quantities of oil, and it doesn't make sense as you will fry one poori at a time). When the oil is hot, but not smoking, slip in a poori and press it down with a slotted spoon. Pressing it down below the surface of the oil, makes it puff up into a round ball. This is an important step. After a minute turn it over and fry for another minute. If the oil gets too hot, the pooris will brown too soon and harden. Pooris should be soft and light brown in colour. Turn down the flame to keep the temperature at a medium-high. Turn it up again if the oil goes too cold and the pooris don't puff up.

makes 20 pooris

Daal

While their staples divide north and south, the whole of India – from toothless toddlers to haggard old men – goes doolally for **daal**. The word daal means lentils or pulses, but mostly people use the specific name of each pulse. More often, daal refers to a wide range of pulse-based dishes.

Where we might refer to our basic living as our 'bread and butter' Indians refer to **daal roti** (daal and bread) as all they need to survive. Whatever your means or connections you'll eat daal at least once a day, either as a side dish or as a main with bread or rice. This might not sound inspiring if your only reference is the souped-up slop served in Indian restaurants around the world, but daal is the foundation of sustenance here. There are countless delicious variations on the theme as you travel between different neighbourhoods, towns and states. Punjab, for example, is renowned for its tandoori cuisine, yet Punjabis themselves go doolally for daal, concocting more versions of it than any other state.

From the thin sambar of the south to the thick **moong** (mung bean) daals of the north, you may encounter up to 60 different pulses including lentils, beans and peas. Whether the legumes are cooked in the skin or husked, whole or split, changes the character of each daal dish. However, it's the **bhaghar** (spices tempered in hot oil or ghee which are then added to the cooked pulses) that gives each one its distinctive zip and will have your mouth watering each time you sample *yet another* daal.

How the pulses are cooked is often a good regional guide. **Maah ki daal**, for example, is Punjab's signature and is made from **urad** (black gram or lentils) simmered for hours over a low fire, rendering it utterly irresistible when combined with freshly baked roti. The simply cooked, lightly spiced daals of Mumbai are characteristic of Maharashtra's rustic cuisine, while the omnipresent sambars of the south go perfectly with rice and, along the eastern coast, you'll find pulses that have been dry roasted before being cooked.

The most common pulses are **chana**, a slightly sweeter version of the yellow split pea; tiny, yellow ovals called **moong daal** (mung beans);

Masoor   *Moong daal*   *Moong*

salmon-coloured **masoor** (red lentils); the ochre-coloured southern favourite, **tuvar daal** (yellow lentils; also known as **arhar**); **rajma** (kidney beans); **kabuli chana** (chickpeas); **urad** (black gram or lentils); and **lobhia** (black-eyed peas).

Finally to farting. Yes, increasing your bean intake all of a sudden is bound to stir things in your stomach, and gusty conditions may prevail. However, you'll probably experience this a lot less in a restaurant in India than you might in an Indian restaurant elsewhere. Indian ingredients are added for their health properties as well as taste, and you'll find that there are dozens of spices and flavourings like caraway seeds, cumin seeds, asafoetida and mint that cooks add to dishes to aid digestion and reduce flatulence.

Maah Ki Daal (Black Lentil Daal)

Though many different daals are cooked in Punjab, this one has taken on a symbolic significance in Punjabi cuisine.

Ingredients

1 cup	urad (black gram or lentils), skin on
3 Tbs	ghee
½ tsp	cumin seeds
4	seeds of 4 cardamom pods, ground
4	cloves
4	garlic cloves, finely chopped
2	onions, sliced
2½cm	piece ginger, shredded
2	ripe tomatoes, chopped
½ cup	full cream.

Soak the lentils overnight. Boil them in plenty of water over a low flame for at least an hour so the lentils dissolve. Heat the ghee in a separate pan. Put in the cumin seeds, cardamom and cloves. Add the garlic and fry until light brown. Next add the onions and ginger and saute until the onions are pale gold. Add the tomatoes and cook further until they become a paste. Pour in the daal and stir well. Simmer for another 5 minutes. Mix the cream in and serve with hot rotis.

serves 6

Daal from the Crawford market, Mumbai

Meat

While India probably has more vegetarians than all other countries put together, it still has an extensive repertoire of carnivorous fare lapped up by the Muslim and Christian communities (and increasingly by the Hindu middle class). Goat, lamb and chicken are mainstays; religious taboos forbid Hindus from eating beef and Muslims from pigging-out on pork.

The Mughals are credited with introducing what would become some of India's favourite dishes, and the Muslim community maintain their carnivorous traditions, receiving enthusiastic support from the Christians of Goa and Kerala, as well as smaller communities such as the Parsis. Even in the predominantly vegetarian inland south you'll have little difficulty finding meat; just keep an eye out for the crescent or the cross.

Many communities have their own signature meat dishes that you should track down. Parsis are gregarious company and zealous carnivores; if you score an invitation to dine with them you'll be impressed by their self-deprecating humour and fusion fare, particularly **dhansak** (a one-pot wonder consisting of meat, usually chicken, and vegetables in a spicy puree of several daals). The Christians of Goa giddily prepare the famous tongue-searing **pork vindaloo** (pork curry in a marinade of vinegar and garlic), a dish that the Portuguese left to soften the blow of colonisation. You'll be spoiled for choice in Jammu & Kashmir because both Hindus and Muslims here depend on meat as a staple. You'll be able to sample authentic **roghan josh** (lamb or goat in a rich, spicy sauce), the curry dish that has been bastardised all over the world.

STAPLES

The meat section of New Market, Kolkata

Pork Vindaloo

Vindaloo tastes equally good with rice or some soft bread such as the Goan speciality, **pao** (see Goa in the Regional Variations chapter). It is never served with Indian breads.

Ingredients

1kg (32 oz)	pork in 5cm dice
10	dried red chillies (slit and the seeds removed)
10	peppercorns
8-10	garlic cloves
5cm	piece of ginger
2 tsp	cumin seeds
1 tsp	mustard seeds
1/2 tsp	turmeric powder (optional)
8	cloves
5cm	piece cinnamon
2 tsp	salt
1 tsp	sugar
1/2 cup	malt vinegar
2	onions, finely chopped
2 Tbs	vegetable or sunflower oil

Put all the ingredients (except pork, onions and oil) in a food processor and grind to a fine paste. Coat the pork with this paste and leave to marinate for 2 hours. Now heat the oil in a heavy-bottomed pan and saute the onions until light pink. Add the pork and stir well. Just about cover the pork with water and cook it until a thick gravy forms (about 30 minutes).

serves 6

Meat is becoming more prevalent among the Hindu majority, especially the middle classes, many of whom identify meat consumption as a modern trend to be whole-heartedly embraced if one is to improve one's status. These days, many Hindus even eat beef in restaurants or non-Hindu homes although very few would ever consider preparing it in their own homes.

The Muslim community does most of the butchering, selling and, of course, cooking and eating of meat. While meat is prepared in a variety of ways throughout the country, perhaps because of the Muslim injunction against eating blood – and the general squeamishness of most Hindus – there's a scarcity of rare, or lightly cooked meat. It often seems that Indians don't care much for the taste of meat, using it instead as a textured carrier for their favourite spices and flavourings. Meat is often processed into mince for kababs, **kheema** (spiced mincemeat) and **koftas** (meatballs).

Goat

Goat is our favourite street livestock and their cheeky food raids provide hours of entertainment. It is also the most commonly eaten meat and you'll see long skinny carcasses dangling from hooks in every market. When the British were here, they called goat 'mutton' and the term stuck. Most international Indian recipe books replace goat with lamb, which has a similar, but far from identical taste.

Poultry

Although you'll see chickens all over India – roaming rural streets and in wicker baskets squashed tighter than Indian commuters on a bus – eating them here is still something of an indulgence. If you're served the bird in a home, you can be sure that you're getting the best treatment. Before cooking, the skin is always removed and the chicken is usually cut into small pieces to ensure that the flavours of the dish reach deep into the meat. Duck, geese and partridge also occasionally feature on restaurant menus, particularly outside cities.

It's something of revelation to find that chicken in India tastes, well, like chicken, unlike the bland matter modern farm practises have come up with all over the developed world. Some popular chicken dishes to look out for are **murgh makhani** (chicken pieces cooked tandoori style, then simmered in a butter sauce), the Goan speciality **cafreal** (chicken with hot chillies), **kashi** (whole chicken stuffed and marinated) and the range of tandoori specialities.

A chicken seller with an abundance of stock in New Market, Kolkata

Mutton Korma (Mutton in a Rich Spicy Sauce)

Ingredients

1kg (32oz)	lamb (shoulder or leg) in 5cm cubes
½ cup	vegetable or sunflower oil
2	onions, sliced
1 tsp	garam masala
2 tsp	ginger paste
2 tsp	garlic paste
2	large onions, ground into a paste
1 tsp	red chilli powder
2 tsp	coriander seeds, powdered
4	seeds of 4 cardamom pods, ground
2	bay leaves
10	peppercorns
4	cloves
1 cup	plain yoghurt or curd

Heat oil in a heavy-bottomed pan. Add the sliced onions, fry until deep brown and drain (but keep the oil). In a food processor, blend the cooked onions and garam masala into a paste and set aside.

In the oil fry the lamb on a high flame for 2-3 minutes. Add the rest of the ingredients (except the yoghurt) and saute for 5 minutes. Pour in 1 cup of water and cook the lamb with the pan covered for 10 minutes.

Open the pan and add the yoghurt. Keep stirring over a medium heat until the water evaporates and the meat takes on a reddish appearance. If you do not stir, the juices will burn at the bottom of the pan.

Add more water according to how moist you want the dish to be – there should be a thick gravy that coats the back of a spoon. As a finishing touch stir in the fried onions and garam masala.

Serves 6

Mutton korma, palak paneer & daal makhani, Oberoi Hotel, New Delhi

Some Indian Ways of Cooking Meat
Kababs

Kabab is a loose term here, applied to marinated chunks or ground meat, cooked on a skewer, fried on a hot-plate or cooked under a grill. In fact, you could probably use the term kabab to describe just about any small cut of meat that doesn't already have a name. The two basic forms are barbecued bits on a skewer and the Muslim specialities made with mince. Falling into the second category, **kakori kababs** are a speciality of Uttar Pradesh and are named after the town near Lucknow (see Uttar Pradesh in the Regional Variations chapter).

Spicy mincemeat kebabs at a streetside stall, Hyderabad

Tandoor

Very few people have a **tandoor** (clay oven) in their homes but tandoori-cooked meats are favourite restaurant fare all over India, especially in the north. In the tandoor, marinated meats are cooked to make kababs, succulent chunks of chicken become the famous tikka and a whole spring chicken surrenders its head and wings in order to emerge as glowing, scrumptious tandoori chicken.

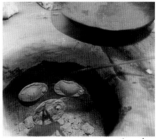

A tandoor

Korma

Another North Indian speciality, korma is a dish in which cubes of goat, lamb or chicken are cooked in a rich, spicy sauce, usually with the addition of onions. Contemporary kormas are often cooked over a stove like stews but if you want the real McKorma, cook it using the **dum pukht** method of steaming, in which the vessel is sealed with dough, placed over glowing embers and 'baked' slowly.

Kheema & Koftas

Kheema means mincemeat but is also the name given to many dishes that include mincemeat, and koftas are meatballs. Both are very popular methods of cooking goat, beef and lamb.

Fish & Seafood

Blessed with a coastline extending 7000km, it's no surprise that fish and seafood are important staples on the subcontinent. Fishing is practised along the entire length of India's coast and on virtually all of its numerous rivers (though you'd hope *not* the Ganges). The types of fish and seafood differ from those found in cooler climes, and popular species include pomfret, mullet, perch, sole, rockfish, catfish, mackerel, trout, prawns, mussels, shrimp, mahseer (similar to the barbel), various carp and hilsa.

As with the rest of India's staples, fish can be cooked in a multitude of ways; fried, stewed, breaded, curried, poached, grilled, steamed or baked, and methods can change from one household to another, let alone state to state.

Dale, Panaji, Goa   *Pomfret, Dadar, Mumbai*   *Kalundra, Panaji, Goa*

India's west coast – from Mumbai down to Kerala – is famous for its seafood dishes showcasing the treasures of the Arabian Sea. Kerala is the biggest fishing state and produces delightful dishes such as **meen** (fish curry), combining coconut, tamarind and fish, the state's three primary crops. Huge, succulent prawns and fiery fish curries are just a couple of highlights of a trip to Goa, where locals claim to have more than 100 types of fish and shellfish. The fishing communities of the Konkan Coast – sandwiched by these two states – are also famous for their seafood dishes. Many of the most popular restaurants in cosmopolitan Mumbai specialise in the seafood cuisines of these regions.

You may also have heard of bombay duck and be surprised to learn that it's not duck at all but a pungent salted fish known as **bombil** which, apart from the curious misnomer, has little to recommend it.

On the east coast, there's hardly a main meal in Orissa which won't feature fish, and in the far northeast, the Assamese go weak at the knees for **tenga**, a sweet-and-sour fish stew made with **rohu** (a type of carp). Punjabis are also keen on scaly snacks and have found that they go particularly well in their beloved tandoor.

A fishing boat off Benaulim beach catches the last of the days rays, Goa

STAPLES

Pomfret fry from the Mezban Restaurant in Hotel Asma Tower, Kozhikode, Kerala

Lads from the Panaji fishmarket show off their latest catch of mackerel

But it is in West Bengal, where seafood is actually spurned, that fish is king. Bengalis don't like the taste of saltwater fish but fortunately their state is puddled with ponds and lakes, and irrigated by rivers teeming with a rich variety of fish. **Hilsa**, a relative of the herring is the most popular despite having lots of small bones with which to contend. Even Brahmins of this state eat fish, while their brethren elsewhere in India are pure vegetarian. Perhaps it was they, in an attempt to retain their pure status, who came up with **jal toori**, the Bengali word for fish that translates as 'fruit of the sea'. Bengali fish curries are typically laced with nose-tingling mustard which could well be the only flavour the first-timer detects.

Fishing nets dry in the sun on the banks of the Brahmaputra River, Guwahati, Assam

Shorshe Maach (Mustard Fish Curry)

Ingredients

500g (16oz)	rohu cutlets (you could substitute it with carp or even a saltwater fish like trevally)
3 tbs	mustard seeds
1½ tsp	salt
1 tsp	turmeric
½ cup	mustard oil (this greatly contributes to the flavour, but you may substitute it with vegetable or sunflower oil)
6	green chillies

Grind the mustard seeds then mix them in ½ cup water with half the salt and half the turmeric. Coat the pieces of fish with the remaining salt and turmeric. In a wok, heat the oil until it smokes. Lower the flame and lightly fry the fish on both sides. You can do it a few pieces at a time. Put all the pieces of fried fish in the wok and pour over the mustard paste. Add one more cup of water (the pieces of fish should just be covered with water) and simmer the fish for 15 minutes. Just before taking it off the fire add the green chillies whole, for their aroma. Bengalis always drizzle a little raw mustard oil over the fish as it adds a wonderful nose-tingling zing. Serve with plain rice.

Serves 6

STAPLES

There is a general shift towards large-scale operations that not too far into the future will threaten the survival of many fishing communities. In fact, overfishing by mechanised vessels is already alarming conservationists who fear the depletion of fish stocks along the west coast. A visit to a traditional fishing village is an absolute must for any traveller (even if you're lounging on a beach and gawking at the locals in some Goan hideaway). In many places fishing is still carried out according to tried and trusted methods, and there are few mechanised fishing craft. Old, toothless men pull the nets next to young, smiling boys; the womanfolk wait on the beach to help with the haul; silvery mounds of fresh fish slap and gasp as tourists soak in the unhurried atmosphere of life by the sea; the men divvy up the catch; cooks rub their hands; and within an hour your fish has joined you for dinner.

There are dedicated fish markets near all major fishing areas and most towns and cities within reach of the coast. There are also usually fish stalls in the regular markets. You won't need to be told but take care when selecting fresh fish: make sure the fish smells fresh and mild, that the gills are red (although not too red because some mongers use red dye to make yesterday's catch look fresh), the eyes bright and the flesh firm.

Vegetables

Indian fruit and vegetable markets are mesmerising, a feast for the eyes and foreplay for the palate. With an estimated 600 million vegetarians, you'd reckon that India had something special going on in the garden, and you'd be right. Indians, even certified carnivores, love vegetables. They are served at every main meal, and **sabzi** (vegetables) is a word recognised in every Indian language.

With its climatic range, India is able to grow more vegetables than most other countries, and because the majority of the population depend on veggies for their vitamins, cooks have come up with zillions of ways to cook them. Without intensive farming or large commercial hothouses, the seasonal variations in Indian vegetables are clear-cut and help shape the menus of restaurants and homes alike. If you travelled around sprightly enough you could follow your favourite vegetable around the subcontinent; cauliflower tour anyone?

There is no meat-and-three-veg here; vegetables play much more than supporting roles. They are rarely just boiled or steamed, instead they're generally cooked **sukhi** (dry) or **tari** (in a sauce). Within these two categories they can be fried, roasted, curried, stuffed, mashed, combined, wrapped in batter and made into a **pakora** (fritter) or **bhaja** (vegetable fritter), made into a kabab or kofta, whatever takes the cook's fancy that day.

A proud spinach seller from Sabzi Mandi, Udaipur

Most of the vegetables you're probably familiar with grow here, although you might see several different species of the same thing. Potatoes are ubiquitous and popularly cooked with various masalas, cooked with other vegetables, mashed, spiced or fried for the street snack **aloo ki tikki**. Onions are fried with other vegetables, ground into a paste for cooking with meats, and used raw in relishes or as garnish. Heads of cauliflower are a surprising feature at the Indian market and are usually cooked dry on their own, with potatoes to make **aloo gobi**, or with other vegetables like carrots and beans. Indian carrots are small, thin and sweet, and are sometimes used in sweet snacks such as **gajar halwa** (sweet made with carrot, dried fruits, sugar, condensed milk and lots of ghee).

Plain okra is usually transformed into a taste sensation by being prepared dry with spices. Likewise, when cabbage gets the sweet and sour treatment from tamarind it is unrecognisable. Bland marrow gets stuffed and joins the party.

In late summer, cobs of roasted corn emerge as a popular street snack in North India. Fresh green peas turn up stir fried with other vegetables in pulaos and biryanis, and in one of North India's signature dishes, **mattar paneer** (peas and fresh cheese). Zesty tomatoes are used across the subcontinent in salads, sauces and even soups. **Brinjal** (eggplant; aubergine) come in all different shapes, shades and sizes and their majestic, passionate, deep purple colour will have you swooning over them at the market. After seducing shoppers, eggplant are often sliced, deep fried and served as a delicious side dish.

All over South India, white pumpkins are smashed outside homes and offices as part of the Dussehra celebrations (see Dussehra in the Celebrating with Food chapter). White pumpkin is an auspicious vegetable and their use is said to bring good luck for the coming year (although if the pumpkin hurled at us from a balcony in Chennai had been on target, there might not have been a next year). When they are not being smashed or hurled at foreigners, white pumpkins make for a very tasty curry.

Dwarf gourds   *Young okra*   *Saijna danta*

Indians are also very fond of their **saag** (a generic term for leafy greens), which can include mustard, spinach, fenugreek, white radish and chickpeas. Each region has its own way of preparing its greens, but you'll often find them made into sauces to accompany your deep-fried street snacks.

India is also home to some lesser-known vegetables. **Drumsticks** (so called because of their shape) are actually the fruit of the moringa tree and mostly grown in the south; locals eat them whole but we found the skin a little fibrous for our taste. **Gochian** is a black, beehive-shaped mushroom that grows only in Kashmir. Most stalls have an array of gourds (including snake gourd, ash gourd, bitter gourd, bottle gourd and white gourd) hanging from the rafters, looking like props from *The X-Files*. Kashmiris cook lotus roots with spinach or fish; Bengalis use the pith of the banana tree as a vegetable; and the **nendraparram** (a large reddish-coloured banana) of Kerala is used as a vegetable when raw. You'll find new and exotic items in every region of India and never think about vegetables the same way again, especially eggplant, ahem.

Palak Paneer (Fresh Cheese & Spinach Curry)

Ingredients

300g (10oz)	paneer (see paneer recipe later in this chapter), cut into 2cm dice
250g (8oz)	spinach, washed
½ cup	coriander leaves, chopped
2	green chillies
4 tbs	vegetable or sunflower oil
2 tbs	onion paste
1 tsp	ginger paste
1 tsp	garlic paste
2	large tomatoes, chopped
1 tsp	cumin powder
1 tsp	salt
1 tsp	garam masala

Puree the spinach with coriander leaves and chillies. Heat the oil in a wok. Put in the onion, ginger and garlic. Saute for 3 minutes – don't let it stick to the bottom of the wok. Add the tomatoes and cumin. Saute until the oil rises to the surface. Now pour in the spinach puree and add a cup of water and salt. Simmer the green spinach gravy for about 5 minutes. Add the paneer pieces and simmer for another 5 minutes. Finish with garam masala and remove from the flame.

Serves 4

Vegetables on the streets of Mumbai, from front to back is eggplant, snake beans, dwarf gourd, white gourd, capsicum, Indian snow peas and ridged gourd

Fruit

A scraggly old woman studies you curiously before walking away, the laden basket remaining steady on her head; a skinny dhoti-clad man stands behind his cart laden with ripe, green bananas; the season's first mangoes are being tended by a young girl who crouches shyly behind her basket; the grizzly, machete-wielding wallah suddenly comes alive and lops the top off a tender coconut; a shady-looking fellow entices passers-by with slices of freshly cut watermelon; a cherubic boy displays five sweet limes, splayed across his tiny hand, he doesn't hear the word 'no'; and the parade of roaming fruit carts dazzle you with the colours of their wares stacked in columns behind glass. And then, of course, there's the colour of the market. It's impossible to imagine Indian streets without the luscious veneer of fresh, enticing fruit.

From the exotic delights of the balmy south to the temperate favourites of the cooler north, India is a paradise for those who like to fruit. Indians relish the bounty when in season and preserve it when it's not. Whatever the time of year, there's always something to entice you, set your heart racing, and make your vitamin count surge.

Balancing paw paw and bananas, Karnataka

Selling coconut juice in New Market, Kolkata

A man and his watermelons, Panaji market

Guava sold on the streets of Bangalore, comes with a sprinkle of salt and chilli powder

Oranges which look a lot like large green mandarins, Colaba market, Mumbai

Sweet limes, also called sweet lemons, look very similar to oranges, Colaba market, Mumbai

There is no fruit sweeter or more flavoursome than fruit ripened on the plant. After all, the sole function of fruit is to entice animals like us to pick it, consume it, and help propagate the mother plant some place else. Therefore, consider the joy for us unfortunate supermarket plebs to come to India and be surrounded by fruit which has been picked from the plant at the perfect point of ripeness and rushed to some street or market for us to devour in all it's sensual splendour.

Everyone eats fruit, either as a refreshing snack or a complete meal in itself (you'll be amazed at how quickly a bunch of bananas can disappear). You'll also find fruit fashioned into a chatni or pickle, or a flavour in **kulfi** (ice cream; see Sweets later in this chapter) or other sweet treats. In most Indian homes, the final course of the main meal is a piece of fruit, peeled and cut by the woman of the house. Different varieties of bananas are found across the length and breadth of the country although Kerala has the most impressive range.

Ripe paw paws in Dadar, Mumbai

All along the southern coast, tropical fruits like pineapples, papaya and mangoes taste like they've fallen from the plate of Vishnu. Pineapple might not seem so exotic but if you've only sampled imported ones before, the sweet, intense flavours of Kerala's tropical beauties will make your head spin. Monstrous spiky, sweet jackfruit ripens in the southern spring.

If you're mad about mango you might consider emigrating; Indians enjoy more than 500 varieties, and supply 60% of the world with what they regard as the king of fruit. The most expensive and exquisite is Maharashtra's **alphonso**, which you'll find in Mumbai's Crawford Market. **Langra**, **dassehri** and **chousa** are among other irresistible varieties.

Citrus fruit such as oranges (which are actually yellow-green), tangerines, pink and white grapefruits, kumquats and sweet limes grow all over India. Himachal Pradesh produces delicious apples in autumn. Juicy and flavoursome strawberries abound in Kashmir during summer. Labour-intensive pomegranates, with their leathery jackets and sweet seeds encased in an inedible membrane, are winter favourites. Reach for a gorgeous guava to slake your thirst or buy a sweet-lime juice from a roaming juice cart.

Ladakh's apricots are prized and commonly feature in Muslim and Parsi cuisine as a symbol of wealth and extravagance. Dates are closely associated with Allah, and are often eaten to break each day's fast during Ramadan. There are two common varieties of starfruit (carambola), one used to add a sour taste to dishes and another sweeter species that's made into chatni.

Pears at Colaba market, Mumbai

Gooseberries at Colaba market, Mumbai

Coconut

In the south, coconut is called **shrifal** (the fruit of the gods) and is used in Hindu ceremonies as a reminder that we should all strive to make our lives full and rewarding. Auspicious occasions often begin with the breaking of coconuts and the offering of the flesh to the gods, and gifts are given with a coconut to symbolise respect.

The coconut tree is appropriately called **kalpravriksha** ('the tree that grants boons') and is one of the most useful trees in existence: the hard shells can be used for bowls; the fibrous outer shell is used for making ropes and nets; the strong-stemmed leaves are used for thatching; and the wood for building. And then there's toddy (see Regional Spirits in the Drinks chapter).

The coconut itself yields meat, milk and oil, and is one of the defining flavours of South Indian cuisine. Every home along the western seaboard has a coconut scraper for shredding the white meat that's made into chatni, garnish, or added to various curries, **appams** or **uttappams** (rice-flour and coconut milk pancakes), daals and rice dishes.

Coconut milk is not the clear fluid found just inside the shell, but the liquid extracted from the flesh of the kernel. This liquid is used for a wide variety of dishes, such as coconut-based curries and appams. **Copra** (dried coconut flesh) is pressed and made into coconut oil, a very popular cooking medium in Kerala.

Selling coconuts in New Market, Kolkata

Pickles, Chutneys & Relishes

No Indian meal – from a packed lunch to a full dinner – is complete without one, and often all, of the above. A relish could be anything from a roughly chopped onion to a delicately crafted fusion of fruit, nuts and spices. The best known is **raita** (yoghurt or curds combined with any number of vegetables or fruit, served chilled) which makes a delicious and refreshing counter to even the spiciest meal. Beyond this familiar staple, there is a mesmerising litany of 'little bits' which can go a long way to changing the flavour of your feast. **Chatnis** (chutneys) can come in any number of varieties, from sweet to salty, and can be made from many different vegetables, fruits, herbs and spices. Most chatnis are made fresh and usually served in small, non-metallic bowls.

But proceed with caution before polishing off that pickled speck on your thali; it'll quite possibly be the hottest thing you've ever tasted and usually the smaller the speck, the bigger the smash.

There are two standout ingredients in the gamut of Indian chatnis: coconut is the base for the ubiquitous coconut chatni in the south, and mint for the mint chatni in the north. Outside this division, each family will have its own favourite relishes, the recipes for which may have been passed down over generations. There are many specialised pickle stores dotted around India but many families still make their own (see the boxed text Thakur Bhrata).

STAPLES

A selection of chatnis, from left to right, onion & red chilli, coconut and coriander from the Bhopathy Restaurant, Chennai

THAKUR BHRATA

The weather and the food are milder in Himachal Pradesh. When locals want warmth, they freewheel down the Himalayan foothills, but when they want to spice up their food, they head to Thakur Bhrata, Shimla's most famous pickle shop.

Selling pickles in Shimla

The evening sun streams in the door of this quaint little shop, off Shimla's mall. It illuminates the tall glass containers holding an array of multi-coloured pickles. Rajinder squints through his spectacles but keeps his hand steady as he pours amber-coloured honey into a plastic bag. He is neatly groomed with grey hair and a soft moustache. He wears a shirt, a cardigan, gentle eyes and an easy smile. He looks like my grandfather, or everybody's grandfather the way we remember him.

"It's from Kashmir", he says breaking my stare.

"Huh?"

"It's from the nectar of wild flowers", says Vijay, the older brother who hands me a sample on a piece of paper. The fragrance and flavour are delicate and sweet. I have to sit down. The Thakur brothers carry on working, just like they have done for the last 30 years or so.

"It's delicious, I'll have some."

"Okay", smiles Rajinder, "in time" as he walks past, handing me a sheet of paper with a selection of pickles to sample.

The brothers move quickly and quietly around their shop, surrounded by 35 different types of pickles and preserves including ones made of cauliflower, carrot, green chilli, lime, mango, yam, radish, mushrooms, red stuffed chilli, garlic, turnip, ginger, lotus stem, apple, rose petals and quince. They live above the shop with their families, and make all these pickles before and after they close each day.

Customers sit on a long bench opposite the activity, unhurried and good humoured. I give up trying to get the undivided attention of either brother, and just talk out loud as I sample each coloured blob in the pickle cavalcade. A customer sidles up next to me and insists I write down the botanical name of each fruit. Vijay passes and hands off a splot of pickled **amla** (Indian gooseberry, considered to be the elixir of good health). It tastes tangy and sweet. Yes, the *emblica officinalis* wasn't bad at all.

Their father and uncle set up the shop over 60 years ago, and they've added only three new pickles to the range. Mushrooms, for example, weren't available in their father's time. You can look forward to kiwi pickle as soon as the fruit becomes affordable.

"Lord Shiva's favourite", says Rajinder, leaning over with a dot of pickled bel fruit (also known as wood apple and, eh, *aegle marmelos)*. It's apparently a great cure for dysentery and a good sweet-and-sour pickle to boot.

"Which is the most popular pickle?" I ask to nobody in particular.

"They're all popular", says Vijay. "Indians are very adventurous when it comes to food, especially spicy foods."

"They'll even go against the advice of their doctors when it comes to spicy foods", pipes in Rajinder.

An elderly woman with a distinctly British air buys a bag of crystallised ginger and offers me one, announcing that she has been shopping here since she was a schoolgirl. The zip of ginger melts in my mouth and just as I'm about to compliment her choice, she leans forward and whispers, "I know, they're not as good as normal" and walks in a huff.

"So, what's your favourite pickle," I ask the wall.

"The big lime", they both blurt through beaming smiles. My botanist friend nods sagely, and we are both offered a sample of 'the big lime', which is quite nice if you're into big limes.

"We eat it every day with daal and sabzi", says Vijay before they go back to ignoring me.

I'm about full by this stage, feeling pretty good, despite having had pickles for an entire meal for the first time in my life. I buy some of my favourites (and the big lime, just so I can bond with the brothers who I like very much) and make to leave when in walks a man who is introduced to me as being from Jammu. I'm polite, as anyone would be when introduced to a man from Jammu, and chat for a moment. Only after a few minutes does it dawn on me that the man from Jammu has made the 12-hour journey from his home specifically to shop at Thakur Bhrata, to get traditional almond oil which his family drink daily as a health tonic.

"Why come all this way?" I ask, incredulously, "do they give you a great discount?"

"No", he laughs. "Almond oil promotes health and long life, and my family have been buying it from this shop for over 20 years. They give me something which is pure and that's why I come."

With a small bottle of almond oil under my arm (which I still have minus a few suspicious slurps) I bid them farewell. At the door, I turn and say, "you'd think they'd give a discount after coming all the way from Jammu!"

Oh yes, got their attention there alright.

Martin Hughes

STAPLES

Dairy

The cow wasn't deemed sacred because of its grace, athleticism and good looks, it was protected because it's worth a lot more alive than dangling from a hook. Milk and milk products make a staggering contribution to Indian cuisine. **Dahi** (curds) are served with most meals and are handy for cooling down food. Many cookbooks use yoghurt instead of curd, but nobody in India uses the word 'yoghurt'. You might be turned off when you're served lumpy, watery curd, so leave your yoghurty preconceptions at home and enjoy healthy, delicious curd in raitas, chatnis, drinks, desserts and on their own.

Roadside curd sellers, Udaipur, Rajasthan

The best Indian sweets, particularly those from West Bengal are made with **chhana** (unpressed paneer), a godsend for the vegetarian majority; other sweets like barfi are made from the whey produced in the production of paneer; popular **lassi** (curds drink) is only one in a host of nourishing sweet and savoury milk-based drinks; **ghee** (clarified butter) is an essential cooking medium; and what would **chai** (tea) be without the half measure of milk? On top of that, cow dung is dried and burnt for fuel all over rural India. Risk all that for a steak and a couple of burgers? Nah, the cow is sacred, case closed.

Outside the bigger cities, to see India at its most relaxed, you should get up at dawn and start walking the residential streets. Besides the joy of baiting bleary-eyed rickshaw-wallahs who are too sluggish to harass you, you'll see the cows finally earning their keep, being milked by the side of the road. Within minutes of the cow's first moody moo, mothers and children emerge from homes with containers of all shapes and sizes, queuing up to get the warm milk. Men take off along the streets on bicycles laden with aluminium urns, selling the cow's frothy goodness to anyone who waves them down.

With their work done for the morning, the cows go back to feeding on whatever they can find and dropping smelly discs of fuel wherever they please. People go back home with the milk and start preparing the day's food. First they might make paneer, a soft, fresh cheese made with curdled milk. Paneer tastes quite mild and has a similar texture to tofu. It also takes-on other flavours well – and is particularly good when browned first and cooked with spinach or peas to make mattar paneer. It's a versatile ingredient, and can also be used to stuff breads, or mixed with grated vegetables to form 'meatballs'. **Gwalas** (milk shops) all over India sell fresh paneer but many people still make their own.

Paneer (Fresh Cheese)

You can buy paneer at any Indian grocery store but it is also very simple to make at home.

Ingredients
450ml	milk
1-2 tbs	fresh lemon juice (or as much as you need to curdle the milk)

Bring the milk to the boil and remove from heat. Stir in the juice until the milk separates into solids and a watery liquid (whey). Once coagulated completely (after a few minutes) strain and place the solids on a plate and weigh it down for several hours until all they whey has drained out and the paneer is compressed. You can then cut the paneer like tofu.

WHITE MEAT & COLOURFUL WEDDINGS

"We rely on milk in Rajasthan because the state is so dry and poor in agriculture, and cow's milk is especially good for physical and spiritual health", says Ravi Khaturia as he hands me my third rose-flavoured lassi. His milk shop sits in the shadow of Surajpole's main temple in Udaipur, Rajasthan. Along with an assortment of uncles and nephews, he runs the shop established by his grandfather more than 50 years ago.

Lunch is the only quiet time so Ravi invites me to chat. The day starts soon after dawn when he receives 200 litres of milk collected from local villages. Their first task is to boil huge vats of the stuff. From 8am, bleary-eyed commuters arrive on foot or by scooter and Ravi's men hand out glasses of white tonic without comment. All day long, women and children pump water from the well opposite the shop, and their exuberance lends the place the giddy atmosphere of a playground.

Ten workers busy themselves making: curd, paneer, **milk badam** (milk flavoured with saffron and almonds, sometimes reduced by simmering), rose-flavoured lassi, fresh cream, **rabri** (reduced flavoured milk, basically cream floating in thick milk) that simmers for a day, **srikhand** (literally, ambrosia of the Gods; yoghurt dessert), **kala kaand** (chewy white squares of reduced milk, like a completely solid rabri) and their very own **milkcake** (a brown version of kala kaand that's pressed and kept in the mould).

A sauntering cow stops by to see what Ravi and his mates are doing with her produce. She seems impressed and carries on. A long procession of colourfully clad women walks past, singing a cheerful song. One holds a stick piled with multi-coloured scrunchies.

"A bridal party out shopping", explains Ravi. "That's the bride with the hair things and they are her relatives and friends."

Ravi sits beneath an image of Krishna, who watches over the counter.

"Krishna is associated with milk. He 's known as the makhan chor, or 'thief of curds', but he's better known for seducing **gopis** (cowgirls)."

I ask him if there is therefore some honour in stealing milk.

"I don't know about honour but we have 10 people working here and they're all makhan chors", he laughs.

A thunderous racket comes down the main street and I rush out to see a wedding procession. A raggle-taggle band, wearing ill-fitting white and red uniforms, blaring trumpets and beating drums. Behind them a gloomy looking groom is bedecked in a turban and brightly coloured robes. He sits on horseback behind a small boy. The horse is draped with colourful and intricate textiles and mirrors, which shimmer in the sun. Scooters weave in and around the procession and it looks so much like Mardi Gras that I'm half expecting some young maiden to flash her breasts.

"It's the marriage season", says Ravi. "We see them all day this time of year. Many, many weddings. Good business."

Martin Hughes

Cooking Mediums

Just as each state uses different ingredients, different cooking mediums are used to give dishes their characteristic regional flavour. Peanut (groundnut) oil is the most common, especially important around Maharashtra and Gujarat. It is high in protein and has a neutral flavour and taste that makes it ideal for visiting palettes. Strong, pungent mustard oil is the preferred medium along the east coast, particularly West Bengal and Bihar as well as in parts of Punjab and Jammu & Kashmir. Discerning cooks in the south use light sesame oil, which imparts a nutty nuance to the food and has a high boiling point, making it ideal for frying. In the south and west, where coconuts grow so abundantly, coconut oil is widely used. To the uninitiated, the flavour coconut oil imparts in many dishes can be incredibly strong and more than slightly unpleasant. If, while in Kerala, you're unable to work out which ingredient is offending your taste-buds, it's probably the coconut oil. Many out-of-state Indians don't dig coconut oil either so there's absolutely no problem with asking the cook to use something else. On your travels, you may also find rapeseed (canola) oil – but never olive oil.

If these mediums divide the country, then **ghee** (clarified butter) brings it together again. Traditionally most cooking was done using ghee. Oils, on the other hand, were considered inferior products. Because ghee is high in saturated fat and expensive it is used more sparingly in Indian homes these days (unlike in Indian restaurants throughout the west). It's commonly used for frying, in desserts, smeared on top of roti, or added to any dish that needs a little lift. Ghee is still highly regarded because of the association dairy products have with purity and every meal prepared for an occasion at home or for a large-scale event will be cooked in ghee. The flavour of ghee cannot be surpassed, a fact known and taken to heart since the 8th century BC when it was first mentioned in historical Indian texts. Refrigerated, it can be kept for years and will last for several months stored at room temperature, no doubt part of its ancient appeal. Buffalo milk is sometimes used in place of cow's as it has a higher fat content and makes for a cleaner flavour.

You will be able to buy ghee at any Indian store. In fact, remarkably, the best product is imported to India from the Netherlands. It's simple to produce a quality version at home. To do so just melt unsalted butter in a heavy pan, simmer on a very low heat for about half an hour until the solids finally settle to the bottom. With a metal strainer, strain the golden ghee (the top layer of liquid) into a glass jar and voila – ghee for every occasion! A decadent version can also be made with pure cream, and Indian cooks, intending to make their own ghee will systematically collect the cream off milk over a couple of weeks and use it for ghee.

Nuts

At first glance, nuts don't seem to make much of a contribution to Indian
food. But, hang on, wasn't that dish fried in peanut oil, the sweet garnished
with the exotic chirongi nut, the stuffing flavoured with almonds and walnuts, and weren't ground almonds the base for that curry? Well, yes. Also,
pine nuts are produced throughout the Himalayan foothills where they are
used extensively to flavour rice, meat and vegetable dishes. Imported pistachios and almonds are used in many sweets (especially ice cream) and in
drinks. And finally, if it weren't for the betel nut, **paan** would be a curiosity instead of a way of life (see Paan later in this chapter).

Unhulled walnuts, Shimla, Himachal Pradesh

Polished and unpolished cashews, Panaji, Goa

Differing grades of cashews and almonds in Kujuwalla, a speciality nut shop, Panaji, Goa

STAPLES

Sweets

Indians have a mind-boggling range of **mithai** (sweets) to satisfy their voracious cravings, although sometimes the most surprising feature of the range is why they bother at all. Most of the sweets are sickly sweet and some of the mass-produced kinds are just plain yuk. Homemade sweets are more refined than the shop-bought sort but even so – maybe you have to have grown up on these 'treats' to really appreciate them. Nevertheless, sweets are an effective form of **baksheesh** (tip/bribe/sweetener) and make popular gifts.

Apart from the Bengalis, Indians only eat sweets on festive occasions. However, such occasions come around so often that there isn't much willpower required (see the Celebrating with Food chapter). The main categories are **barfi** (a fudge-like sweet made from milk), **halwa** (sweet which can be made with vegetables, cereals, lentils, nuts or fruit), **ladoos** (sweetmeats, usually ball-shaped) and those made from **chhana** (unpressed paneer) such as **rasgulla** (literally, ball of juice; cooked briefly in syrup before being served chilled) **cham cham** and **gulab jamun**. **Mysore pak** (a shortbread made with either gram flour and ghee, cashews and ghee, or just ghee) is almost a category of its own, although North Indians tell us it's a type of barfi. There are also simple sweets like **jalebis** (orange-coloured whorls of fried batter dipped in syrup) that you will see all over the country.

Every Indian has their favourite sweet shop, some of which are so famous you'll be lucky to get through the door during festival times. If you do, you'll see slabs upon slabs of these colourful sweets going into big gift boxes. By a long shot the best Indian sweets are the milk-based concoctions from West Bengal, where sweet making is an art (see West Bengal in the Regional Variations chapter).

Gulab jamun   *Paan bhog*   *Jalebis*

Barfi

Ladoos

Mysore pak

Kheer

Kheer (called **payasam** in the south) is India's favourite dessert. It's a rice pudding made with reduced milk to which rice is added while boiling. Unusual for Indian sweet things, it has a light, delicate flavour. Depending

on where you are, your kheer might be flavoured with cardamom, saffron, pistachios, flaked almonds, cashews or dried fruit, but the base remains the same. You can bet your sweet tooth that communal gatherings will conclude with delicious, creamy kheer or payasam, often served in earthenware cups or bowls.

Vermicelli

Yes the Italian pasta, is another common dessert, popularly made into a milk pudding or fried in ghee with raisins, flaked almonds and sugar to make a sweet, dry treat.

VARK – The Silver Lining in Indian Sweets

Many sweets come shimmering with a foil that you might presume to peel off and throw away; well you shouldn't because it's edible silver. It has no flavour or taste and is added to sweets for decoration. Small balls of silver are placed in leather pouches and hammered down into sheets of paper-thin foil. If you visit Tunde ke Kabab in Lucknow you'll get an idea of how much banging takes place and how loud it can be. Each year, more than 13 tonnes of pure silver are converted into this edible embellishing foil.

Sweet paan wrapped in vark, Hyderabad, Andhra Pradesh

JAGGERY

Indians have an unrivalled penchant for sweet things and there's no way that plain old sugar could meet all their sweet cravings. They extended their culinary range by coming up with another sweetening agent, known as **jaggery** (or **gur**) which is made at the first stage of sugar production. Enormous cast-iron pots of sugarcane juice are simmered for hours until the juice thickens. It's then poured into moulded trays where turns into the hard fudge-like bricks you'll see piled up at markets and street stalls throughout the country, attracting various black and yellow insects. In West Bengal, a speciality jaggery is made from date juice.

Although it's sometimes used interchangeably with sugar, jaggery has a distinctly musky flavour of its own. Jaggery can be crumbled and added to lentils and sweets, and it melts down into a thick, syrupy liquid that is added to drinks. It is also slightly alcoholic and used to make liquor in central and southern villages.

Gulab jamun

These golden delights are deep-fried balls of milk dough soaked in rose-flavoured syrup. You'll see them in homes, restaurants, and street stalls (although you might lose your taste for them once you've seen flies floating around in the syrup of the street kind).

Cashew kulfi, Chennai

Kulfi

This is a delicious, firm-textured Indian ice cream made with reduced milk and flavoured with any number of nuts, fruits and berries. It's our favourite Indian sweet thing but, disappointingly, hard to find outside summer (unless you're invited to an Indian wedding). Western-style ice creams are taking over in a big way and kulfi is getting squeezed out. You can find kulfi on sticks like western ice-lollies, but nothing competes with the fresh, homemade kind. There's a terrific kulfi store opposite Chowpatty Beach in Mumbai.

Paan

Don't be put off when you find yourself having a conversation with a chap who refuses to open his mouth. He'll talk all right, but through clenched teeth. His lower lip will jut out to stop him dribbling. Every now and then, he'll decorate the pavement with blotches of red spit. He's not mad and doesn't have a disorder, it's just that you're interrupting a paan moment.

Paan is a sweet, spicy and fragrant mixture of betel nut, lime paste and spices such as aniseed, cloves and cardamom, wrapped up in a betel leaf. It's eaten as a digestive and mouth freshener, although that's just half the story. The betel nut is mildly narcotic and, while most people chew it only after meals, some paan aficionados go through paan the same way heavy smokers consume cigarettes. The tobacco content is also a major reason for paan addiction. If you chew a lot of this stuff, and over many years, the betel nut will rot your teeth red and black. This accounts for the number of men you'll encounter who look like they'd had their faces kicked in the night before.

There are two basic paan types; **mitha** (sweet) and **saadha** (plain, often with tobacco). All over India men and women will confide in you that they have one vice which they can't resist, and it invariably turns out to be paan. Well, it should be easy for you to resist the foul tobacco version but a small parcel of mitha paan is an excellent way to finish a satisfying meal and short-term use is of no harm at all. You'll soon find yourself walking out of restaurants and immediately heading for the nearest paan wallah, whom you'll find in a jiffy, for they are as common here as bumpy roads. The wallahs make paan to order and there are dozens of different ingredients that can go in the mix – it may even include opium if you've got enough cash and contacts. Some wallahs have made fortunes through the quality of their product and the extravagance of their rich and famous patrons. You're probably neither, so just ask for the mitha paan and be on your way. Pop the whole parcel in your mouth and chew slowly, letting the juices secrete around your gob. When you've chewed the flavour out, spit the remains onto the street (there really is no point in trying to be discreet).

A paan wallah at Howrah Station, Kolkata

STAPLES

Making unsweetened paan

Betel nut

The nuts of the betel palm – no relation to the tree that provides the betel leaf – hold special significance in Indian life. Historically, kings would place a betel nut in their court and anyone willing to accept a challenging task would pick it up. To give somebody paan is a mark of great respect (although you should check that the person eats paan beforehand, otherwise it could be a mark of simple ignorance). Shah Jahan, he who built the Taj Mahal, once caught his daughter with a man he didn't care for. He smiled and offered the unapproved beau a betel leaf. The betel leaf was packed with poisonous ingredients but the beau – although suspicious – could not risk offending the emperor, thanked him, started to chew and commenced dying.

drinks
of india

Sweet, milky **chai** (tea) is the drink of the nation and is the perfect antidote to the rigours of travel. Coffee provides comfort in the south and there is a tempting host of juices and dairy drinks to slake your thirst. Times are tougher for tipplers, although there is a plethora of beers as well as fine local whisky, fiery **feni** from Goa and terrifying illegal spirits.

Alcoholic Drinks

Considering other Indian traditions, it's surprising to learn that many Indian men drink. And most of them drink with the sole intention of getting blotto. Women don't, for they are society's standard bearers (and other such vague 'complicated' tosh made up by Indian men). Only prostitutes imbibe or pour drinks, and most Bollywood movies are packed with heaps of supporting imagery.

Most Indians don't stock booze at home, instead they duck into dimly-lit bars, drink in a hurry and return to sulking wives. More than three quarters of India's drinking population quaffs 'country liquor' such as the notorious **arrack** (liquor distilled from coconut palm sap) of the south. The same rot comes with quaint names like **Amanush** (Inhuman) and **Asha** (Hope) in the north. This is the poor-man's drink and millions are addicted to the stuff. It is cheap, gives an instant high and tastes ghastly. If you're a glutton for punishment or feel compelled to sample some, make sure you drink the government-distilled variety. Each year, hundreds of people are blinded or even killed by the methyl alcohol in illegal arrack.

Only rich, educated high-fliers keep well-stocked cabinets, drink five days a week and throw parties on weekends. The focus here is on anything foreign, and the latest international trends are tracked and adopted (a bootlegger's dream).

"Fear thou not, for I am with thee", divine assistance in a Panaji bottleshop, Goa

Spirits

About a quarter of India's drinks market comprises Indian Made Foreign Liquors (IMFLs). You'll probably notice that well-known brands taste vaguely familiar but somehow unpleasant.

The base of most spirits manufactured here is Extra Neutral Alcohol (ENA; rectified spirit). This is a clear, flavourless spirit made from molasses, a by-product of the thousands of sugar mills that dot the Indian landscape. Rum is therefore the only authentic Indian spirit as it's the only one that's supposed to be made from molasses.

Cheap whisky is made from ENA and artificial whisky flavour, mid-price whisky is ENA and scotch for flavour, high-price whisky is ENA and lots of scotch for flavour. This applies to every spirit on sale except the higher-end dark rums like Old Monk, Contessa or Royal Treasure. Cheaper ones are, you guessed it, ENA and artificial rum flavour.

Peter Scott Whisky, Khody's Rum and Blue Riband Gin at the Victoria Hotel, Bangalore, Karnataka

THE PATIALA PEG

The night before the England cricket team was to play the Maharaja of Patiala's side, he got them drunk by pouring whopping 120ml spirit measures. After a generous pour, you may hear people say "Oh God, he's poured a Patiala!"

Fernandes and Filhos' bottleshop, Panaji, Goa

Bagpiper – hold your breath (you have to when you're drinking it) – is India's largest-selling whisky, and the 14th most popular whisky in the world (even though it's only sold in India). India's other 'millionaire' brands (those which sell more than a million cases a year) come with dignified names like Gilbey's Green Label, Director's Special, McDowell No 1, Aristocrat, Officer's Choice and Diplomat. They all taste pretty much like the IMFLs.

However, it's not all doom and rectified spirit gloom for the whisky drinker. Peter Scott, Antiquity and Solan No 1 (in that order) could all stand proudly in the international drinks cabinet. They've all got a little rectified spirit but there's enough malt to kill its taste. Lots of low-end international brands are imported in bulk and bottled in India; regulations will be relaxed from 2002 making premium brands available, to the few who can afford them.

BAM BAM BOLE!

Shiva, one of Hinduism's two most important gods, spent a good deal of his time off his rocker on **bhang** (form of cannabis). Today his followers partake in this perfectly legal pastime and get their supply from government-run bhang shops. The very strong, mind-altering, and frequently sick-inducing pot is added to drinks like **lassi** (curds drink) and is particularly popular during Hindu festivals.

DRINKS

Regional Spirits

Tribal communities have a rich history of local alcohol production, and what they traditionally brewed and distilled was much more palatable and healthy than the rot they are forced to drink by the government today.

The best-known drink is a clear spirit with a heady pungent flavour called **mahua**, distilled from the flower of the mahua tree. It's brewed in makeshift village stalls all over Central India during March and April, when the trees bloom. Mahua is safe to drink as long as it comes from a trustworthy source. The flower ferments naturally and animals like bears, monkeys and even elephants have a ferocious thirst for it. We've seen inebriated monkeys trying to jump across trees (missing them completely) and we've listened to a herd of elephants singing *Old Lang Syne*, although we were also on the mahua.

Rice beer is brewed all over east and northeast India (see the boxed text A Laopani Party later in this chapter). In the Himalaya you'll find a grain alcohol called **raksi**, which is strong, has a mild charcoal flavour and tastes vaguely like scotch whisky. Raksi is a delightful drink in cold weather, especially when it is being distilled drop by drop in front of you.

Wherever you find palm trees (as in Kerala), you'll see strong, skinny men scaling trees with large pots. Then you'll hear the rhythmic tapping of buffalo bone against the palm bud. These chaps are called toddy tappers and if you befriend one, you'll get to taste **toddy**, a delicious natural wonder, straight from the source. The evening toddy is stronger in alcohol (around 15%) than the morning variety. Toddy shops usually mix the drink with water to extend it, and add cucumber, pumpkin or chemicals to preserve it. Sample it straight from the toddy tapper's pot if you can (after he's strained it for red ants).

Toddy, Kerala

Coconut and cashew feni, Panaji, Goa

Ferocious, fiery **feni** is the preserve of Goa's fun-loving Christians, and our primo Indian spirit. Coconut and cashew are the two main varieties. Coconut feni is light and unexceptional but the much more popular cashew feni – made from the fruit of the cashew tree – has a smooth intense flavour that's worth bringing home. Like any spirit, quality depends on the producer, but even the stuff you get in back-street bars in Panjim is palatable, warming and full of buzz. If you're in Goa for an extended stay, or you're just plain lucky enough, you'll find a good source of this sippable sensation. Goan feni aficionados can make feni from a variety of ingredients, and the most refined drink we had on the subcontinent was Patrick's "rutsanerbs" feni in Palolem. Some time after tentatively tasting this mysterious feni creation, we found out it was made from "roots and herbs".

DRINKS FROM THE RAJ

While much is made of Anglo-Indian cuisine, British drinking patterns had a more far-reaching impact. The local drink, **arrack** (liquor distilled from coconut palm sap), was too rough for refined British palates and it was combined with citrus juice, spices, water and sugar, a concoction that apparently had existed in India for thousands of years. The British called it 'punch', after the Hindi word **panch** (five; the number of ingredients in the mix) and brought it to lawn parties around the world.

British colonists had been instructed to drink quinine tonic water as protection against malaria. In the hunt for a more agreeable flavour, they mixed this sharp-tasting liquid with one of their favourite tipples, and the gin & tonic was created.

And finally, Indian Pale Ale (IPA) was a bright and hoppy pale ale brewed specifically to survive the long journey from Britain to thirsty beer drinkers in India. A ship carrying IPA was wrecked soon after it left Liverpool and some casks of the beer were recovered and sold in the local market. The new drink was keenly received and later became popular as 'bitter' throughout Britain.

Beer

Most travellers look forward to a beer at the end of a hot, dusty day, but the quality of Indian brews generally isn't worthy of your thirst. Indians don't go in much for beer, and as government taxes push the price up, a bottle usually costs a few times more than your entire meal. Despite the fact that there is a plethora of local and national brands, there's little to tell them apart as most are straightforward pilsners around the 5% alcohol mark and contain glycerine as an emulsifier.

But this certainly doesn't stop us from drinking it. No, we'd gladly pay through the nose for a cold beer. Outside the cities and tourist centres, you'll struggle to find a beer cold enough to slake your thirst. Make sure you feel the bottle first before letting the waiter open it, for the only thing worse than drinking lukewarm Indian beer is blowing your budget in the process.

Most travellers champion Kingfisher, which is available nationwide, although Royal Challenge, Dansberg, Golden Eagle, London Pilsner and Sandpiper are our favourite national brands – all reasonably quaffable. Solan, from Himachal Pradesh and the highest-altitude brewery in the world at 8000 feet, is also a reasonable choice. Goa has several top-notch brews; look out for King in particular. Fosters and San Miguel are now also manufactured and bottled in India, but sold only in two states: Goa and Maharashtra. In Bangalore, Mumbai, and Chandigarh, draft lager is widely available. (See the Where to Eat & Drink chapter.)

Kingfisher Premium, a popular Indian beer

Wine

Oh dear, it seems like we're being very hard on Indian alcohol. Anyway this is no place to stop. Indians will tell you that Grovers from Goa is the best wine in India, which to our mind is like claiming to be the best slalom skier in the desert.

Tom's Wine shop, Panaji, Goa

DRINKS

A LAOPANI PARTY

"So, what's the local drop around here?" I asked innocently as we drove through rural Assam. Our guide barked instructions to the driver, who yanked into a U-turn and drove down a side road.

"You'll see," he said.

Scrambling along the narrow dirt tracks running through villages, chickens fled from our path while children ran into it. We stopped to ask directions, and two young men jumped into the car. We drove whichever way the boys pointed, the car heating up with all the anticipation of a Friday night on the town.

Within minutes of mentioning alcohol, we were in the village of Marra Kuchi, being ushered into Labandu's house and a dim room where rice was spread out on a tarpaulin.

"Fermenting" he said, brushing the flies from his face and showing us into another room where about six of his friends sat around on the mud floor.

"Laopani?" said Labandu, placing a jug of cloudy liquid in front of Greg and me. Suspicious of the hygiene, Greg rubbed his belly and pulled a sick face. For my part, I was determined to drink his share as well as my own.

"Cheers" I said, raising my glass to the company who were already drinking. Alarm spread across their faces and they stopped smiling. Maybe it was the dead heat in the room, but having gone this far in my cultural tutorial, I insisted on clinking everyone's glass. One chap wrapped both his hands around his vessel to protect it, while the others pensively submitted to the loopy foreigner. The beer was warm but pleasant, and it improved after each sip. It tasted like Tibetan rice beer, if that's any guide.

"So, do you get drunk on this", I asked through the guide.

"No, we grow up drinking it. Even our children drink it. It makes them strong. We've been drinking all day. Do we look drunk?" They smiled more than was strictly normal but, no, they didn't seem drunk. While the men and women around the village looked strong, they moved slowly and with grace, and they spoke in much softer tones than other Indians we'd met.

We arrived in the middle of a religious festival – about a one-in-ten chance at anytime in India – which is why they had been drinking all day. They said they were honoured by our visit and made us promise to join them for their big festival, Kati Bihu in March/April, an Assamese festival in honour of Lakshmi, the goddess of their harvest. One fellow said he would kill a chicken, another promised a pig.

Labandu brought another tall glass and several small ones. "Nice" he said, handing me the tall glass and filling it to the brim with a rice spirit also called laopani. It tasted a little like a wood cordial if there were such a thing, or diluted retsina. Anyway, it was very easy to drink and I necked it. The others got small glasses but they seemed very pleased all the same. Labandu whispered to our guide who whispered to me "yours is the true spirit, there is no water added." I was thrilled with the VIP treatment, which made me feel all fuzzy inside. Or perhaps that was the spirit …

"So, is this illegal?" I asked. The drinkers laughed but Labandu shrugged his shoulders.

"Ah, a few rupees to the police."

"They're his best customers!" another piped in.

When it was time to go, we headed out in the fresh air and hot sun, both of which immediately confirmed that I had been drinking. They insisted we go look at their temple. We weren't allowed inside but they opened the door and we peered through from a distance. Well actually, I hung at the back of the group, trying to get my bearings in the dazzling sun and studying the bottle of laopani that Labandu had given me. I think I was smiling a lot. I joined the palms of my hands and said "namaste" to everyone who had come out to see the foreigner.

"Namaste, namaste, namaste!"

Greg pointed out that I was bowing the way the Japanese do, which looked "odd".

After I had bowed to everyone in the village, Greg decided it was best to take my laopani-laced body back to the hotel.

"Group photograph!" I announced before Greg bundled me into the car, which was probably for the best.

Martin Hughes

The author with Labundu (centre) and the guide, Moira Kuchi near Guwahati

Non-Alcoholic Beverages
Tea

Legends abound about the origin of tea, India's national beverage. Our favourite – and, even for a legend, the least plausible – is that the Buddha once fell asleep during meditation and decided to cut his eyelids off in an act of penance. The lids grew into the tea plant which, when brewed, banished sleep.

Tea growing really took off under the British and now India is the world's largest producer, exporter and consumer of the stuff. There are two tea plants, the original *camellia sinensis* from China (cultivated in Darjeeling and the Nilgiri Hills) and *camellia assamica*, discovered in Assam.

Tea workers pick on a plantation near Guwahati, Assam

DRINKS

Of the three main tea-growing regions, Darjeeling (in West Bengal) and the Nilgiri Hills (in the Western Ghats; Nilgiris means 'blue mountains') produce the best tea, while Assam grows a strong-flavoured variety that is only really good for blending or in chai. If Darjeeling' is the 'champagne of teas', then perhaps the Nilgiri is a palatable whisky, and Assam could be considered the mixer.

But while the hills of Darjeeling and Nilgiri grow tea for the world's connoisseurs, you won't find many porcelain cups and dainty pinkies among India's tea drinkers. **Chai** is Hindi for tea but the similarities with the familiar beverage stop there.

Glasses stacked ready for service at a streetside chai stall, Udaipur, Rajasthan

Chai

Chai is the drink of the masses. It transcends cast, creed and class, and an invitation to share it is on the first page of India's guide to hospitality. Chai won't be for everyone, but if you give your discerning taste-buds a rest and immerse yourself in its culture, you'll experience the very essence of this mad and magical country.

Chai is made with more milk than water, more sugar than you'd care to think about, and is spiced with cardamom in winter and ginger in summer. A glass of steaming sweet milky and frothy chai is the perfect antidote to the heat and stress of Indian travel and, not only is it a tonic for body and soul, sharing chai provides gilt-edged opportunities to meet and befriend the locals. Even if you meet somebody away from the chai stand, you'll be invited to seal the acquaintance over a cup or two. On top of all that, it is also one of the safest beverages for us travellers to drink (just don't look too closely at the smudges on your vessel).

As chai is always served hot enough to scald fingers and tongue alike, sip slowly or even better, ask for another glass and pour a little bit into the cold glass at a time. Or you can do as the locals do and pour it from one glass to another to make it froth up. Many Indians, particularly in restaurants, drink their chai from an accompanying saucer.

Chai for six, Orissa

A chai wallah taps his trusty teapots, Lucknow, Uttar Pradesh

DRINKS

Wherever chai is served, men gather to rile one another, discuss politics, gossip, read newspapers and debate. Every stall is like a little oasis for the traveller, an instant retreat from the frantic, dusty pace of life on the streets. There will be jars of various sweet biscuits to choose from and a place selling fried snacks won't be far away. If you like you'll be left alone but if you're willing you can answer questions relating to your good name sir, your country of origin, your marital status, and how often you 'make' sex with your partner.

The disembodied voice droning 'chai, chai garam' (hot tea) will become one of the most familiar and welcome sounds of your trip. You can have a 'boy' bring it to even the most basic hotel room – whether he's 10 or 80, if he fetches tea or carries your bag, he's the boy – although without the company or the respite, it tastes just like sickly sweet, milky tea instead of the very essence of India.

If chai's not your cuppa, you'll be able to find the familiar formula of black tea, milk and lumps of sugar in multi-starred hotels and in the planters clubs of tea-growing regions. You can order 'tray' or 'separate' tea just about anywhere but if it's not the establishment's usual offering, you'll wish you hadn't.

Darjeeling Tea

The fragrant, light tea produced in Darjeeling will be familiar to even part-time connoisseurs. But in reality how many of us have actually tasted it? The startling fact is that while there are 12 million kilograms of tea produced in Darjeeling per annum, more than 60 million kilograms of 'Darjeeling' is sold around the world each year! All this should change in the next few years, though, as Darjeeling tea will soon need to have an authenticity trademark to be sold under that name.

There are many shops in Darjeeling selling local tea, predominantly to tourists. Many are rip-off merchants charging outlandishly high prices for cheap brews. Avoid teas in fancy boxes because they are often stale and not even from Darjeeling. The best way to judge the quality of the leaves is by their aroma. Take a sample of tea in your closed fist, breath moisture in to it, open your hand and assess the fragrance. You might have no idea what you're looking for, but you'll at least look like you do.

The highest quality Darjeeling tea is graded as SFTGFOP, which stands for Special Fine Tippy Golden Flowery Orange Pekoe. Apparently a guide-book writer mistook the 's' for 'super' and, fed up explaining the mistake to disgruntled travellers insisting on the super fine stuff, many local shops changed their labels to agree with the error. Every estate has this grade available, which only means that it is that particular garden's best tea. As the first letters of the grade are dropped, you come down in quality, until you eventually end up with OP, just no-frills orange pekoe. In theory, the OP from one garden could be as good as the SFTGFOP from another.

Quality also depends on the season. The most expensive and eagerly-awaited teas are from the 'first flush', which are harvested from late February. The young leaves give the lightest, most delicate and fragrant Darjeelings. Then there is spring's 'second flush', 'summer flush' and 'autumn flush' and the teas get stronger and flatter each harvest.

You'll want to bring some Darjeeling tea home as a souvenir and, naturally, you'll want the best. However, Castletown Estate in Darjeeling sold 1kg of its tea for US$220 so you might think about pulling your neck in a little. Lipton's Green Label is a reliable Darjeeling; it costs around Rs 80 for 500g and is available at all grocers.

A visit to a tea garden is a must and lots of them open their doors to tourists. Try to get to a garden away from the town; the more remote the better. Drop into the Planters Club to say hello, seek advice, and enjoy a nice cuppa (see the Darjeeling map). If you wouldn't mind, apologise for the metal tea strainer we stole as a souvenir. If you can make it out to Marybong Estate far up in the remote Himalayan foothills you'll be able to savour one of the finest teas you've ever tasted while looking out over a precipice of paradise. Bring some sweets for the field workers!

A tea worker plucks tips from a Darjeeling tea bush, Duncan's Marybong Tea Garden

DRINKS

DARJEELING

Lloyd Botanical Gardens

Chowk Bazaar
Catch glimpses of the Himalayas from this low-key fruit and vegetable market.

Old Super Market complex

Chowrasta

Chowk Bazaar

Sadar Hospital

Windamere Hotel
Afternoon tea with cucumber sandwiches, spectacular views, warm hospitality and toffee-nosed tourists.

JN Mirai Rd

Hill Cart Rd

HD Lama Rd

DB Thapa Rd

(The Mall)

Dr Zakir Hussain Rd

Planter's Club
A pleasant place to hang out, talk tea, ping pong and bounce billiards.

RN Sinha Rd

NC Goenka Rd

NB Singh Rd

Clubside

Nehru Rd

Dekeling
Tibetan restaurant with friendly mamas and good momos.

Hill Cart Rd

Laden La Rd

JP Sharma Rd

Park Restaurant
Where the locals go for terrific North Indian grub.

Tenzing Norgay Rd

Laden La Rd

Joey's Pub
A very ordinary bar, perhaps the best in India.

Gandhi Rd

Nathmull's Tea
Informative connoisseurs of Darjeeling tea and reliable merchants with a mail-order system.

0   50   100 m
0   50   100 yd

DRINKS

1. Plucking tea bushes

2. Loading leaves into 'withering troughs'

3. Tea leaves being processed through a 'roller' otherwise known as a mangle

4. Fermented leaves coming out of the dryer

5. The sorting room where tea is, well,...sorted

6. Choice tea being poured from a contraption known as 'Andrew's breaker'

7. Tea ready for examination by a tea master

8. Packed tea, Duncan's Marybong Tea Garden, Darjeeling, West Bemgal

DRINKS

CHAI & CRICKET IN KOLKATA

The term 'seething mass of humanity' makes sense once you've been in peak hour at Kolkata's (Calcutta's) Howrah station. Tides of people swirl around a yellow sea of waiting cabs while cops angrily lash out at reckless drivers. Beggars compete with sadhus; scrums form around ticket desks; passengers squeeze themselves onto trains; porters hiss to clear the way. All human life is here and, amid the maelstrom, there's a chap making chai.

His name is Umesh and he laughs in embarrassment when Himmat, my guide, asks if we can speak to him. He serves his chai in **kullarhs** (biodegradable earthenware cups), which you just discard after use. These cups impart a pleasantly earthy taste to the chai and, before plastic, they were used all over India. They are extremely cheap and of course, environmentally friendly, but still the nation chokes in polymers.

Squatting by a kerosene stove, Umesh answers questions – through Himmat – while making and selling chai: "Ten years ago, he lost his office job in Bihar and came to Kolkata looking for work. His friend gave him this job and he works every day from 4am until midnight, and gets paid Rs 40 a day. His friend, Bhola, had the money to buy the pots so he's the boss."

Himmat's bleeper goes off, for about the third time that hour.

"Sorry," he says meekly. "Cricket."

India is playing New Zealand in the final of the world knockout competition and he's receiving score updates on his pager. Indians are fanatical about their cricket and the crowd we've attracted is eager to know the score.

"None for 80" he says to nods and raised eyebrows.

Umesh hands us two more chais and continues talking: "He lives here" says Himmat, pointing into the station. His pager bleeps again.

"Tendulkar's gone." The crowd gasps. Umesh shakes his head and bangs the remains of the last batch of chai from the blackened pot, wiping it with a dirty rag. He fills the pot with water and milk and puts it back on the stove.

Himmat continues: "Every four months he goes back to his wife and family in Bihar and stays for two months. He couldn't do this job in Bihar because the people are too poor."

The milk comes to the boil and Umesh adds several pinches of tea leaves and sets it to brew. A sadhu walks up to our group, peers inside the circle and walks away dipping into his bag of puffed rice.

"He was shy and inexperienced when he first started [beep] one for 100, but now he enjoys it. He meets people and it passes the time."

I notice Umesh straining the tea through the same dirty rag he used to wipe the pot. He adds a heaped spoonful of sugar, then another, and another, and … I have to turn away.

"All of these people" says Himmat, pointing to the food and drink stalls

Bhola at his chai stall at Howrah Station, Kolkata

surrounding us, "come from the same village in Bihar. Everyone's here under the same circumstances, and they all support one another. That's what makes this tolerable." The people in the crowd begin to cheer themselves when the sound of Himmat's bleeper hushes them again.

"Dravid's been run out, two for 132."

I take my leave and go back to my hotel to watch the cricket with the assortment of porters, cooks, and receptionists assembled around a portable television at reception. 'Boys' are sent out all afternoon to fetch chai, and consumption increases with the tension as New Zealand put on an exciting run chase. I'm an honorary Indian when the match swings in India's favour, and a pesky foreigner when it doesn't. When the Kiwis win in a cliff-hanger – two balls to spare – a hail of polystyrene cups are hurled at the television, and I slink off to my room.

Martin Hughes

DRINKS

Coffee

While chai is the drink of the nation, South Indians share their loyalty with coffee – although it's often made with so much milk and sugar that you couldn't tell them apart. That said, in the more discerning establishments, you'll be pleasantly surprised with Indian coffee, most notably beans like Mysore Nuggets and the enchantingly named Monsoon Malabar.

If you like any of the coffee here, you've got Baba Budan to thank. In the 17th century, this pilgrim-cum-smuggler is believed to have left Mecca with seven coffee seeds strapped to his belly. Baba's beans bore fruit and Mysore (formerly a princely state, now the name of the charming city in Karnataka) became the birthplace of coffee outside Arabia. The British East India Company was the first to commercially cultivate the crop in India, which is now one of the world's largest coffee producers. There are coffee plantations all along Karnataka's hills and many people grow the beans in their own gardens.

Mysore Nuggets grow on the west-facing slopes of the Western Ghats at an altitude of 1000m. With extensive shade growth and favourable temperatures, these oversized nuggets are grown for extended periods and ripen slowly, resulting in a rich, thick and distinctly syrupy brew. Monsoon Malabar – named after the region in Kerala and the rainy season that shape its character – is another large bean with a unique flavour. Green coffee is stored and exposed to tropical winds for 2-3 months, during which time the beans absorb additional moisture that, after the beans are roasted, yields a rich, mellow beverage.

Water & Ice

You don't need to be told but only drink water that comes from a sealed bottle. Some travellers refuse bottles that don't have the additional plastic covering but if the cap is sealed, it's sealed, and there's no need to get neurotic about it. If you do, you'll miss out on blue-capped Bisleri, our favourite brand. Coca-Cola has it's own brand of mineral water and runs scare-mongering ads inferring that other brands aren't safe. Most of the mineral water is actually just treated tap water but is safe to drink.

Disposing of plastic is a huge problem for India so if you don't want to contribute to the crisis you could bring your own water bottle and purify the local supply (see the Fit & Healthy chapter). Also, look out for tourist places that supply purified water.

Freezing does nothing to kill the harmful bacteria in dodgy water so be cautious before going on the rocks. Indians will rarely use ice to chill soft drinks so unless it is an integral ingredient – like in the delicious lassis of Varanasi – you're best to go without.

Soft Drinks

Coca-Cola and Pepsi are in a race to paint their name on every available surface across India, and the bombardment of their advertising is suffocating. Young 'with it' locals are lapping up their sickly sweet concoctions. One day, we asked a shopkeeper for mineral water. He came with a coke and a smile.

"Mineral water", we corrected.

"But we have Coca-Cola", he said incredulously.

These – and local brands such as Thums Up – are generally safe to drink as long as you're not diabetic. **Masala soda** is the quintessentially Indian soft drink available at all drinks stalls. It's a freshly opened bottle of soda (thus safe), pepped up with a lime, spices, salt and sugar.

A few empties, Panaji, Goa

DRINKS

Taking a refreshing Limca break, a lemon-flavoured soft drink

Fresh lime and soda drink

Fruit Juices

Most of India's mind-boggling range of fruit is blended into juice at some stage. Restaurants think nothing of adding salt and sugar to intensify the flavours but if you just want vitamins, tell the waiter to leave them out. On the streets there are multitudes of fresh fruit vendors, tempting you with colourful fruit. Be very prudent about which ones you patronise and follow a well-heeled crowd. If the juice is ridiculously cheap, then it's probably been adulterated and you might just get a combo of water, ice and essence. If the watermelon looks too luscious, it has probably been coloured with dye. Indians have no problem with preservatives – that's why they embrace Coca-Cola et al.

The most popular street juices are made from sweet lemon and sugarcane, which is pressed in front of you by a mechanised wheel complete with jingling bells.

A juice seller makes sweet lemon juice, also known as sweet lime, Chandni Chowk, New Delhi

Jal Jeera

This is perhaps India's most therapeutic and refreshing indigenous drink, made of lime juice, cumin, mint and rock salt. It's sold in large earthenware pots by street vendors but if you're not feeling game, you'll also find it served in restaurants.

Tender Coconut

The juice from the green tender coconut is a safe and healthy alternative to the sometimes risky street juices. You'll find them all over the south and much of the north, and watching the machete-wielding wallah whop the coconut into a drink is half the fun. After you've drunk the juice, he'll whop the coconut some more, providing you with chunks of tasty coconut meat.

Milk-Based Drinks

Sweet and savoury **lassi** (curds drink) is popular all over India although the best are in the north. Some places give their lassi a little twist of their own flavour, something subtle like rose, but beware of places with dozens of flavours because it is probably a tourist joint and the lassi won't be any good. (For the best lassi in India, see the Varanasi map). **Falooda** is a rose-flavoured Muslim speciality made with milk, cream, nuts and strands of vermicelli. Hot or cold **badam** (milk flavoured with saffron and almonds) is an invigorating breakfast drink.

Badam milk with almond and pistachio

Rose Lassi

The quintessential Indian drink couldn't be simpler to make. You can experiment with flavours like saffron and cardamom, and garnishes like slivered pistachios or almonds. You can also make a savoury lassi with the likes of coriander and mint, replacing the sugar with a pinch of rock salt.

Ingredients

300ml (10 fl oz) plain yoghurt
                or curds
150ml (5 fl oz) water
1 tsp   rosewater
                 sugar to taste

Blend ingredients and chill before serving.

Lassi wallah, Varanasi

home cooking & traditions

The family is the fabric of Indian life, and each home its haven. While life's most important bonds are fastened in the privacy of each family fortress, doors are always open to visitors. Hospitality is an honour for the bestower, and as soon as you cross the threshold you become an honorary family member, wrapped in warmth and good cheer and treated to the treasures of India's finest cuisine.

If the home is shelter, then the kitchen is sanctity. Millions of Indians – traditional Brahmins and other upper castes – won't let food that's not prepared in their own kitchen pass their lips. Even those without such taboos cherish home-cooked food above all else.

Many rural homes keep livestock – 'pets' as they call them – and any space surrounding a house is used to grow fruit, vegetables, herbs and spices.

Women are the homemakers and cooking is their exclusive craft. Unless men learn how to cook formally or for business, they are utterly hopeless; lucky if they even know a few 'survival dishes' to sustain themselves when left alone.

The typical Indian woman works harder than her husband, with dual responsibility for earning money and keeping home. In public, she is expected to be demure and subservient, to maintain a low profile and avoid any situation or behaviour that could possibly bring shame on the family, like getting ideas above her station. The situation is "complicated and not easy to explain or understand" according to most Indian men. At home, away from the harsh realities of a largely prejudiced society, she feels most liberated and willing to share the intimacies of her life.

Home kitchen, Udaipur, Rajasthan

In this context, cooking is a vital form of expression and her cooking skills go a long way to defining her status and worth. She takes pride in what she prepares and knows the culinary keys to the hearts of all her extended family and friends. She doesn't own a cookbook and is unfamiliar with the concept. She learned the art from her mother and grandmother, a science that is passed down orally, instinctively and affectionately. She jealously guards her culinary secrets and the special touches she has acquired.

Millions of Indian women struggle to feed their families. Limited by lean daily wages, there is never a stock of food in her larder. The evening meal depends on how much can be bought on that particular day. Sometimes it might be **daal roti** (daal and bread) or even roti and onions; on a better day she could muster up a dish of spicy greens, and on the rare day that a fish or cut of meat is bought, she creates a curry with sheer ingenuity and the barest minimum of spices. She will be the last one to eat, after she has served and watched her family demolish the frugal meal. Sometimes she doesn't have enough to fill her stomach, but the others would have left the kitchen (where the meal is normally eaten) and there won't be anyone to commiserate her fate.

Above this stratum is the bulk of the rural and urban middle class. Though it's a struggle for them to make ends meet, a woman here has a chance to show her culinary skills. She is always on the lookout for fresh vegetable and bargains in the meat and fish market, and when prices fall she buys in bulk to make pickles and preserves to stock her larder. Planning economical and creative meals parallels the complicated managerial activity that this woman will never get a chance to test on professional turf. A majority of Indian women are still full-time homemakers, pandering to the different demands and tastes of her extended family – cooking and serving hot food to children and working people whenever they return home.

The contrast with the modern, urban affluent woman could hardly be more stark. She is educated, career-oriented and, in many cases, married for love and not by arrangement. She likes foreign cuisine and buys Tarla Dalal's cookbooks featuring Indianised versions of Italian, Mexican and Chinese food. She goes to special markets and pays way over the odds for foreign brands. She thinks going to TGI Fridays is a good night out. She watches Hollywood movies and finds out about the latest exfoliating techniques in lifestyle magazines. If she hasn't travelled she knows somebody who has.

She thinks that life is very hard for western women, and cannot fathom how they can simultaneously work and tend home. But she would never trade places; she has hired help (perhaps a poor village girl who lives in and takes care of the washing, childcare and cooking). Someone else drives her and perhaps somebody else comes in for an hour each day specifically to make roti or chop vegetables.

Strolling back to the kitchen in Barada near Udaipur, Rajasthan

She doesn't cook but talks as if she does. She does the shopping – perhaps over the telephone – because the help cannot be trusted. She knows what she likes and usually coaches the cook. Away from the table her main focus is keeping up with the Singhs and what she will do when it's her turn to organise the kitty party, the high point in the social lives of most urban housewives (see the boxed text Kitty Parties). In this Indian version of Ladies Who Lunch, groups of women get together regularly, contribute to a pool, and draw lots to see who will get the kitty and the responsibility of hosting the next lunch.

The middle class is expanding in pursuit of this lifestyle. They clamour to be seen as modern and thus elevate their status. This is a danger zone for traditional Indian cuisine as many consider their indigenous food to be old-fashioned and inferior. Mothers aren't cooking so daughters aren't learning, and grandmothers are lamenting the loss of tradition. It is unthinkable but a great many young modern Indian women can't cook and the foundations of Indian cuisine are looking more rickety by the modern minute.

KITTY PARTIES

At last my great day has come to end. I didn't know how I would go through it. Twenty ladies including two great cooks like Mrs Punjwani and Sheila Datta. After all, organising a successful Kitty Party is the greatest proof of your efficiency. And our group is so large and unmanageable. But of course as Mala says, the larger the numbers, the larger the kitty! So if 20 ladies put in Rs 1000 each month, it's Rs 20,000 a go! Mala is so wicked, she worked to get 20 ladies because she's determined to buy some diamond tops at Tribhovandas Bhimji. Sunny is too stingy to dish out the amount. But saving Rs 1000 from the household money is no big deal – no one notices so it quietly goes into the kitty. Put up with the expense of the lunch when it's your turn to host it, and then wait for the draw. If you're the lucky one, you get such a whopping sum. I realised the sense of this and agreed to join – even though I don't make good conversation like the others, let alone produce grand lunches!

My day of reckoning was drawing closer. And I was getting more and more panic-stricken – especially after the Tex-Mex spread Laila Shah dished out last month. What's all this Tex-Mex business? It looked like roti, chicken and **rajma** (kidney beans) to me, but the rajma was called 'chilli' and the roti 'tortilla' (don't make the mistake of pronouncing the 'l' – I went quite red when Laila corrected me). And then there was that fancy dip called 'guacamole' made of a fruit called avocado. It seems they sell for Rs 80 each at Khan Market and come from God knows where. It's only ladies who want to show off their cooking (and who have enough household help) who host parties at home.

I can't go through all that – so I took the easy way out and booked two tables at Thai-Chai. And I think the idea was brilliant because Thai food is such a hit nowadays. It's so much tastier than Chinese which is so bland and boiled-boiled. People just pretend to like Chinese – it's more likely that their husbands want to keep the weight off with that steamed stuff. Give me spicy curry and rice any day! Sangita Sharma told me about Thai-Chai and it was a hit – people were impressed with my restaurant knowledge! Of course ladies who live in posh places go to five-star restaurants – but that's for the business class. With husbands like ours who are middle-class lawyers and officers, middle-class restaurants are fine. And nowadays heaps of restaurants offer discounts for Kitty Parties – it's a good way to get business on weekdays.

I told Mala it's her responsibility to keep the conversation going. But when 20 women get together, you don't have to worry about that! Everyone was talking up their husbands' promotions and their sons and daughter's grades at school. And of course there is the evergreen topic of new saris and jewellery. Kitty parties are nice, but you must keep up with the times – you can't be labelled a 'boring suburban housewife'.

Sheema Mookherjee

Kitchens & Utensils

You'll be surprised at the simplicity of modern Indian kitchens and the sparcity of poorer ones. Resources influence the characteristics of each kitchen more than any religious differences.

Up to 30 years ago, kitchens looked and worked the same way they had for centuries. Women prepared food while crouching on the floor and cooked in a blackened, reliable pot over an earthen fireplace in the corner of the room. Grains and spices were ground in querns.

Food was eaten while sitting on the ground in another room. Sensibly then, shoes were forbidden indoors and nobody was allowed in the kitchen before they had bathed.

Little has changed for the majority of rural folk, but the kitchens of India's expanding middle class have evolved dramatically. Most now have kerosene or gas stoves, women cook while standing at workbenches and families eat at tables. Electricity has come to most homes, flanked by indispensable mod cons such as rice cookers, blenders and pressure cookers. Other important utensils include the **kadhai** (common Indian cooking utensil, similar to a wok) for deep-frying and sauteeing; several spatulas, spoons and ladles for stirring and serving; a **tawa** (hotplate) for making roti; **dekchis** (heavy-bottomed pots with user-unfriendly lids) of several sizes; a **paraat** (a round base for kneading dough); **ghada** (plastic and steel vessels for storing water), and **chanis** (sieves; generally plastic or aluminium but also bamboo baskets in rural areas). Meat-eating families have big wooden chopping boards and cleavers.

Most cooks grind spices just before cooking; this is done with a mortar and pestle in the south, and a flat slab and rolling pin in the north. Those who can afford it make sure they have coffee grinders on-hand that are used specifically for preparing spices.

Every South Indian kitchen has a coconut scraper, a serrated iron disc mounted on a wooden board. Customised steaming equipment designed to fit inside pressure cookers is available in the various special shapes required for such foods as **idlis** (spongy, steamed cakes of fermented rice flour and daal).

Thalis (indented plates) are still the most popular serving dishes. Traditionally, the material they were made of – gold, silver, bell metal – was a mark of family wealth and status, but these days everyone apart from the painfully pretentious use stainless steel because basically it's just easier to clean. The accompanying little bowls that fit in the thali's indentations are called **katori**.

Very few homes have their own **tandoor** (clay oven), which is partly the reason for why tandoori food is such popular restaurant fare.

HOME COOKING

Kadhai and tawa of all sizes, Bangalore City market, Karnataka

COOKING TRADITIONS & PRIMETIME TELEVISION

It was with the sight of me skimming across soggy paddy fields in my flip-flops that Srinivasan decided he liked me.

"Yes, snakes," he enthused with wide-eyed amusement, as I kicked my way through stumpy acres of sugarcane. When he read the response in the expression on my face, he bent over in hysterics, slapping his thighs for effect.

This was the first time he'd laughed since we met hours earlier in Mysore, where he works as head of the tourist office. When I asked him to recommend a guide for me, he volunteered himself. At first I wished he hadn't. Bumping along in a rickshaw from his office to the bus stand, he squinted through two-stroke fumes and snarled, "I can't bear the city. The pollution, the traffic, everyone rushing around, people way too busy to talk".

"Riiiight", I said softly, nodding, the way you do when you've nothing to say. I could hardly have disagreed with him more. In Indian terms, Mysore was exactly the opposite (even the scammers make you smile as they empty your pockets). "Hang on, isn't it your job to promote Mysore?" He said nothing.

After a silent 20-minute bus journey through lush paddy fields and lively villages, we got off at a quiet dusty village called Srirangapatnam.

He comes to life once we're in the countryside.

"Now, do you understand?" he says, smiling and filling his lungs deeply with fresh air. With the mood lightened, I take the liberty of calling him 'Sri', deciding that my botched pronunciations of his name were embarrassing us both.

We take a rickshaw and tour the rural villages, stopping to talk to field workers on the way. We both chew big sticks of sugarcane, which he said would strengthen my teeth. I'm feeling pretty tough until I graze my gum on one of the gnarly bits. Among a group of workers in a paddy field, Sri meets an old school friend who he hasn't seen in 20 years. They only live 10 minutes apart. We chat about food and farming, and one of the children passes me a handful of red-brown **ragi** (finger millet), the staple of rural Karnataka. The locals call ragi a miracle food and they eat it more than rice as it provides excellent fuel for working long hours in the fields.

As dusk approaches we head back towards Sri's home and, finally, after I have dropped all the hints at my disposal, he invites me to have dinner with his family.

On the terrace outside his home, Sri's beautiful 12-year-old daughter is practising **bharat natyam** ('dance of India', the classic dance of Tamil Nadu). Grace and poise turn to panic and she runs into the house to inform her mother about the guest. I linger outside while Sri explains the

Cherubic faces from Guwahati, Assam

aberration. The terrace is bare apart from a sacred **tulsi** (holy basil) tree, found outside every Hindu home, and a **kolam** (Hindu symbol of welcome) made with rice flour.

Invited in, I follow perceived protocol and leave my shoes outside.

"No" Sri waves, "the monkeys will take them".

I look around and, sure enough, behind the gable of the next house two cheeky monkeys wait in ambush. I'm introduced to Rani and Swathi, Sri's wife and daughter. I say hello and smile, but know not to offer a hand. They have the same hazel-coloured eyes, beaming smiles and radiant complexions. They look and act like sisters as they hold one another giggling, looking at the foreigner, giggling some more. Sri can't help himself, shakes his head and sighs a smile of his own.

The living room is empty but for a television, a photograph of Swathi, and a **kolo** (altar) featuring a colourful display of dolls. Among the stern-faced Hindu gods, I notice Barbie with a ponytail. Sri explains that the dolls are for the Dussehra festival (see Dussehra in the Celebrating with Food chapter). Rani hovers around the kitchen preparing dinner and Swathi follows, platting her mother's hair.

Sri keeps offering me chai, sweets and snacks. Eager to sample everything, I don't refuse; but it's poor Rani who is summoned each time and scampers around following Sri's instructions. Sri takes me on a tour of the neighbourhood to see much grander kolos. The entire living room of one house is stacked wall-to-wall with dolls, and the family beam proudly from an adjoining room. As we enter each house, the warm, welcoming smell of spices engulfs us. Each neighbour gives us sweets that I eat and Sri holds in his hand. Outside each home, he offloads the sweets to me, saying that as a traditional Brahmin he only eats what is prepared in his own home. Meanwhile I've eaten enough for two or three and worry about how I'll get my appetite back for dinner.

Back on the terrace, Sri tells me about an Australian man who came to their home several years earlier. Robert Cook, as we'll call him, made quite an impression and an old letter from him was treated like a precious family heirloom. As we chat, groups of children rush past us into the house, making their Dussehra collections, just like our trick-or-treat.

Just before dinner, Swathi splashes herself with a mixture of turmeric, red colouring and rice while she sings a song in front of the kolo. This is **Araathi**, Sri explains, the conclusion of the day's **puja** (literally, respect; offering or prayers) and Swathi is drawing out the evil eye.

The mat is removed and the spotlessly clean living-room floor is swept spotlessly cleaner. Four place mats are laid out and we're each given a metal tumbler of water. I won't be touching that, I think to myself.

Rani places pots full of rice, **sambar** (vegetable and daal stew), **rasam** (spiced daal broth), **dahi** (curds) and pappadams (daal wafers) right in the centre of the floor. She kneels upright filling everyone's thali, except her own. In fact, she doesn't even have a thali and Sri explains that she will eat what is left. If they'd ever seen me eat before, they might have made an exception in this case, but I resolve to leave enough for the cook.

I pause, waiting to gauge any other unfamiliar protocol. Swathi eyes me keenly, waiting for me to eat. Sri is already shovelling handfuls of food into his mouth with the grace of a wild goat so I feel quite relaxed and begin to eat. Swathi blurts, "remember the time Robert ate with his left hand!" and everyone laughs. Ah, humour at my expense was what she was after.

The delicious, hearty fare summons my appetite back when a sudden power cut casts us into darkness. I continue eating while Rani fetches the lamp. I am lowering food into my gaping mouth when the lights return and the gazes of the family are fixed on me.

"We stop eating when the power goes", Sri says solemnly. "Only the devils eat in the dark."

Oops.

While the rest of us devour what she has made, Rani watches our thalis, diligently adding more of this and that as required. She gives Sri some brown balls, which I guess are made from the ragi I had seen earlier. With my confidence back, I brazenly ask for a sample.

"You want to try this?" asks Sri with the kind of smile that clearly said I did not. I take a chunk from the ball, called mudde, and put it in my mouth, quickly realising what chewing wet plasticine must be like.

Sri throws his hands up. "No, don't chew, swallow!"

Spit it out would have been a more welcome command because I've taken too much and begin to choke. My foot twitches and I kick the tumbler of water across the floor into the kitchen (I wasn't going to drink it but, I'll admit, this was a tad drastic). I'm given another full tumbler which I down without hesitation.

As the colour of my face gradually fades from puce to red to its regular pale, Sri rises to answer the door. They have been way too busy laughing to notice the knocking. Sri doesn't bother introducing the man who enters, just saying he is the landlord. Another knock, another guest and soon there are eight of us. Rani sets out a row of red plastic chairs behind me, as I sit alone on the floor clearing my thali.

"Every night these people come to watch a program on television", Sri explains. I'm intrigued; what could be so popular? A serialisation of the epic Ramayana perhaps, an Indian version of *Seinfeld?*

"No, it's *Kaun Banega Crorepati"* Sri says with oratory flourish.

Ooh, it sounds quite grand and, captured by the excitement in the room, I wait for the cultural adventure, pen and pad ready to record the details. Sri flicks through the channels before settling on ... wait for it ...

the Indian version of *Who Wants to be a Millionaire?* It is identical to the version I know from home, but this one is hosted by the Bollywood immortal, Amitabh Bachchan.

Rani clears the dishes and serves herself what is left of dinner. Around me, the home contestants lean forward in their chairs to hear the first question read out in a combination of Hindi and English.

"What is the capital of Himachal Pradesh?"

"Shimla!" the group choruses. "Shimla ... yes, Shimla ... it's Shimla ... definitely Shimla ... I think Shimla" they repeat to leave the others in no doubt that they are right and very clever.

After the first few easy questions, the group seems to lose interest. Sri stands among us cutting an apple into slices and handing one first to each of the diners and then to the assorted guests. Faced with a tricky question, the studio contestant grabs her 'phone-a-friend' lifeline. Her first choice is unavailable because the telephone lines are down. Her second choice becomes hysterical when he hears Bachchan's voice. Play is delayed for a few minutes while the contestant regains his composure, and gets the answer wrong.

After an hour or so, I make to leave. I am dreading the thought of going back to the city, even Mysore. I feel truly enriched by the experience: an ordinary family meal without any special treatment. Then I think of the next traveller lucky enough to befriend these warm, generous people. Maybe you'll be sitting around with an Indian family and one of them will laugh "remember the time that chap with the big ears choked on the ragi ball and kicked the tumbler of water all over the house?"

Martin Hughes

Honoured Guest

Indian hospitality can be overwhelming and it's always extended with warmth and affection through the medium of food.

The ancient Sanskrit idiom **atithi devo bhava** (a guest is equal to God) underpins this philosophy and whether your hosts live in a lavish mansion or a mud-brick hovel, they will do their utmost to make you feel welcome. In affluent homes they might throw an elaborate banquet; meat-eating rural families might slaughter a chicken in your honour; and few hosts will let you leave before you've at least had chai and something sweet.

When your host offers you refreshments, it's normal to decline a few times before accepting. You won't be expected to bring anything, but sweets or fruit are always appreciated. If you cannot accept an invitation it's best to avoid an outright 'no' – Indians may consider it impolite. Just do as the locals do. Even if you're going to be flying home at the time, say "I will try".

Sambar (Vegetable & Daal Stew)

Ingredients

1 cup	**tuvar daal** (yellow lentils; also known as **arhar**)
1 tsp	turmeric
2 tsp	salt
¹/₂ tsp	sugar
100g (3¹/₂oz)	eggplant, cubed
100g (3¹/₂oz)	pumpkin, cubed
1 tsp	sambar powder (available in most Indian grocery stores)
¹/₈ tsp	asafoetida
2 tbs	tamarind paste
1 tsp	vegetable or sunflower oil
¹/₂ tsp	mustard seeds
10-15	curry leaves

Boil the daal in 5 cups of water, with the turmeric, sugar and salt. If a white scum forms around the sides of the pan, skim it off.

When the daal is half done (about 10 minutes) add the vegetables and cook them along with the daal. (If you do not like squishy vegetables you can substitute these with carrots and French beans cut into small pieces). The grains of daal should dissolve and you should be left with around 3 cups of liquid – though it's not necessary to be so precise.

With the daal simmering, stir in the sambar powder, asafoetida, and tamarind paste.

To finish the sambar, heat the oil on a separate flame in a small frying pan. Add the mustard seeds. Once they crackle turn off the flame and add the curry leaves. Pour hot oil and spices over the daal and stir.

Serves 6

Vegetable sambar, idlis and vada and coconut chatni,
Woodlands Restaurant in Chennai, Tamil Nadu

An Indian Banquet

Indian mothers never cook just enough for the family; the unexpected guest is always expected. A stream of visitors could pour in all day and no one – invited guests, casual visitors or beggars – who came past the gate should ever leave hungry. In fact Indians issue dawat (dinner invitations) like others offer greetings. When people meet unexpectedly on the street or in the supermarket, they're assured of being invited home for dinner within the next five minutes. It is this sense of warmth and generosity that makes the Indian dawat so special.

When you host an Indian dinner party, the meal itself can range from a basic pulao or roti and daal combination to an elaborate feast with a number of side dishes. If you're not used to cooking Indian, you should keep it simple. While the cooking techniques are straightforward, seasoning is an art perfected only with practice. Spices can be used whole and ground to a fine powder, individually and in combination to produce stunning flavours. Opt for locally made spice blends rather than imported ones if possible – spices retain maximum flavour when they are freshly ground.

Carefully selecting the ingredients can transform a simple meal into something dramatic and memorable. Take basmati rice for example; it is aromatic, looks fantastic, tastes delicious and rarely loses its shape. Infuse the grains with a hint of saffron, garnish them with a handful of roasted nuts and you have a dish fit for royalty (see the recipe).

Saffron Pulao

Ingredients

2 cups	basmati rice
2 Tbs	butter or ghee
3 cups	water
	a few strands of saffron
1/4 cup	unroasted cashews or almonds

Wash the rice thoroughly, drain and spread on a kitchen towel to remove excess liquid. Heat 1 Tbs butter/ghee and slowly add the rice. Stir carefully to avoid breaking the grains. When all the moisture has dried up, pour in the water. Stir in the saffron. Cover the pan and cook on a low heat, stirring occasionally until all the liquid is absorbed and the rice is cooked. Separately heat the remaining butter/ghee and roast the nuts until golden brown. Dish the rice onto a serving platter and garnish with the roasted nuts.

Serves 4-6

Rotis require a little bit of extra planning. Traditionally, the woman of the household makes them fresh as the family dines and the rotis go straight from the **tawa** (hotplate) to the plate. While some varieties can be made in advance and wrapped in aluminium foil to prevent them drying out, others such as pooris are best consumed as they are made. You could persuade your friends to make their own pooris and pass it off as a hands-on dinner.

Stick to recipes hailing from around the same region, otherwise the flavours of your meal may clash. A raita or plain natural yoghurt is a must, especially to cool the palate in case you have overdone the chilli. **Chatnis** (chutneys), pickles and pappadams add flavour and crunch to the meal. While Indian meals are usually served up all at once, snacks such as samosas and pakoras make great appetisers. Seasonal fruits, especially tropical ones like mangoes, pineapple, guavas and bananas, are a refreshing and authentic last word.

Fruit juice and lassi are the traditional drinks but alcohol, beer and white wine are also suitable. Chai is the perfect winter after-dinner drink. Add a bit of grated fresh ginger and a pod or two of green cardamom for flavour (see the boxed text Chai & Cricket in Kolkata in the Drinks chapter). Alternatively, good quality ready-made spiced tea is available in specialist grocery stores.

Indian music caters for many tastes and moods. As with food, music is regional and you could marry the food with the music of its home. Classical music is broadly classified into two styles: Hindustani (north) and Carnatic (south). The popular sitar maestro, Ravi Shankar, is a wonderful exponent of the Hindustani style. If mellow classical is not your speed, folk music from any part of the country is sure to add energy. The rhythm of Bhangra music from Punjab is particularly lively, being specifically designed for celebrating joyous occasions, such as weddings and bountiful harvests. If you're into contemporary fusion, you can't go past Talvin Singh, Nitin Sahwney or Asian Dub Foundation.

Couch throws, napkins and brightly coloured tablecloths (perhaps with traditional motifs) are a must-buy while you're in India and will go some way to giving your soiree an Indian flavour. Also look for small, lightweight items such as coasters decorated with intricate handiwork. These can be purchased in most cities at the Government Cottage Industries Emporium. If possible, serve the meal on steel plates rather than ceramic ones and persuade your guests to use their fingers (of their right hands) instead of cutlery. You could serve the meal in true Indian fashion by seating everyone on mats on the floor although this is comfortable only when your guests are wearing loose clothing.

In keeping with the tradition of equating the guest with the Almighty, the welcome at the door is very important. A **namaste** (joining of the palms), broad smile and enthusiastic ushering into the home are the norm. Usually the entire family comes to welcome the guest. Since the first impression is often the lasting one, a special effort is made to ensure it's a warm and happy moment. With this in mind, remember that even if you walk through the door blindfolded, you can identify a home as Indian merely by the aromas wafting from the kitchen. Some people burn incense sticks to mask this – sandalwood, rose and jasmine evoke a distinctly Indian atmosphere – although there can hardly be anything more Indian than the inviting smell of spices heralding the feast to come.

Unless the dawat marks an occasion like a religious ceremony, the atmosphere is informal. Usually, there is activity in the kitchen right up until the guests are seated at the table. Nobody is too finicky about punctuality and, remember, Indians tend to eat their evening meal very late.

Make sure you have plenty of water on hand during the meal, as it is customary to refill glasses regularly. The hostess scurries between the kitchen and the dining room with dishes of hot food while the host sits in command at the table – a tradition you may wish to ignore at home. As a host, you should not take 'no' for an answer when offering more food. The guest is expected to be courteous and refuse second helpings and the refusal is ignored. Skip a meal before you tackle the Indian banquet.

Malini Jayaganesh is a cookery presenter and food writer
based in Melbourne, Australia

celebrating
with food

India seems to be in a perpetual state of celebration. There's always some community celebrating a harvest, a special god's birthday or an auspicious date in the Hindu calendar. Personal celebrations like birthdays take a back seat in the pantheon of occasions, and the most important events are those shared by the whole community, young and old, rich and poor.

Hindu Festivals

Most festivals have the sheen of religious reverence but, essentially, they are occasions for high spirits, laughter and gay abandon. Whatever the occasion, people gather, exchange gifts, forget their differences and escape their worries. And feast. Food is the medium through which they celebrate and each festival will have its own special dishes, which change form according to the region.

Sweets are considered the most luxurious of foods and every occasion is celebrated with a staggering range prepared by women striving to outdo one another with their sugary flourishes. In religious festivals, each sweet is first offered to the associated gods before being shared with family and friends. If you visit during a festival, you'll be smothered in a mountain of sweet offerings. Make the most of it because homemade sweets are vastly superior to the shop variety.

Orange marigolds, yellow chrysanthemums and white Indian jasmine, New Market, Kolkata

Holi

Holi is the most boisterous Hindu festival and falls on the full moon in the Hindu month of **Phalgun** (usually around March). It's a time when people join nature in casting off their winter coats and rejoice in the arrival of spring. People greet each other with colours, everything from a gentle smearing of coloured powder on someone's cheek to a deluge of dyed waters tipped over their heads. It's also an occasion to celebrate nature's bounty, and an abundance of special foods are prepared for the feast. **Karanjis** (crescent-shaped flour parcels stuffed with sweet **khoya** (milk solids)) and nuts are synonymous with Holi, and the festival wouldn't be the same without **malpuas** (wheat pancakes dipped in syrup), **barfis** (fudge-like milk sweets) and **pedas** (multicoloured pieces of khoya and sugar).

Many traditionally celebrate Holi with generous quantities of **bhang** (cannabis) mixed up with vegetables and fried into pakoras or drunk in lassis. With the riot of colours and half the town in a state of bhang-enhanced exhilaration, this will be one of the most memorable festivals you'll ever witness. It's celebrated most in the north because southerners don't have much of a winter to get through.

A range of sweets including malai barfi, kamala barfi, saffron sandesh, Mysore pak, cajew, bafir, kesar, coconut barfi, pineapple barfi, kala khan and son papri

Pongal

Pongal (Tamil for 'overflowing') is the major harvest festival of the south and takes place on or around 14 January each year. During this time people worship the gods responsible for the weather, most importantly the sun. The festival is all about the community giving thanks to the gods for the gifts of food, nature, the cow and kinship.

Spring cleaning is the focus of the first three days, and worn-out household items – particularly utensils – are slung into community bonfires as a symbol of people starting anew. The outside of every home is decorated with intricate **kolams** (Hindu designs symbolising welcome) traditionally made from rice flour or powdered limestone.

Pongal is most closely associated with the dish of the same name, made with the season's first rice, along with jaggery, nuts, raisins and spices. On the second day of the festival, every home makes pongal, which is first offered to the gods then traditionally offered to cattle and crows (believed to be returning souls) before being shared among the village or community as **prasad** (blessed food). Huge dinners are organised and people from all castes and classes dine together and thank the gods for their good fortune. It's important to cook pongal but more important to *let* it pongal (overflow) as the ritual is primarily about celebrating abundance. Traditionally people build mud stoves or circular pits to hold firewood outside their homes to cook the pongal and let it spill over in a glorious mess.

The third day is Matu Pongal (matu means 'cow'). Working beasts are given the day off, bathed, painted in bright colours and paraded around town with garlands of flowers hung around their necks.

Pongal (Festive Sweet Rice)

Ingredients

1 cup	rice
1/2 cup	**moong daal** (mung beans)
2 cups	milk
2 cups	water
1 cup	sugar (or jaggery)
15-20	cashews chopped
1/2 cup	ghee
2-3 tbs	raisins
1 cup	fresh grated coconut
6	seeds of 6 cardamom pods, ground
1/4 tsp	ground nutmeg

Dry roast the daal lightly over a low heat, in a heavy-bottomed frying pan or skillet. Mix daal with the rice and wash thoroughly. Put the milk and water in a heavy-bottomed pan and bring to the boil. Add the rice and daal and cook, stirring until it's a soft mass and the liquid is fully absorbed. Add the sugar and cook over low heat until dissolved. Add 4 tsp of ghee and stir until the pongal acquires a sticky consistency. Heat remaining ghee in a frying pan and lightly fry the coconut, cashews and raisins for 2-3 minutes. Sprinkle this mixture over the pongal along with the nutmeg and cardamom and serve warm.

Serves 6

Sankranti

This is the northern version of Pongal, and takes place on the same date. Hindus believe that someone who dies on this day escapes the cycle of rebirth and their soul makes a beeline straight to heaven and eternal peace. There are many different rituals and celebratory dishes for Sankranti throughout the country but many communities make sweets made with sesame seeds. They are often made into sweets, particularly **ladoos** (sweetmeats; usually ball-shaped), and offered to people while saying "eat sesame and speak sweet words". Many women also exchange different kitchen utensils bought on this day, as an expression of respect for each other.

An enticing tray of ladoos

Diwali

Diwali, the festival of lights, is the most widely celebrated national festival, and takes place during October or November. The name is derived from the Sanskrit word *deepavali* (a row of lamps), and families set out lanterns on every available surface and float flickering candles down rivers. Shops are decked out in mercilessly bright lights creating – literally at times – an electric atmosphere. After sunset, landscapes are awesomely illuminated, providing a twinkling welcome to Lakshmi, the goddess of wealth.

Legends abound about the origins of Diwali. One recounts that a young prince had been destined to die from snakebite today, the fourth day of his marriage. He was resigned to his fate but his young wife kept him awake all night by singing songs. She laid all her jewellery at the door to the chamber and lit lamps throughout the room. Yam, God of Death, arrived in the

Garlands of marigolds for Diwali

As part of Diwali, candles set the waters of the Ganges ablaze, Dasawamedh Ghat, Varanasi

form of a snake but was so dazzled by the bright lights that he couldn't enter. Instead, he sat on the jewellery, listened to the sweet melodies and slithered off in the morning granting the young prince a reprieve.

Houses and business premises are renovated, decorated and given a fresh lick of a brightly coloured paint leading up to the festival. Homes are adorned with **rangolis** (the northern term for kolams), only here they are drawn with brightly coloured powders (see Pongal earlier in this chapter). This is the most upbeat Hindu festival; everyone is in buoyant mood, dressed in their best clothes, exchanging gifts and feasting. Of course, there would be hardly be a festival if it weren't for sweets and consumption reaches festive frenzy during Diwali. Some regions have specific Diwali sweets and if you're in Mumbai fill your face with delicious **anarasa** (rice-flour cookies).

Diwali feels like our New Year. In fact, it is traditionally regarded as the beginning of the financial year so it's not far from the truth. Primitive fireworks and crackers are set off throughout the five-day event, and exuberant children delight in terrorising livestock and foreigners with their ear-splitting mischief. While women spend this time buying jewellery and kitchenware.

A flower stall in New Market, Kolkata

LEARNING THE ART OF INDIAN COOKING

My apprenticeship in the kitchen started when I was eight, and so began my journey into the fascinating world of Indian food. It was considered imperative for every girl to be an accomplished cook as a prerequisite to married life. It seemed to me that for years all I ever did was chop vegetables in specific sizes and shapes. Then there was the grating of the coconut, in fine shreds for garnishing and in thicker pieces for curry pastes. When I got this wrong, my grandmother would shake her head and reprimand me as if I was letting down the family name.

Despite more than a decade of learning, I was never allowed to be a part of the kitchen on major festive occasions because as a daughter of the house, I would be considered a child until I got married. The training continued until I got hitched at the age of 24.

My earliest memory of Diwali is at my grandmother's house in Coimbatore in Tamil Nadu. She presided over her retinue of married daughters and daughters-in-law like a football coach. The kitchen was abuzz as I stood on the threshold watching with growing excitement, the aromas wafting from the stove. The huge cauldrons and steaming vats beckoned me to take a closer look but I didn't dare venture forward – tempers could be sharp when there was work to be done.

Even as a young adult, my involvement was peripheral. I was allowed to accompany my uncle to the market to select the vegetables and the freshest spices but my place in the kitchen was in the corner, out of everyone's way. My protests were met with promises from my aunts that the one day the time would come when I would be included as an equal in the proceedings.

After years of anticipation, the opportunity finally came a few weeks ago when I returned to the ancestral home to celebrate the Tamil New Year. In my grandmother's absence my eldest aunt, **Periamma** (Tamil for 'elder mother') took charge. She gave me directions as easily as if I had been a part of the select tribe for years. There was room for me at the kitchen bench and the women accepted me as if I'd always been there.

Preparations started the day before the festival. My uncles went to the market and came back with baskets bursting with colourful gourds, pumpkins and other vegetables. I sat on the floor with the other women grating and peeling well into the night, energised by laughter as we playfully teased one another.

We retired at 2am, but awoke two hours later. Periamma applied oil on my hair and turmeric on my forehead, and I was sent off for a purifying bath before I could enter the kitchen, a festival custom. Being my first-time, I was allowed an extra hour's sleep – the only concession afforded to me – and by the time I entered the kitchen, it was already a hive of activity. Lentils were bubbling away on one stove while milk was being boiled down on another to make sweets. The menu would consist of rice, two types of **sambar** (vegetable and lentil stew), nine vegetable accompaniments, two fresh **chatnis** (chutneys), three sweets and of course, pappadams. **Athai** (father's sister) was asking **Chithi** (younger mother) if another measure of rice was required from the storeroom; **Amma** (mother) was reminding **Akka** (elder sister) to stir the milk before it started to stick to the pan. Every now and then one of my uncles would pop in on the pretext of checking if we required assistance and walk away with a cup of freshly filtered coffee. My two-year-old nephew wandered into the kitchen in tears, collected his due share of hugs and kisses and wandered out again clutching a lump of sticky jaggery.

I could have watched this animated scene for hours but there was plenty to do. There were whole spices to be roasted and powdered into different blends, and fresh coconut and chillies to be ground. Positioning myself at the grinding stone with my aunts passing ingredients in quick succession, I set about making the wet curry pastes, moving on then to the dry spices that I pounded in the mortar and pestle.

One of my aunts called me over to the stove to watch over the rice that was bubbling away in a huge brass pot. Stirring it with the metre-long ladle was a balancing act. My sister-in-law, Deepa, broke out into a comic song about a wedding feast and everybody joined in. I was asked if Australia, my adopted home, had any songs about food. The only song I knew was 'Waltzing Matilda' so I sang about the swagman waiting for his billy to boil, which was met with raucous laughter.

As I worked I was conscious of being part of a colourful, ancient scene: women in vividly colourful sarees working feverishly to make an elaborate meal for 30 people and still finding time to laugh. The aroma of sweet and savoury dishes swirled around and enveloped me.

I heard a sigh at my elbow. Standing across the threshold, with a wistful look on her face, was Nitya, my 10-year-old niece. I bent over to whisper comfort, echoing my aunts to assure her that her turn would come to join us in the kitchen. And as I straightened up, I caught my mother's eye. She smiled in acknowledgement. At last, I am on the other side.

Malini Jayaganesh is a cookery presenter and food writer based in Melbourne, Australia

Dussehra

Dussehra is another fascinating festival celebrated in different ways throughout the country but always lasting for 10 joyous days around September and October.

Indian women especially celebrate Dussehra as it celebrates Goddess Durga, the Eternal Mother, who is as mild and protective as she is brutal and destructive. She was created when the gods needed an all-powerful being to kill the demon king Mahishasura, who was set to attack them. All of the other gods gave their special weapons to Durga, who destroyed the demon. She is the ultimate form of feminine beauty and strength – her smiling face, with large outlined eyes, exudes a protective, maternal glow, but her body, with 10 hands splayed around her, each holding a different weapon, takes a totally martial stance. The vanquished demon cowers at her feet while her vehicle, a fierce lion, snarls at him.

People from all over India (except West Bengal where the festival takes a different form) spend **navaratri** (the first nine nights) in the worship of Durga. A strict vegetarian diet is followed, and many only eat sweets and fruits. Celebrations are largely focused around the home and local neighbourhood. It's a sociable time when people visit each other's houses and exchange gifts. Different sweets are made each day and are first offered to the gods and then eaten by the family and given away to neighbour's children, who sometimes go on house collections similar to trick-or-treat.

CELEBRATING

In Maharashtra and Gujarat community dances called **dandiya** take place all night. In South India, each house builds a **kolo** (altar) to Durga, featuring dolls that they have amassed over the years. Some kolos are so huge that they take up entire rooms, and it is often a source of friendly competition to see who can build the most impressive display. Any dolls can be used, as long as the gods go on the top shelf or step.

The 10th day, Dussehra itself, is in honour of Durga. It is considered a most auspicious day among Hindus, who believe that any venture started on this day is bound to succeed.

People traditionally worshipped their weapons today but in modern times, they worship the implements from which they earn their living. You'll see rickshaws, buses, cars, offices, machines, pens and household articles, all decked out in bright flowers, tinsel and the long, green leaves of the Ashoka tree.

In the days leading up to Dussehra, you'll see special flower markets set up all over the city, seas of dazzling marigolds and jasmine. No work is done on Dussehra; it's a day for giving thanks to all the people who support you in business. We spent a cheerful morning in a travel agency in Bangalore, where the computers and maps of the world wore garlands of marigolds. They wouldn't give us a train ticket but we got the warmest welcome along with a plate of savoury snacks and a sweet, delicious drink they called **payasa** made from banana, milk, jaggery, sugar and ghee.

The Chowk flower market, Varanasi, Uttar Pradesh

Durga Puja

In West Bengal, Dussehra takes the form of Durga Puja, a jamboree of merriment and feasting that lasts for 10 days. Though the devout concentrate on worship, the general emphasis is on feasting. Bengalis take any excuse to binge, and as always with these epicures, sweets are the focus in this carnival of calories.

The most typical Durga Puja food is **bhog**, the ceremonial food served to Durga and later had as a community meal. It consists of a delicious **khichri** (rice cooked with daal; popularised by the British as kedgeree), along with eggplant and potato fritters, **labda** (a spicy mixed vegetable dish) and a sweet, runny tomato chatni.

The people of each area get together, pool funds and organise a sculpted idol of Durga for their locality, and there are competitions to judge which neighbourhood has the best. Artistic licence is pushed to the extreme and there have been Durgas made of glass shards, wood shavings, shells, daals and even plastic bottles. The idols resembled Princess Diana and Mother Teresa the year the two celebrities died, and often she looks like the reigning film diva. After nine days of celebration and worship, the idols are submerged in a nearby lake or river, occasionally to the dismay of the sensitive sculpting artistes.

The actual celebrations in Bengal start from the sixth day and from then on there are bhog-focused community lunches like the one described above. Sometimes on the eighth day of worship, **mangshor jhol** (mutton curry) and **luchi** (fried flour puffs) are served. Traditionally on this day a goat was sacrificed to Durga but these days the symbolic sacrifice is done by beheading a banana plant.

Pilgrims carry an effigy of Durga down to the Hooghly River, Kolkata

Ganesh Chaturthi

The smiling elephant-headed god, Ganesh, is a most popular deity and his festival (in September) is celebrated with cheer throughout the country. The most spectacular celebrations take place in Mumbai, where giant idols of the god are constructed, feted in processions around the city and worshipped for 10 days before being carried by crowds to be immersed in the sea.

And because of Ganesh's fondness for sweets – he is rarely depicted without a bowl of **modaks** (sweet rice-flour dumplings filled with a delicious paste of coconut, condensed milk, sugar and cardamom) – he feasts on lots of different sugary offerings each day of the festival. These will include modaks, of course, as well as karanjis, **kheer** (rice pudding), and the magnificent range of ladoos for which Mumbai is renowned. Once pot-bellied Ganesh has taken his spiritual nourishment, the sweets are shared among his mortal devotees. There are also savoury items associated with the festival although they proved so popular that they have also been adapted as everyday fare (see Maharashtra in the Regional Variations chapter).

Janmashtami

This festival commemorates the birth of Krishna, who is popular with Hindus of all castes. He is best known as the charming, flute-playing seducer of **gopis** (cowgirls) and is regarded as the God of Song and Dance. Especially in Uttar Pradesh where he was born and raised, this festival is marked with colourful pageantry and **ras-lila** (the re-enactment of Krishna's dances with the gopis). **Naivedya** (a sweet made with puffed rice, milk, curds and sugar) is the most popular offering.

Krishna is also known as **Makhan Chor** (Thief of Butter) because of his childhood pilfering of butter, milk and curds from earthenware pots hanging outside houses. His mischievous pranks are gleefully recreated today, and provide some of Bollywood's most popular images. People hang pots of curds, sweets and coins out high on the streets. Gangs of young men, called **gopalas** (cowboys), form human pyramids to reach the pots and then smash them with whoops of joy before divvying up their bounty.

It's believed that it must rain on this day, as Krishna was born during a great deluge and smuggled out of prison by his father to be given to his foster parents; the skies never disappoint the faithful. People actually stay awake fasting until midnight to mark the moment of his birth.

Narial Purnima

This festival is celebrated by all those who depend on the sea for their livelihood, and takes place on the full moon of the Hindu month of **Shravan** (around July). The sea god, **Varun**, is worshipped and coconuts are thrown into the sea to invoke his blessing for fruitful and safe fishing.

Beguiling portraits of various Hindu gods, Dasaswamedh Ghat, Varanasi

Raksha Bandhan

In this ceremony – which usually takes place around August – a sister ties a **rakhi** (amulet of coloured thread or beads) around her brother's wrist to symbolise the deep love between siblings. In return the brother gives the sister a gift or money. Such is the importance of this ritual that many women will travel great distances to fulfil it. Even if a girl ties a rakhi around the wrist of a stranger, it is an auspicious moment and a symbol of great respect that forms an instant and deep bond. The brother is expected to protect his sister throughout his life, under all circumstances. Food also features, as the sister gives her brother a special lunch or dinner, and the brother provides sweets for her.

Onam

This is Kerala's spring festival and, although Hindu in origin, it is celebrated by absolutely everyone in Kerala. The celebrations last for 10 days in April, with the final day being the most festive. Houses sparkle, people wear bright, new clothes, there are dragonboat races on the backwaters and colourful folk dances abound. Most of the community goes vegetarian for the day and sumptuous meals of up to 18 courses are served on banana leaves and merrily devoured.

The food is served in a fixed order and the display of white, yellow and orange dishes on the green leaf is a visual feast in itself. Dishes include **payasam** (rice pudding), raita, **toran** (stirfried greens), **erasseri** (yellow vegetable curry), **avial** (vegetables in curds and coconut), **olan** (potatoes in coconut milk), banana chips, sweet banana fritters, and chatnis made of ginger and lime.

Non-Hindu Festivals
Navroj (Parsi New Year)

While Parsis are small in number, many people celebrate Navroj because Parsis are popular, generous and gregarious hosts. They are passionate about food, and it plays a starring role in all their occasions. Fish, mutton, chicken, nuts, spices and fruit are bought the day before and cooked up into lavish spreads. The first meal of the day is traditionally **ravo** (semolina, milk and sugar) or **sevai** (milk pudding with vermicelli), after which each family visits the fire temple.

Lunch can consist of any number of items, including pulaos with nuts and saffron, fish masalas, mutton or chicken curries, and daal. **Falooda** (the sweet drink made from milk, vermicelli and rosewater) is made in every home and pressed on visitors. Parsis are always supportive of the community's poor and on this day children pass on food and gifts to remind them to always share with others.

Sevai (Milk Pudding with Vermicelli)

Ingredients

1 tbs	pistachios
1 tbs	almonds
¼ cup	raisins
¼ cup	ghee
1 cup	vermicelli
6 cups	milk
1 cup	sugar
4	seeds of 4 cardamom pods, ground
1 tbs	rosewater

Soak the pistachios and almonds in warm water, peel and cut into slivers. Soak the raisins separately so they swell. Heat the ghee and fry the vermicelli on a low heat until golden brown. Add both the almonds and pistachios and saute for 30 seconds. Turn off the flame.

In a heavy-bottomed pan, boil the milk and reduce it to ¼ the original quantity. Add the sugar and stir until it dissolves. Add the vermicelli, nuts and raisins and cook on low heat for 5-10 minutes. The vermicelli should swell and absorb the milk.

Remove from heat and sprinkle with rosewater. Serve warm or chilled.

Serves 6

Ramadan & Id-ul-Fitr

Ramadan is the Muslim month of fasting. The holy book, the *Quran*, was revealed during this month and Muslims are enjoined to fast so they can understand the suffering of the poor.

During the fast, Muslims abstain from eating, smoking or drinking even water during daylight, replenishing themselves only before daybreak and at night. Each day's fast is broken with dates – the most auspicious food in Islam – followed by fruit and juices. The evening meal is called **iftehar**, which the women of the house start preparing in the afternoon and the family eats together once the men return from the mosque. If they can afford it they will eat non-vegetarian food, including pulaos and biryanis, every day. For **sehri** (the last meal before sunrise) each family eats different foods, commonly roti, meat gravy, rice, and curds (curds help prevent thirst).

On the 26th night of Ramadan, Muslims make extra food and deliver it to mosques and shrines for the community's poor. These dishes must be non-vegetarian, with mutton pulaos the most common offering. **Zakat** (the giving of alms) is a fundamental Islamic belief, and Muslims are encouraged to give at least 5% of their personal incomes to the needy.

Id-ul-fitr is the final (30th) day of Ramadan, and follows the appearance of the new moon. This is the only day when women go into mosques. When they return home, an extravagant feast is prepared to celebrate the end of the fast. Non-vegetarian biryanis are a festive staple and there's a proliferation of sweets including sevai and **shrikhand** (see the recipe).

If you thought Ramadan was only about austerity and fasting, check out the Muslim parts of town for Id-ul-Fitr – a party of fun, feasting and flesh that will quickly overhaul your perceptions.

Shrikhand ('Ambrosia of the Gods')

Ingredients

1kg (32oz)	full-cream yoghurt or curds
¾ cup	castor sugar
	few strands of saffron
2	seeds of 2 cardamom pods, ground
1 Tbs	pistachios, finely chopped

Tie up the yoghurt in a large, clean cheesecloth and hang it over the sink for 5 hours. Untie the cloth and place the yoghurt in a glass bowl. Stir in remaining ingredients and serve.
  Serves 6

Id-ul-Zuhara

This Muslim festival commemorates Abraham's obedience to Allah. Abraham was commanded to sacrifice that which he held dearest and, with unwavering faith, he set to sacrifice his son. Impressed with Abraham's devotion, Allah switched the boy for a lamb and Abraham's son was spared.

On this day, every Muslim family is required to sacrifice a healthy animal and divide the meat between the poor, relatives and the family itself. A full-grown camel, cow, goat or sheep is considered the best offering and on the days leading up to the festival, Muslim areas are completely packed with livestock tethered to every available post. Halal butchers come around in the morning to slay the animals in baths and backyards although sometimes the men of the house take it upon themselves to slaughter the animal, ending up with nasty injuries. If you go to a Muslim area at this time, you're sure to see men in bandages. Biryanis of every conceivable concoction are prepared for this day.

The dates of Muslim festivals do not correspond to the Gregorian calendar, but are based on complicated lunar reckoning. The calculations are best left to astrologers.

Goats nibble on birdseed, Dasaswamedh Ghat, Varanasi

Christmas

December 25 is a national holiday because it's the biggest festival among India's Christian population. Christmas is celebrated mainly in Kerala and Goa but the celebration infects many big cities as well. Santa Claus, turkey and christmas cake complement regional specialities and, in Kerala, the season is given an Indian twist with processions of musicians and caparisoned elephants. Interestingly, the Syrian Christians of this state thumb their noses at Rome and celebrate yuletide on 7 January.

Personal Celebrations
Weddings

Marriage is the most important social occasion for families here, and Indian weddings are the stuff of legend. They are famously lavish and colourful affairs and can last for days. Even poor families spend money they haven't got to ensure an elaborate feast which will go a long way to validating their status in the community.

It's normal to have around 500 guests at a wedding reception and affluent families cater for thousands in the banquet rooms of five-star hotels. The ceremonies differ all over the country, from the Kerala's traditional five-minute do to the elaborate Bengali and Punjabi marriages that can last all night.

During the various wedding seasons of North India, you'll see brocaded grooms with swords in scabbards being paraded around town on horseback, preceded by raggle-taggle brass bands belting out popular film tunes – 'Come September' is a favourite, and you'll probably return home humming it. If you follow the procession, and then peer into the wedding long enough, you'll stand a good chance of being invited to join in the celebrations.

Children party in the streets during a local wedding, Hyderabad, Andhra Pradesh

CELEBRATING

Sugar crystals given to guests as part of a wedding celebration, Chennai, Tamil Nadu

Weddings here are much more sensuous and relaxed than the rather dry and stuffy ceremonies of the west. Because they can last for hours, only the immediate families are expected to watch the formalities, and many guests wander off towards the food before the couple have even been married. The feasts are usually sumptuous multi-coursed versions of all the classic specialities of the region (see the Regional Variations chapter for details).

Food is also symbolically important in wedding rituals. At various stages of the ceremony the bride and groom offer rice, milk or ghee to the holy fire (which is the witness to their marriage). The marriage vows are also taken round this fire, circling it seven times to represent seven blessings: food, strength, wealth, progeny, happiness, devotion and cattle. Sweets and fruits are offered to the gods and later various symbolic foods are also given to the bride and groom to eat – honey to the bride, so that she always speaks sweet words, and a fish head to the Bengali groom, as it is the most prized bit!

Muslim nuptials can be even more elaborate, and typically last for three or four days. The first day is **mehendi**, when the families get together for the first time in a celebration of singing and dancing. In a typical wedding in Bangalore, the bride's family offers the groom's family such symbolically rich dishes as **sharbat** (milk, almonds and rose petals) and **malinda** (ground wheat mixed with dried fruit and ginger then deep-fried) by way of welcoming the union of the two families.

Checking out the buffet, Hyderabad, Andhra Pradesh

Shukrana is the second day; the two parties meet in a large hall and exchange gifts, which are often accessories that the couple will wear on the wedding day. Dozens of sweetmeats are prepared along with at least two types of biryani, whole fried or grilled chickens and fried fish. A special sweet poori, made with grated coconut, dried fruit, ginger and poppy seeds, is given by the females of the bride's party to the men of the other side. There is more singing and dancing and friendly competitions between the two families.

The third day, **nikah** (marriage), features variations of the same food, along with tea, coffee and ice cream. **Gajar halwa** (sweet made with carrot, dried fruit, sugar, condensed milk and lots of ghee) is a Muslim speciality commonly served on this day. The bride's family host nikah and give each of the guests packets of dried fruit (usually dates, which are very auspicious in Islam and regarded as Allah's favourite food).

The wedding itself takes place on the evening of the fourth day (**valima**), normally hosted by the groom's family. Once a certain verse of the *Quran* is read out during the ceremony, the bride is showered with trays of dried fruit, almonds, walnuts and sugar candy.

Exquisite gold and silver embroidery on a wedding sari, Dadar, Mumbai

Funerals & Anniversaries of Deaths

Myriad different eating rituals follow a death in the family, but generally no food is cooked in the house for a few days and friends and relatives supply meals to the bereaved. Brahmins often don't cook for up to a week and the first meal prepared in the home following the departure of a loved one is first offered to crows – believed to be returning souls. Many people fast on the anniversaries of family deaths.

Birthdays

Birthdays are very low-key affairs, usually celebrated by preparing the individual's favourite meal. Birthday cakes are increasingly popular although payasam is the traditional birthday sweet.

regional
variations

India is divided into 29 states, each a culturally distinct entity with unique customs, language and cuisine. As though 29 states weren't enough, each comprises myriad ethnic groupings. The cauldron of Indian cuisine overflows with such an immense variety of dishes that no Indian could taste them all in a lifetime.

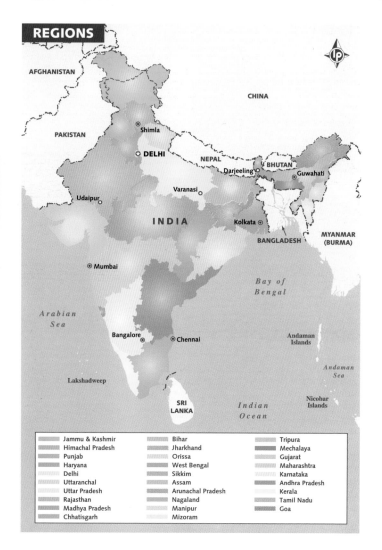

REGIONS

AFGHANISTAN

CHINA

PAKISTAN

Shimla

⊙ DELHI

NEPAL

BHUTAN

Darjeeling ○

⊙ Guwahati

Varanasi ○

INDIA

Kolkata ⊙

Udaipur ○

BANGLADESH

MYANMAR
(BURMA)

⊙ Mumbai

Bay of
Bengal

Arabian
Sea

Bangalore ⊙

⊙ Chennai

Andaman
Islands

Andaman
Sea

Lakshadweep

SRI
LANKA

Indian
Ocean

Nicobar
Islands

Jammu & Kashmir	Bihar	Tripura
Himachal Pradesh	Jharkhand	Mechalaya
Punjab	Orissa	Gujarat
Haryana	West Bengal	Maharashtra
Delhi	Sikkim	Karnataka
Uttaranchal	Assam	Andhra Pradesh
Uttar Pradesh	Arunachal Pradesh	Kerala
Rajasthan	Nagaland	Tamil Nadu
Madhya Pradesh	Manipur	Goa
Chhatisgarh	Mizoram	

North India
Jammu & Kashmir

The Kashmir Valley, with its lush meadows, bubbling streams and beautiful lakes, is a magical land tucked away at the northern tip of India. Vested political interests have so accentuated this region's cultural differences that Kashmiris no longer feel a part of the nation's mainstream. Over the last decade a violent movement demanding autonomy has gripped this landlocked valley making it dreaded territory to which few 'outsiders' dare go. However, many Kashmiri migrants have moved to Delhi and other cities, where you can sample their unique cuisine.

Few vegetables grow in the Kashmiri climate and most people here eat meat. Mutton (in this case sheep, unlike goat meat known as mutton throughout India), chicken and fish are eaten in abundance. **Paneer** (fresh cheese) is a staple as is rice, cabbage, turnips, radish, lotus roots and **haak** (a leafy green vegetable). Daal, including **rajma** (kidney beans), **moong** (mung beans) and **urad** (black gram or lentils) is also eaten.

Kashmiri cuisine is identified by its spice mixes and meats cooked in curds or milk, giving them a whitish colour and smooth texture. Chilli or powdered cockscomb flowers is added to give curries a fiery red tinge, as in the famous **roghan josh** (lamb curry). Even Brahmins here eat meat and fish, although they replace garlic and onions with spices like **hing** (asafoetida), **saunf** (fennel or aniseed), **dhania** (coriander seeds) and **sonth** (dry, powdered ginger). **Succh badi** is a Kashmiri masala made of hing and spices ground with urad; dried then pressed into 'tablets' that are crumbled into food.

Kashmiris are famous for **wazwans** (banquets) held to celebrate weddings, festivals and other festivities. Guests sit in groups of four around **thramis** (enormous silver platters). Rice is piled onto these and two **sheekh** (mincemeat wrapped around iron spikes) are laid over it to form a cross, demarcating each guest's quarter on the plate. Served along with this is **dum kokur** (chicken cooked in saffron-scented curds), **alu bokhara korma** (lamb korma with almonds and dried plums), **aab gosht** (milk-simmered goat or lamb with garam masala), **tabak maaz** (crunchy rib chops), **goshta-ba** (balls of pounded meat simmered in a curds gravy) and roghan josh.

For adventurous travellers who actually make it to Kashmir, a stay in a **shikara** (houseboat) on Dal Lake is a must. Most shikara owners dish up an impressive Kashmiri meal which, will be a highlight of your trip. For Kashmiri food outside the state, visit the Chor Bizzare restaurant at Daryaganj, Old Delhi (see the Delhi map).

Jammu cuisine is an extension of Punjabi food. The people of Jammu are known as the Dogras, and live on the plains. Here you'll find roti, fresh vegetables and milk products, lentils, kidney beans and other pulses.

REGIONAL VARIATIONS

DON'T MISS

- Dining with devotees at the Golden Temple in Amritsar, Punjab
- A stay in a houseboat on Dal Lake, Kashmir, or sampling roghan josh at a traditional Kashmiri **wazwan** (banquet)
- Eating naan fresh from the tandoor
- Exquisite Mughlai fare of Lucknow and Delhi
- Tasty street food, lassis and sweet chai sold along the ghats in Varanasi
- Rajasthan's rustic and rich cuisine; delicious food created with meagre resources
- Wandering Udaipur's colourful Mandi Market
- Udaipur's Lake Palace Hotel, perhaps the world's most romantic setting for a meal

Punjab, Haryana & Delhi
Punjab

Nestled in the shadows of the Pindari Ranges and irrigated by five major rivers, the state of Punjab is a lush green bowl of prosperity. Though it occupies only 1.5% of India's landmass, Punjab is one of the richest states and its people earn double the Indian average. This is partly down to nature's bountiful blessings, but also due to the industrious and resilient character of its cheerful people who are mainly followers of Sikhism. You'll be familiar with Punjabi food because many of its staple dishes have come to represent Indian food internationally.

Following Indian Independence Punjab became famous for its 'green revolution' by adopting new methods of farming and irrigation. This prosperity is evident all over the countryside. There is a joke that Punjabis use old washing machines to churn gigantic quantities of buttermilk, but judging from their generosity you couldn't put it past them. Enormous glasses of fresh, frothy buttermilk or **lassi** (curds drink) are invariably pressed upon a visitor; if you offer money in return your host will be deeply offended.

Punjab contributes over 60% of India's wheat. It also produces basmati rice, corn, sugarcane, mustard (mainly for oil), and a variety of pulses and vegetables. Every rural home has cows and buffaloes, and milk products are a part of every meal. The food of these hard-working, fun-loving people is basically wholesome and simple; it's said it takes just 'home-cooked daal and roti' to satisfy a true Punjabi.

For the women of the household, the day begins with the chanting of morning prayers while churning buttermilk (often consumed instead of tea). Fresh vegetables are picked from the backyard and the day's cooking begins. The main meal consists of hot rotis with dollops of unsalted butter, a generous bowl of daal and a vegetable dish such as the favourite **aloo gobi** (curried cauliflower and potato), spicy **baingan bharta** (roasted eggplant fried with onions and tomatoes) or **aloo mattar** (a delicious curry of potatoes and green peas). Farm-fresh cucumbers, tomatoes, onions and radishes are roughly chopped and served-up with a good squeeze of lime to add tang.

In Punjabi cooking, a paste of onions, garlic and ginger forms the basis of most dishes. Chillies, tomatoes, cumin, garam masala, dried fenugreek leaves and **kalonji** (a black, tear-shaped seed similar to caraway; also called onion seed) are added in varying combinations.

The variety of daals used here outnumbers that in any other state. Urad is simmered for hours over a low fire for the famous **maah ki daal**, delectable with fresh roti. The most satisfying Punjabi meals are available at the **langars** (communal dining halls) within Sikh temples (see the boxed text All You Can Eat at the Golden Temple in the Where to Eat & Drink chapter).

A Sikh chef prepares chicken tandoori pieces in the Surjit Chicken House, Amritsar, Punjab

An integral part of Punjabi cooking is the **tandoor** (clay oven), open at the top and fired by charcoal below. Originally introduced by the Turkish invaders, the tandoor can now be found at every restaurant front and out in the courtyard of many homes. To watch fresh naan being made in a tandoor is a poetic experience. Enormous mounds of dough are kept ready, covered by a damp cloth. A small ball is broken off and expertly patted into an oval shape between the palms. This is deftly stuck onto the side of the glowing-red tandoor wall. In the twinkling of an eye the dough puffs up and becomes speckled with brown patches. Every cook knows the magical moment when the bread is ready, and out it comes with the help of an iron spike. This very same tandoor turns marinated meats into a gamut of kababs: **sheekh** (mincemeat on iron skewers), **tangri** (plump chicken drumsticks), **boti** (spicy bite-sized bits of boneless lamb), **chicken tikka** (succulent chunks of chicken on skewers) and of course the ubiquitous **tandoori chicken**, which goes in whole.

In winter, Punjab's mustard fields are a riot of yellow flowers, and corn from the summer harvest is ground into golden cornmeal. Mustard greens and cornmeal team up in the quintessential rural Punjabi meal of **sarson ka saag** (a divine-tasting spiced puree of tender mustard greens and spinach) and **makki ki roti** (cornmeal roti). Breakfast throughout winter consists of vegetable-stuffed **parathas** (flaky flat breads) and a bowl of cooling curds, and can keep you going the whole day. Parathas in North India are what sandwiches are to packed lunches in the west. You can get them at any of the **dhabas** (roadside eateries) which dot India's rural landscape (see Dhabas in the Where to Eat & Drink chapter).

Haryana

The food eaten in Haryana is much the same as that in Punjab. In fact Haryana was part of Punjab until 1966 when it was designated a separate state. The Surajkund Mela, which takes place every February, is a colourful cultural fair with handicrafts and food stalls from all over India. Surajkund is just 20km from Delhi.

Pilgrims noshing on a free meal from the Golden Temple, Amritsar

Delhi

India's capital is the country's third largest city. It is more conservative than it would care to admit and food here ranges from authentically wholesome at the top to ethnically pretentious and downright gaudy at the very bottom. Delhi has seen the rise and fall of several empires and absorbed various cultures, including Hindu, Muslim and now 'global'. Its cuisine is commonly labelled as North Indian although more accurately; it is really a combination of neighbouring Punjabi and Mughlai (Muslim) food. The Mughals left a lasting impression on Delhi's culture, including its food.

In Old Delhi these Muslim culinary traditions continue as they have for centuries. Dominating this area is the Jama Masjid, built by Emperor Shah Jahan, around which you'll find several authentic restaurants and roadside food stalls. These are definitely worth a try, notwithstanding the surrounding squalor. One reliable place that's synonymous with this area, is Karim's, a restaurant that has been nourishing patrons for more than 150 years (see the Delhi map). Regulars swear that Karim's **burra kabab** (medium-rare lamb chump chops) and **raan** (roasted leg of lamb) are the best in the country. The **bheja** (brain curry), **kheema** (mince curry) and **mutton stew** (yes, this is the Hindi name but it's nothing like the British version) defy imagination. Karim's has two branches in South Delhi – Nizamuddin and East of Kailash – for those not adventurous enough to venture into the congested lanes of the old city.

The Punjabis who came to Delhi as refugees after the India-Pakistan partition introduced the tandoor and, as you can tell from the number of restaurants with orange tandoori chickens in their window displays, it was enthusiastically embraced. These same restaurants also serve a signature dish known to Indian food fans the world over as **butter chicken**: tandoori chicken is jointed and put into spicy red gravy (the colour comes from pureed tomatoes and red chillies) with dollops of white butter on top. Vegetarians can try **palak paneer** (fresh cheese in a spicy spinach puree). Each of these dishes goes well with fresh, hot roti.

So many different communities have ventured to Delhi in search of a living that it's difficult to identify the original inhabitants; those families who were here to greet the Mughals in the 16th century. They are the Hindi-speaking **Kayasths** – the educated, trading community, who later became the official administrators of the Muslim rulers. There are also the Urdu-speaking Muslim families, who can trace their lineage from the Mughals. Nowadays most of their children have adopted a pan-North Indian identity, though the older generation still bemoan the loss of Delhi's glorious heritage, culture and etiquette.

If you do happen to visit Kayasths or Muslims, you'll be told that Delhi food is quite different from what you'll find in all the restaurants. The food

REGIONAL VARIATIONS

Butter Chicken
This favourite is delicious with freshly baked roti.

Ingredients

1kg (32oz)	cooked and jointed tandoori chicken
200ml (7fl oz)	tomato puree
1 Tbs	ginger paste
1 tsp	garlic paste
1 tsp	red chilli powder (use paprika if you do not want it hot)
2 tsp	salt
100g (3¹/₂oz)	butter
¹/₂ cup	thick cream

Simmer the chicken in tomato puree, ginger and garlic paste, chilli powder and salt for around 10 minutes (until the chicken is tender). Add the butter and simmer for another 5 minutes. Mix the cream in and serve.
Serves 5-6

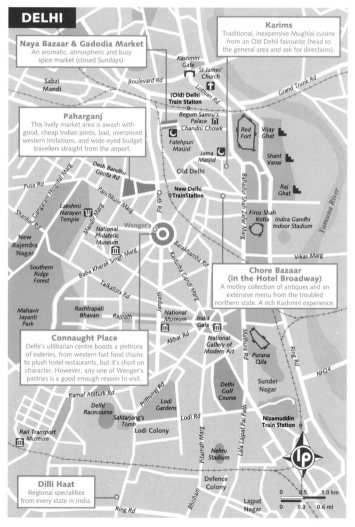

DELHI

Karims
Traditional, inexpensive Mughlai cuisine from an Old Dehli favourite (head to the general area and ask for directions).

Naya Bazaar & Gadodia Market
An aromatic, atmospheric and busy spice market (closed Sundays).

Paharganj
This lively market area is awash with good, cheap Indian joints, bad, overpriced western imitations, and wide-eyed budget travellers straight from the airport.

Chore Bazaar (in the Hotel Broadway)
A motley collection of antiques and an extensive menu from the troubled northern state. A rich Kashmiri experience.

Connaught Place
Delhi's utilitarian centre boasts a plethora of eateries, from western fast food chains to plush hotel restaurants, but it's short on character. However, any one of Wenger's pastries is a good enough reason to visit.

Dilli Haat
Regional specialities from every state in India.

Kashmiri Gate
St James's Church
Lothian Rd
Boulevard Rd
Grand Trunk Rd
Sabzi Mandi
(Old) Delhi Train Station
Begum Samru's Palace
Chandni Chowk
Red Fort
Vijay Ghat
Fatehpuri Masjid
Jama Masjid
Shant Vanai
Old Delhi
Raj Ghat
Desh Bandhu Gupta Rd
Panchkuin Marg
Pusa Rd
Qutb Rd
Canggram Hospital Marg
Lakshmi Narayan Temple
Madir Marg
New Delhi Train Station
Firoz Shah Kotla
Indira Gandhi Indoor Stadium
Sharkar Rd
National Philatelic Museum
Wenger's
Bahadur Shah Zafar Marg
Yamuna River
New Rajendra Nagar
Baba Kharak Singh Marg
Barakhamba Rd
Vikas Marg
Southern Ridge Forest
Kasturba Gandhi Marg
Talkatora Rd
Janpath
Mahavir Jayanti Park
Rashtrapati Bhavan
Rajpath
National Museum
India Gate
Mathura Rd
Purana Qila
Ring Rd
NH24
National Gallery of Modern Art
Akbar Rd
Kamal Ataturk Rd
Prithviraj Rd
Delhi Racecourse
Lodi Gardens
Delhi Golf Course
Sunder Nagar
Rail Transport Museum
Safdarjang's Tomb
Lodi Rd
Lodi Colony
Pilamah Marg
Lala Lajpat Pai Path
Nizamuddin Train Station
Nehru Stadium
Defence Colony
Bhisham
Lajpat Nagar

0   0.5   1.0 km
0   0.3   0.6 mi

prepared in a 'purist' Kayasth home would likely have strong links to Uttar Pradesh food, with certain distinguishable Muslim touches. Elegant meat dishes like **mutton do piaza** (literally 'two-onions mutton'), **khare masale ka gosht** (mutton in whole spices) and **aloo mutton ka salan** (mutton and potatoes in a rich gravy) take pride of place at the table. Several elaborate vegetable preparations are also enjoyed, including **bharva sabzi** (stuffed spiced vegetables). Bland vegetables like bitter gourd, marrow and baby squashes are magically transformed with a tasty stuffing of powdered coriander, aniseed, **amchur** (dried green mango) and chillies. These are then fried and curried with browned onions, spices and tomatoes. Another traditional Delhi dish is **mangodi** (little fried golden balls of mung-bean paste). Cooks fry these with amazing dexterity and arrange them in pyramids. They are then served with spicy **chatnis** (chutneys) or in a gravy base. The traditional Muslims (most of whom live in the walled city of Old Dehli) have food very close to that had by the Mughals, although the amount of spice and ghee used nowadays is considerably curtailed.

Cooked and uncooked pomfret, Oberoi Hotel, New Delhi, Delhi

There is an enormous choice of international fare in Delhi. In most of the posh South Delhi markets or in the central Connaught Place you will find a plethora of Chinese, Thai, Italian, and European restaurants although the hybrid fare of these joints is almost certain to disappoint. International pizza and burger chains are easy to find (if that's what you want) with a few Indian touches livening up their homogenous menus (see the Where to Eat & Drink chapter).

If you won't have the chance to try regional cuisines in their natural setting, you can get a crash course at the open-air shopping arcade called Dilli Haat (see the Delhi map). This government-run plaza gives you a wide choice of handicrafts, as well as authentic inexpensive food from all the different states. This place should definitely be supported for its ambition even if the execution of it is a little half-hearted.

Uttar Pradesh & Uttaranchal

India's most populous state is a haven for trekkers, wildlifers, hill station enthusiasts, history lovers and foodies. It showcases a variety of cuisines including pure Hindu vegetarian, majestic Nawabi Muslim, and rugged and simple hill fare.

In Hindu homes here, food is treated with a kind of ritual sanctity. The kitchen must be washed clean twice a day, the person who cooks it must be of a high caste (usually called a **Maharaj**), and the ingredients must be unadulterated, without a trace of meat. So much is made of the **pucca pundit** (pure upper-caste) tastes in these homes, that you have to wonder if they enjoy their food at all.

However, the ordinary street food of Varanasi, Agra, Lucknow and Allahabad is so delicious that you're instantly reassured that everyone here eats well. For example, breakfast bought from a **thela** (pushcart) where for a song you'll get hot **kachoris** (corn or daal savoury puffs), delicious potatoes in a daal gravy, and **nukti ka raita** (curds with droplets of fried gram flour).

A neighbouring thela will sell hot **jalebis** (orange whorls of fried batter dipped in syrup) that you can crunch on to complete your meal. If you're in Varanasi, start your day by watching the sun rise over the Ganges on a bathing ghat (preferably listening to an early morning classical raaga on your headphones) and follow it up with breakfast from a thela, and you would have attained the deepest insight into Hindu spirituality!

Places of pilgrimage like Varanasi are predominantly vegetarian and it's a revelation how the simple food can taste so delicious without onions, garlic or meat. For special dishes a touch of **khoya** (milk solids), **malai** (cream) and **mewa** (dried fruits) is added. The humble potato is a perennial and versatile favourite. Other popular vegetables include pumpkin, cauliflower, okra, eggplant, spinach and a variety of gourds.

A standard meal comprises **phulkas** (delicate, small roti), **daal chaval** (daal and rice) and a seasonal **sabzi** (vegetable) dish. A wedding lunch here is naturally more elaborate, and would be served on a **pattal** (a large plate made of leaves pinned together with tiny sticks). Such a lunch includes three types of **poori** (deep-fried bread) along with four dishes: **rasedaar sabzi** (vegetable with watery gravy – a potato-pumpkin combination is a great favourite), two dry sabzis and a dish made with paneer, served on special occasions. There would also be **pulao** (aromatic fried rice), **raita** (yoghurt or curds combined with any number of vegetables or fruit, served chilled) and fried **papads**, the North Indian term for **pappadams** (daal wafers). A choice of several sweets would follow and the meal always ends with **paan** (see Paan in the Staples & Specialities chapter).

The people of Uttar Pradesh & Uttaranchal have a soft spot for sweets, and an abundance of milk and sugar caters well to their craving. The basic

REGIONAL VARIATIONS

Bhatti Ka Aloo (Potatoes with Spicy Gravy)

Ingredients

500g (16oz)	potatoes
1 tsp	cumin seeds
5	cloves
4	seeds of 4 cardamom pods, ground
1	cinnamon stick, broken in two
2	bay leaves
1/8 tsp	asafoetida
3	tomatoes, chopped
1 tsp	ginger paste
1 tsp	turmeric
1 tsp	cumin powder
1 tsp	salt
1 tsp	garam masala
2 tsp	amchur (dried green mango – though it gives a very special touch, don't go crazy finding it)
4	green chillies
1/2 cup	coriander leaves, chopped
4 tsp	ghee or vegetable oil

Peel and boil the potatoes. Crumble them into bite-sized pieces with your hand (cutting seals the edges and the flavours won't soak in).

Heat the ghee in a wok or deep pan. Add the cumin seeds, cloves, cardamom, cinnamon, bay leaves and asafoetida. When the spices release their aroma (don't let them burn), add the tomatoes and cook them until they dissolve. Now add the ginger, turmeric, cumin powder and keep sauteeing until you see the ghee on the surface. The paste should leave the sides of the pan. Add the potatoes and salt and stir well. Pour in 2 cups of water and simmer for 15 minutes. A couple of minutes before removing from the flame, add the garam masala, amchur, green chillies and coriander.

Serves 6

ingredient in Uttar Pradesh's sweets is **khoya** (milk solids). **Peda** (round pellets of khoya with sugar, pistachios, saffron and cardamom) is popular, as is **barfi** (a fudge-like sweet made from milk). Ramasrey Sweets in Hazratganj, Lucknow, is a good place to try all these delicacies.

As Varanasi is the centre of Hindu culture, Lucknow is its Muslim counterpart. Under the rule of the Nawabs, the city's culture and etiquette reached an unparalleled peak and Lucknow is associated with the most majestic cuisine. The culinary tradition was meat all the way, cooked in pure

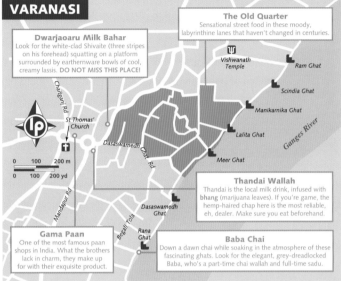

VARANASI

The Old Quarter
Sensational street food in these moody, labyrinthine lanes that haven't changed in centuries.

Dwarjaoaru Milk Bahar
Look for the white-clad Shivaite (three stripes on his forehead) squatting on a platform surrounded by earthernware bowls of cool, creamy lassis. DO NOT MISS THIS PLACE!

Vishwanath Temple

Ram Ghat

Scindia Ghat

Manikarnika Ghat

St Thomas' Church

Chaitganj Rd

Dasaswamedh Ghat Rd

Lalita Ghat

Ganges River

0 100 200 m
0 100 200 yd

Meer Ghat

Mandapur Rd

Thandai Wallah
Thandai is the local milk drink, infused with **bhang** (marijuana leaves). If you're game, the hemp-haired chap here is the most reliable, eh, dealer. Make sure you eat beforehand.

Begzi Tola

Dasaswamedh Ghat

Rana Ghat

Gama Paan
One of the most famous paan shops in India. What the brothers lack in charm, they make up for with their exquisite product.

Baba Chai
Down a dawn chai while soaking in the atmosphere of these fascinating ghats. Look for the elegant, grey-dreadlocked Baba, who's a part-time chai wallah and full-time sadu.

ghee. Kormas and **kalias** (gravied meats), koftas and kababs, biryanis and pulaos prepared with spices, saffron, nuts and raisins, were prepared daily and laid out on the **dastarkhwaan** (ceremonial cloth) for a shared meal on the floor. Though Lucknow has become modernised in many respects, some families proudly hold on to this last vestige of grandeur and go through the daily ritual of sitting down at the dastarkhwaan. Nowadays, however, vegetarian dishes are also prepared as a staple diet of meat is so costly.

Lucknow is famous for its kababs, made with mincemeat or meat paste (while the kababs in Punjab and Delhi come from the barbecue tradition or skewered bits). The **shami kabab** (boiled mincemeat, ground with chickpeas and spices) is the mainstay in Uttar Pradesh homes. Raw papaya is added to make the meat so tender that it melts in your mouth. Other common kababs are **galavat** (balls of mincemeat), **sheekh** (mincemeat wrapped around iron spikes) and **ghute** (mincemeat stirred into a fine paste in the pan). **Kakori kababs** are a speciality named after the town near Lucknow. The meat is pounded into a fine paste, which is then spiced, wrapped around a skewer and quickly charred until crispy on the outside and almost creamy within.

Rajasthan

The stark, arid landscapes of this desert state have led to extraordinary forms of survival: enormous and imposing rock-hewn fortress-towns; ancient methods of water conservation; vibrantly coloured fabric worn by the local people to protect them from the sun; and a hot, spicy cuisine derived from meagre resources. Boosted with limited fresh vegetables, fruits or fish, Rajasthanis make the best of cereals, pulses, spices and milk products to produce a cuisine that is surprisingly elaborate and reflects the lifestyle of the **Rajputs** (warrior clans) who originate here.

Cereals form the backbone of Rajasthani food. Wheat-flour is used to make rotis, pooris and parathas, and the state's most remarkable dish, **bati** (baked balls of wholemeal flour). These are broken up by hand – in your case, probably your waiter's – soaked in ghee and mixed with a spicy daal. This very unusual, rustic dish is a tasty testament to survival in hard times. Along with bati goes **churma** (fried wholemeal flour balls pounded with sugar and nuts) to make the classic Rajasthani combination, **daal bati churma**.

Daal bati at the Lake Ghat Guest House, Udaipur, Rajasthan

REGIONAL VARIATIONS

Other grains like barley, millet and corn are used to make thick rotis called **bhakri**. A working-class meal would comprise bhakri, spicy pounded garlic, red chilli chatni and raw onions (eaten to prevent sunstroke). Powdered barley is dissolved in curds and made into **kadhi** (a sour, spicy soup) and corn is boiled with lentils to make **khichdi**.

Besan (gram or chickpea flour) is another staple, and is used to make **pakora** (fritters), **sev** (savoury nibbles), and other salted snacks generally known as **farsan** (see the Gujarat section later in this chapter). The most distinctive besan-based dish is **gatte ki sabzi** (also known as **besan gatte**); spiced besan dough rolled out into 'snakes' – there's a better description but you might not appreciate the imagery – and steamed. These are cut up and cooked in spicy gravy. This classic dish is delicious but can be pretty heavy so don't indulge every day.

The Brahmins and traders in Rajasthan stick mainly to a vegetarian diet but the Rajputs enjoy a variety of meats, including game. Hunting is a favourite pastime of this warrior caste when they've got nobody to fight. In

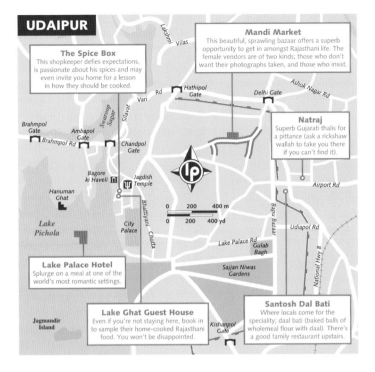

UDAIPUR

The Spice Box
This shopkeeper defies expectations, is passionate about his spices and may even invite you home for a lesson in how they should be cooked.

Mandi Market
This beautiful, sprawling bazaar offers a superb opportunity to get in amongst Rajasthani life. The female vendors are of two kinds; those who don't want their photographs taken, and those who insist.

Natraj
Superb Gujarati thalis for a pittance (ask a rickshaw wallah to take you there if you can't find it).

Lake Palace Hotel
Splurge on a meal at one of the world's most romantic settings.

Lake Ghat Guest House
Even if you're not staying here, book in to sample their home-cooked Rajasthani food. You won't be disappointed.

Santosh Dal Bati
Where locals come for the speciality; dal bati (baked balls of wholemeal flour with daal). There's a good family restaurant upstairs.

Lakshmi Vilas · *Hathipol Gate* · *Delhi Gate* · *Ashok Nagar Rd* · *Vari Rd* · *Swaroop Sagar* · *Silawat* · *Brahmpol Gate* · *Brahmpol Rd* · *Ambapol Gate* · *Chandpol Gate* · *Bagore ki Haveli* · *Jagdish Temple* · *Hanuman Ghat* · *Lake Pichola* · *Bhattiyani Chotta* · *City Palace* · *Airport Rd* · *Bapu Bazaar* · *Udiapol Rd* · *Lake Palace Rd* · *Gulab Bagh* · *Sajjan Niwas Gardens* · *National Hwy 8* · *Jagmandir Island* · *Kishanpol Gate*

0 200 400 m
0 200 400 yd

the deserts of Jaisalmer, Jodhpur and Bikaner, meats are cooked without water, using milk, curds, buttermilk and plenty of ghee. Cooked this way, they keep for days without refrigeration. In fact, for special occasions, some dishes are left to steep for a few days to intensify the flavours. **Murgh ko khaato** (chicken cooked in a curds gravy), **achhar murgh** (pickled chicken), **kacher maas** (dry lamb cooked in spices), **lal maas** (red meat) and **soor santh ro sohito** (pork with millet dumplings) are classic Rajasthani desert dishes.

Milk is important all over India but it is vital in Rajasthan (see the boxed text White Meat & Colourful Weddings in the Staples & Specialities chapter). Laxmi Mishthan Bhandar (better known as LMB) in Jaipur is a sweet shop where you can taste the rich variety of milk-based treats, as well as daal bati churma and other Rajastani specialities. (See also the Udaipur map.)

A farmer weeds his murli patch, Udaipur, Rajasthan

Madhya Pradesh

This large, sprawling state is literally at the centre of India. Madhya Pradesh is home to a melange of cultures, although its cuisine is typically North Indian. The original inhabitants were tribal but over time they've come to be outnumbered by migrants from neighbouring states. Each community brought along its own cuisine adapting it to local ingredients. Today 'non-tribal' and 'tribal' are the two broad culinary divisions.

The dry belt that runs from Gwalior to Indore is influenced more by the neighbouring states of Maharashtra, Rajasthan, Gujarat and Uttar Pradesh. The food here, known as the **Malwa** cuisine, is grain and daal based, with few vegetables and a lot of oil and ghee. The city of Indore has a large Jain community (see Jains in the Culture of Indian food chapter).

The capital Bhopal, however, a long tradition of Muslim rule and shares dishes with the elite of Uttar Pradesh and Andhra Pradesh. Korma, **rizala** (a chilli flavoured mutton dish), **ishtu** (spicy stew), **achhar gosht** (a famous pickle-like meat dish of Hyderabad), **boorani** (raita made with chopped tomato, cucumber and onions; another Hyderabadi speciality), kababs and **rumali roti** (large, thin roti) are cooked in most Muslim homes. The most delicious biryani can be bought from pushcarts in the crowded lanes of old Bhopal, near the Taj-Ui-Masjid and Moti Masjid.

A distinctive feature of Bhopali Muslim cuisine is the emphasis on fragrances: fresh herbs, ginger, garam masala, nutmeg, mace and an aromatic essence called **kewra**, extracted from the screwpine flower. No Bhopali meal is complete without paan, the making of which is a fine art in this city.

Chhatisgarh

The tribal belt was declared a separate state called Chhatisgarh, with Raipur as its capital, in late 2000. The food here features unusual fruits, vegetables and tubers. Flowers of vegetables like pumpkin and gourd are fried and eaten. Monsoon is mushroom time – the most delicious among these, the bracket mushroom, grows under teak trees after first rain.

Chhatisgarhis make a variety of **baris** (sun-dried pellets of daal paste), which are combined with curried vegetables like eggplant and bottle gourd. Another popular dish is **karhi** (curds with okra, yam, carrots, horseradish, or seasonal vegetables). Tender neem leaves fried in ghee are considered an ideal start to a meal (see the boxed text Neem in the Fit & Healthy chapter).

Among the state's forest dwellers, the staple food is **pannia** (cornbread cooked in palash leaves) and a thick, maize gruel. Locals compensate for an austere diet with locally brewed liquor, either toddy or **mahua** (see Regional Spirits in the Drinks chapter). Elephants have developed a taste for this spirit and their binges have had disastrous consequences when they've trampled through villages in search of it.

Pitthi Ki Kachori (Flour Puffs with Lentils)

These are delicious when served hot with curried potatoes (see the Bhatti Ka Aloo recipe earlier in this chapter).

Dough

500g (16oz)	wholemeal flour
1 tbs	ghee
1 tsp	salt
	enough water to make dough firm but malleable (about ½ to ¾ cups)

Filling

1 cup	**urad** (black gram or lentils – in Indian shops you can ask for the daal used to make dosa)
1 tsp	red chilli powder
2 tsp	coriander seeds, powdered
2 tsp	aniseed or fennel powder
⅛ tsp	asafoetida
½ tsp	salt
	vegetable or sunflower oil for deep-frying

Make a semi-stiff dough (that you can roll out fine) with the three dough ingredients. Soak the daal for 4 hours. Drain and grind it coarsely in a food processor. Mix the remaining ingredients (but not the oil) with the daal.

Form 3cm balls with the dough. Pat these into little cups in your palms and fill in a teaspoon of daal filling one at a time. Stretch the dough over the filling and pat into a ball again. Flatten each ball in your palm and dust with flour and roll back into a circle.

Once you have rolled all the kachoris, heat the oil in a wok. Slip in the kachoris one at a time and fry, 2 minutes to each side for the daal to cook inside (adjust the heat so the kachoris are golden brown). The kachoris should puff up. Drain on a paper towel.

Makes 20 kachoris

East India
West Bengal

Bengalis, the inhabitants of the state of West Bengal (and the country of Bangladesh) comprise 3% of the world's population. Fondly referred to as 'Bongs' – which has nothing to do with a penchant for water pipes – Bengalis are highly articulate, and can be heard debating art, politics and culture wherever they roam. This is a hangover of the colonial past when the British fostered a class of well-educated Bengalis, known as **bhadralok** (gentlemen) to prop up the Raj. In fact Bengal saw a renaissance that gave rise to several significant reformist movements and towering intellectual figures. Two centuries later the people of this highly literate state bask in that glory and believe they are still at the vanguard of art, literature and culinary prowess. For most non-Bengalis all this can be encapsulated in the single term: arrogance, but no amount of poverty, extreme overpopulation, and political and economic stagnation – which have slowly been engulfing the state and its capital, Kolkata – can dampen the Bengali spirit.

There are few sights more picturesque than the West Bengal country-side. Even if you land in the maddening maelstrom of Kolkata, you'll get glimpses of this scenic beauty while driving out of the airport to the city. Palm trees sway harmoniously in the breeze and clusters of mango trees shelter little mud cottages, built in artistic symmetry. Creepers bearing vegetables trail the neatly thatched roofs and almost every patch of land has a pond full of fish.

All Bengalis are fiercely proud of their heritage and their state has produced some of India's most eminent figures, including poet Rabindranath Tagore and film director Satyajit Ray. Bengalis are equally proud of their cuisine, which they believe is the epitome of refined taste. Probably for this very reason, you'll find very few restaurants totally specialising in Bengali food, as a matter so close to the heart cannot be turned into a commercial business.

For many men, shopping for food is a daily adventure and a challenge to start the day – the early **babu** (sir) gets the best fish. The fertility of the surrounding countryside provides for a profusion of fresh fish and vegetables in the markets. Each day the kitchen basket boasts a variety of at least 10 different vegetables, as well as fish (and chicken and mutton on special days). Along with rice and daal, these are cooked into nutritious four- or five-course meals.

Whether you have to beg, flirt or cajole, you must get yourself invited to a Bengali home for a meal – it's nothing to be embarrassed about because hospitality is the next most important thing to a Bengali after food. At first a mountain of steaming rice will be piled on to your plate. Your hostess will tell you that the courses are to be had in a special order, and cannot be mixed up on the plate "as the philistines in other parts of

India do". You'll make a healthy start with a bitter dish of crisply fried bitter gourd or neem leaves. Then you'll be invited to crunch into a vegetable fritter with hot daal mixed in rice. One or two tasty seasonal vegetable dishes will follow: cauliflower curried with potatoes, cabbage cooked with shrimps, minced banana flowers fried with spices and grated coconut, gourd cooked in a poppy-seed paste. Really, the possibilities are endless.

Next will come fish, the food closest to a Bengali's heart. A plethora of fish is found in the rivers and ponds of Bengal. They are fried, curried in onions, stewed lightly with vegetables or made into spicy **jhaal** (fish with ground mustard seeds and chillies). No part of the fish is thrown away and Bengalis dextrously make short work of the bones by sifting them out with their fingers or teeth. But when there's a special guest, fish alone will not suffice. There will also be gravied chicken or mutton – to be eaten with more rice or maybe **luchi** (the Bengali version of poori). The meal will end with a chatni prepared with some sour fruit like green mangoes, plums or pineapple, cooked in spices and sugar, and then some **misthi doi** (sweetened curds) and a **mishti** (sweet) will be the final seal. Special occasions like weddings, anniversaries or festivals only give an excuse to serve more elaborate meals, with multiple courses.

Nepalese tea pickers, Marybong Tea Garden, Darjeeling, West Bengal

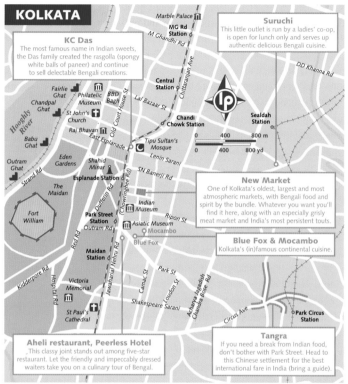

KOLKATA

KC Das
The most famous name in Indian sweets, the Das family created the rasgolla (spongy white balls of paneer) and continue to sell delectable Bengali creations.

Suruchi
This little outlet is run by a ladies' co-op, is open for lunch only and serves up authentic delicious Bengali cuisine.

Marble Palace
MG Rd Station
M Ghandhi Rd
DD Khanna Rd
Chittaranjan Ave
Central Station
Fairlie Ghat
Philatelic Museum
BBD Bagh
Lal Bazaar St
Chandpal Ghat
St John's Church
Old Court House St
Raj Bhavan
East Esplanade
Hooghly River
Babu Ghat
Chandi Chowk Station
Sealdah Station
Tipu Sultan's Mosque
Lenin Sarani
0   400   800 m
0   400   800 yd
Outram Ghat
Eden Gardens
Shahid Minar
SN Banerji Rd
Strand Rd
Esplanade Station
The Maidan
Chowringhee Rd
Indian Museum
Ripon St
Asiatic Museum
Mocambo
Blue Fox
Fort William
Park Street Station
Outram Rd
Red Rd
Dufferin Rd

New Market
One of Kolkata's oldest, largest and most atmospheric markets, with Bengali food and spirit by the bundle. Whatever you want you'll find it here, along with an especially grisly meat market and India's most persistent touts.

Blue Fox & Mocambo
Kolkata's (in)famous continental cuisine.

Maidan Station
Kidderpore Rd
Hospital Rd
Victoria Memorial
St Paul's Cathedral
Jawaharlal Nehru Rd
Camac St
Park St
Loudon St
Acharya Jagadish Chandra Bose Rd
Shakespeare Sarani
Circus Ave
Park Circus Station

Aheli restaurant, Peerless Hotel
This classy joint stands out among five-star restaurant. Let the friendly and impeccably dressed waiters take you on a culinary tour of Bengal.

Tangra
If you need a break from Indian food, don't bother with Park St. Head to this Chinese settlement for the best international fare in India (bring a guide).

There is a **mishtir dokan** (sweet shop) on every street corner in Kolkata, and locals buy their sweets in weekly supplies. Bengali sweets are the best in India, delicious creations made out of such ingredients as evaporated milk, sugar and paneer. The number of sweets they produce increases every day with each innovation. The best known Bengali sweet is **rasgolla** (spongy white balls of paneer) oozing out sugar syrup in which they are boiled. Rasgollas are available in sweet shops all over India, and are even sold in tins by the venerable KC Das (see the Kolkata map). The Das family are credited with creating rasgollas and several other Bengali favourites.

Many other sweets are made based on the basic rasgolla recipe. Some are deep fried, some are tinged with saffron and contain pistachios, and others are coated with crystallised sugar. A new name is given to each invention and some of the more inspiring are **abaar khaabo** ('eat again'), and **praan haara** ('stolen heart').

Another generic group of sweets is **sandesh**, made of paneer paste cooked on a low heat with sugar or **jaggery** (see the boxed text Jaggery in the Staples & Specialities chapter). These are put into clay moulds that shape them into fruits, fish and flowers. Sandesh can be flavoured with palm jaggery, orange zest, mango, chocolate, rose-water or saffron, each of which will change its colour and taste. Unlike elsewhere in India, sweets are eaten year round in West Bengal. However, their consumption reaches frenzied proportions during Durga Puja, the most important Bengali festival (see the Celebrating with Food chapter).

Kolkata has a few good outlets for authentic Bengali cuisine. There are also several restaurants dishing out Continental and Anglo-Indian said to be reminiscent of the Raj. You'll find them on or near Park Street but if they are truly representative of the Raj then that era was expensive and seriously overrated. Decide for yourself: Blue Fox and Mocambo are the most popular (see the Kolkata map).

The familiar blur of a Kolkata taxi

DON'T MISS

- Dusk on the banks of the Brahmaputra River in Guwahati, surrounded by unhurried fishing folk
- Dinner at Aheli restaurant and a visit to New Market in Kolkata (Calcutta), West Bengal's sophisticated capital
- The sublime milk-based sweets of West Bengal
- The patchwork of cultures, customs and unique cuisines of the tribal northeast
- A visit to a tea garden in the Himalayan hill station of Darjeeling, home to some of the world's finest teas
- **Bhog** (special offerings) cooked in earthenware pots piled on top of one another and placed inside massive coal-fire ovens at the Jagannath temple in Bihar – you won't be allowed inside the temple but you can taste the divine food

Orissa

For years, life in historic Orissa was dominated by the intellectually and economically advanced Bengalis just next door, but the state has recently come of age – it is even beginning to get a good share of the lucrative tourist market with visitors entranced by its stupendous temples and boundless natural beauty.

Oriya food is an interesting combination of flavours from East and South India. Like the Bengalis, the Oriyas are used to a generous kitchen basket in this fertile land that has both rivers and a coast. Vegetables are cooked in combinations of four and five, both saltwater and freshwater fish are staples, prawns caught in Chilka Lake are a popular ingredient, and of course rice is the staple grain.

Oriyas, especially the womenfolk, are deeply religious and fervently observe the rituals and customs of traditional Hindu life. Mondays and Thursdays are auspicious and therefore vegetarian days. Families are always congregating due to some special **puja** (religious feast) and, of course, that also means good eating. **Ghanto tarkari**, a mix of colocasia (similar to taro), yam, peas, potatoes, cauliflowers and eggplant that's spiced up with whole gram and slivers of coconut is a must for such occasions. **Pitha** is the favourite sweet all over East India and women at home were making these long before sweet shops became so immensely popular. In Orissa, pithas are made from rice flour or semolina. The dumplings are stuffed with delicate coconut filling, and sweetened with jaggery and raisins. The way of wrapping the batter in turmeric leaves and steaming it makes for a favourite pitha.

One of Orissa's everyday dishes is the quaintly named **tatiya basa** (sitting in a bowl). Not wont to waste, mothers chop up vegetable peels and leftovers like cauliflower stems and leaves, which are placed in a closed bowl and cooked over a slow fire. **Dalma** (mung-bean daal) is a favourite, given the eastern touch of dry roasting before it's cooked. Most of the daals and vegetables in Orissa are garnished with coarsely ground cumin and red chillies roasted on a griddle. This mix is made-up and then stored in bottles for convenience.

Fish is given pride of place in any meal. Some of the many preparations include it being fried, curried with onions or cooked with a mustard and curds paste. **Ambul** is a popular mustard fish preparation that gets its impressive tang from the inclusion of dried mangoes. Tamarind adds a sour touch to dishes and okra is often cooked in sour gravy of tamarind and tomatoes. The use of coconut, tamarind and a lot of red chillies, gives Oriya food a kiss of southern influence, as does the very occasional use of curry leaves.

Bihar & Jharkhand

In step with a flurry of state changes across India, the area formerly called Bihar has recently split into two states: Bihar and Jharkhand. However, because cuisine boundaries remain unaffected by administrative distinctions, for our purposes, Bihari cuisine refers to nosh found in both states.

Bihar was once a thriving ground of intellectual and spiritual wisdom. Just 50km from the capital, Patna, are the ruins of the 5th Century AD Nalanda University. Fifty km farther, Buddha reached enlightenment under a bodhi tree at Bodhgaya. While rich in history, the largely rural population of Bihar & Jharkhand is among the poorest and most underprivileged in India, having faced generations of feudal oppression. Administrative mismanagement and corruption are part of life – a popular chief minister has been imprisoned under several charges of graft but the people still back him because he belongs to the 'lower castes' and identifies with the masses.

Bihari cuisine is rustic, simple, wholesome and wonderfully satisfying. It resembles the cuisine of neighbouring states but with uniquely local touches. **Sattu** (roasted chickpea flour) is the unifying theme; it is cheap, filling and nutritious. Its preparation ranges from coarse to subtly refined, and there are few smells more tempting than sattu being roasted in earthenware pots over coals. A labourer carries it in his **gamchha** (handloom towel) and mixes it with onion and chilli for a quick meal. A middle-class housewife dips Bihar's well-known **littis** (balls of spiced sattu covered in dough and coal-baked), in warm ghee before serving. Littis are prepared everywhere, from roadside tea stalls to affluent homes.

Biharis are fond of meat although economics generally restricts their carnivorous diets. **Meat saalan** (lamb curry in garam masala and cubed potatoes) is a favourite, but daily fare mainly consists of roasted, boiled, fried or curried vegetables. **Chokha** (mash) is popular and very easy with eggplant, potato, bitter gourd, ash gourd and pumpkin. It is served with a garnish of mustard oil, chopped onions, garlic, green chillies and coriander leaves. If this is served sour it is considered a chatni. A hot favourite is **bachka** (crunchy vegetable fritters in a gram flour batter). Sliced potato, onion, eggplant, pumpkin and gourd are all fried this way.

Sweets from here retain their earthy, rustic flavours. During the festival of Chhat (Sun God festival) **thekua** (sweets made of ghee, jaggery and wholemeal flour, flavoured with aniseed) are popular. In winter after the **til** (sesame) harvest, the little white oil-seed is made into balls sweetened with jaggery for **til laddoos**. Another favourite is **tilkut** (thin rectangular wafers of crushed sesame and sugar). The town of Gaya is famous for scrumptious **anarasa** (sweets of sesame, rice, sugar and evaporated milk).

Though snobbish Bengalis next door turn their noses up at Bihari food, it retains a lot of natural goodness missing from 'refined' Bengali cuisine.

Northeastern States

In the far-flung northeastern corner lie the seven sister states of Assam, Meghalaya, Tripura, Mizoram, Manipur, Nagaland and Arunachal Pradesh. Sharing international borders with Bhutan, China, Bangladesh and Myanmar, these areas are quite apart from the Indian mainstream, and home to several ethnic insurgent movements. Assam is the largest state and at the forefront of affairs. Here, and in neighbouring Tripura, you'll find pockets of urbanisation. Otherwise, the region is a sparsely populated collage of stupendous natural beauty, with swiftly flowing rivers, emerald green valleys, dense virgin forest, rugged stretches of the Himalayan foothills, bounteous flora and exotic fauna. Societies here are largely tribal and Nagas, Kukis, Khasis, Jaintias, Garos, Angamis are the main groups although there are many sub-tribes within these. The culture of each is rich and varied, making the region a veritable treasure-chest of art, dance, music and food.

Women are the linchpins of society here, while men are known to be laid-back and quite often unoccupied. The tribal markets, run by women, are spectacular affairs with fresh vegetables and silvery fish competing with intricate handiwork and textiles vying for your attention. Khwairamband market at Imphal, Manipur, is India's largest women's market.

Simplicity and an emphasis on natural flavours are the cornerstones of this region's cuisines. The variety is enormous, with each tribe or community developing its own signature dishes. Obvious common threads are the predominance of rice, fish and boiled or char-grilled vegetables, with ingredients like pickled bamboo shoots or fish used to add flavour. The use of spices and oil are kept to a minimum because of lack of availability.

A divine sunset over the banks of Brahmaputra River, Guwahati

Assam

The Assamese are fond of sour tastes and, like the Thais, use lots of lime and lime leaves in their cooking. **Tenga**, the favourite Assamese fish stew, is made of pieces of sweet-tasting **rohu** (a type of carp), sauteed with onions and simmered in a watery gravy that's zested with lemon juice. Other sour favourites are **kharoli** (fermented mustard paste) and **khorisa** (fermented bamboo shoots), both eaten with rice. As if to counteract their highly acidic food Assamese eat **khaar** (an alkaline by-product of burnt banana tree stems). This ash is sprinkled on daal or vegetables, as part of the daily meal.

The Assamese version of pitha, the sweet popular all over India, is made during the Bihu (harvest) festivals held four times a year. **Aroya pitha** (rice dumplings filled with coconut or sesame), **gur pitha** (fried balls of fermented rice batter flavoured with jaggery, nigella and aniseed) and **anguli pitha** (finger-shaped dumplings boiled in milk and jaggery) are the most popular.

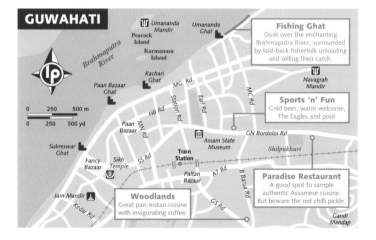

GUWAHATI

Umananda Mandir
Peacock Island
Umananda Ghat
Karmanasa Island
Brahmaputra River
Kachari Ghat
Paan Bazaar Ghat
MG. Rd
Station Rd
Earl Rd
MC Rd
HB Rd
Paan Bazaar
MN Rd
Sukreswar Ghat
Assam State Museum
GN Bordoloi Rd
Shilpukhuri
Fancy Bazaar
Sikh Temple
SS Rd
Train Station
Paltan Bazaar
AT Rd
B Barua Rd
Jain Mandir
Kedar Rd
GS Rd
Gandi Mandap
Navagrah Mandir

0   250   500 m
0   250   500 yd

Fishing Ghat
Dusk over the enchanting Brahmaputra River, surrounded by laid-back fisherfolk unloading and selling their catch.

Sports 'n' Fun
Cold beer, warm welcome, The Eagles and pool.

Paradise Restaurant
A good spot to sample authentic Assamese cuisine. But beware the red chilli pickle.

Woodlands
Great pan-Indian cuisine with invigorating coffee.

Meghalaya

Meghalayan food resembles Assamese cuisine in many ways. The major community here, the Khasis, make rice-based specialties, such as **putharo** (rice-batter crepe fried in a pan with a porous earthenware lid). This tastes sublime with syrupy liquid jaggery. **Pukhen** are sweet fried rice cakes, while **pusla** are steamed rice cakes wrapped in leaves. **Pudoh**, a dumpling similar to dim sum is also made with a covering of rice flour around mincemeat.

Tripura

Tripura has 17 tribes, which are now outnumbered by the large immigrant Bengali population. You'll find an eclectic culinary mix here, as the locals have adopted Bengali sweets and fish dishes, such as **shorshe maach** (mustard fish curry). Tripuris are passionately fond of both fresh and dried fish dishes. **Nona ilish paturi** (salted pieces of hilsa fish, wrapped in an edible leaf and fried) is a great favourite, as is **pithali** (dried fish stew). **Shidol** (a fermented preserve made of tiny freshwater fish) is quintessentially Tripuri and an essential ingredient in every kitchen.

From the northeastern states onwards starts the trend throughout South-East Asia of using various preserves and sauces made of dried fish. Other common elements are the use of fresh green herbs like basil, coriander and lime leaves, and sticky rice (called **binni chaval** in Tripura), many strains of which are found all the way up to Japan.

Manipur

Fish is equally important in Manipur, and the fish preserve made here is known as **ngari**. Two unusual vegetables you'll find here are the fibrous and crunchy lotus stem (which grows profusely in the ponds and lakes) and a perennial tree bean called **yangchok**, which has an overbearing smell sure to take over any meal. **Chemfut** is a favourite sweet made by boiling pumpkin or cucumber with jaggery, and an unusual purplish version of **kheer** (rice pudding) is made with the sticky rice grown here.

Nagaland

As it is in neighbouring Myanmar, rice is paramount here and is eaten with all meals including in the form of gruel for breakfast. Nagas have a taste for pork and several other similarities exist with Chinese food such as the use of spring onions, garlic, ginger and monosodium glutamate. They also make a colourless soybean sauce and another sauce extracted from mustard leaves known as **gan nang tam cha**. Mashing up burnt dried fish with **raja mirch**, an exceptionally hot chilli, makes a fiery pickle. Vegetables including potatoes, cabbage, beans, yam, gourd or different greens are boiled and served with rice along with either dried fish, smoked beef or even pickled bamboo shoots.

Arunachal Pradesh

You'll come across many typical Tibetan dishes this far northeast, including **momos** (similar to dim sum), **churpee** (chewy bits of dried yak cheese) and **thukpa** (a rich noodle soup). People here also have salted tea with yak butter like their neighbours. Arunachal Pradesh's variety of sticky rice is reddish in colour and it is eaten with a chatni made of soybeans and sesame seeds. Millet and barley are other staples.

West India
Gujarat

Think of Gujarat and various images appear: Mahatma Gandhi, Jain temples, rich diamond merchants, the last of the Asiatic lions, intricately carved temples, devastating earthquakes, spectacular beaches and seaside temples to name a few. Now you can add spellbindingly pure vegetarian food.

Vegetarians form almost 90% of Gujarat's population, largely thanks to the huge number of Jains who call this state home. A typical Gujarati thali is by far the most balanced, light and nutritious meal you'll enjoy in India and locals have them for lunch and dinner. The meal consists of rice, roti, a salad (could be finely diced tomatoes and cucumbers) or vegetable relish (shredded cabbage or bean sprouts with grated coconut), raita, a dry vegetable (like stir-fried beans), a curried vegetable (like potatoes or eggplant), daal, **kadhi** (a sour daal-like dish made of curds and besan), **farsan** (crunchy snack), pickle and a **misthan** (any sweet item). All the items are served at once and savoured a little at a time.

Phapda, a besan flour snack, at a roadside stand, Mumbai, Maharashtra

To a certain degree Gujarat's healthy culinary image is undone by an abundance of deep-fried snacks and breakfast foods, which are part of the daily diet. Neighbourhood farsan stores sell mounds of different shaped crunchies, made from **besan** (gram or chickpea flour) – much as Italians fashion different shaped pasta out of flour. Instead of running down to buy freshly baked bread for breakfast, Gujaratis buy hot **gathia-fafda** (thin, hard sticks of fried besan and a softer, broader version of the same), which they have with a relish of raw grated papaya and green chillies, and sweet milky tea spiced with cardamom. The same store sells a variety of other savouries including **dhokla** (spongy squares of steamed besan), **khandvi** (melt-in-the-mouth rolls of cooked besan paste), **sev** (fried besan sticks), **patrel** (neem leaves lined with spicy besan paste, tightly rolled up, sliced like jam rolls and steamed), fried peanuts, cashew nuts, potato wafers, roasted chickpeas and anything else than can be snacked. These are had for breakfast, tea or tiffin.

Winter specialities include **undhiu** (vegetables such as broad beans, yams and eggplant stuffed with a spicy daal, and baked in earthenware pots buried in the earth) and **rotlo** (millet roti) eaten with ghee and freshly made jaggery.

Gujarat's non-vegetarians are mainly **Bohris** (a Muslim sect found around Surat) and Parsis, both of whom speak Gujarati. The Bohris have rich meat curries and kababs and a variety of soups including the very non-vegetarian **siri-paya** made of goat's head and trotters. The family normally sits down to a meal on clean white sheets and eats from an enormous **thaal** (common plate).

The street food of Ahmedabad is astoundingly good and can be found in two main areas. Manik Chowk, the older and more congested precinct also has a jewellery and cloth market, and you can see some beautiful, old carved wooden **havelis** (mansions). The newer food area is Law Garden near the Law College. Hygiene standards are reassuringly higher here although the prices are also pretty steep (well, by Indian standards). Here you'll get traditional Gujarati snacks as well as Jain pizzas and noodles, minus onions and garlic, of course.

Gujaratis love to take after-dinner walks with their favourite ice creams, and this seems to be the main form of casual socialising. The indigenous flavours based on dried fruits and nuts like **kesar-pista** (saffron-pistachio) and **kaju-draksh** (cashew-raisin) will probably be the best ice cream you'll ever taste.

A Jain pizza, Mumbai, Maharashtra

DON'T MISS

- Kulfi (ice cream) along Chowpatty Beach, the travellers' cliche
- The sublime vegetarian fare of Gujarat, the home of the thali meal
- The meaty dishes, warm hospitality and sharp wit of the Parsi community
- Exploring the many regional cuisines found in Mumbai's excellent restaurants (Mangalorean, Parsi, Gujarati, to name a few)
- The vibrant cuisine and exuberant mood of Goa
- Finding a good source for Goan feni, India's finest spirit
- A visit to any fishing village, where fish are caught according to ancient techniques

Maharashtra

In a way, Mumbai – Maharashtra's capital – can be seen as a point where the contrasting cultures of North and South India converge. Here, for example, they rely on both rice and bread and not predominantly one over the other. It has traditionally been a buffer between the two radically different Aryan and Dravidian cultures although it's the height of political incorrectness to put it in such simple terms. Butter chicken, palak paneer, **sambar** (vegetable and lentil stew) and **dosa** (fermented rice-flour and lentil crepe) are all enjoyed equally by these people who comprise a happy mix of North and South Indian cultures, epitomised in the easy-going, cosmopolitan life of Mumbai.

Mumbai is a cosmopolitan jungle considered to be the country's commercial centre. Part of the city's skyline is Marine Drive, also called the Queen's Necklace, a glittering row of lights lining the curved sea face. Along this posh causeway you'll find a wide variety of international cuisines and the most contemporary fast food frauds. It will be much more rewarding exploring the ethnic tastes in the congested lanes of Colaba, Kala Ghoda and the Fort area. Tucked away here you'll find busy little eateries serving Maharashtran, Mangalorean and South Indian food.

Marathis (who consider themselves to be descendants of Shivaji, the great nationalist king) are a simple, hardworking lot. Much of their wealth comes from a professional attitude towards work and a basic philosophy of austerity, bordering on thrift. In Mumbai it is considered quite normal for just ice cream or aerated drinks to be served at a wedding reception, where as most other Indian communities would consider anything short of an elaborate dinner a slur on their status. This is the practical, no-nonsense approach Marathis have to major issues in life, including their food.

The Deccan Plateau, the heart of Maharashtra, yields cotton, peanuts and sugarcane. But much of it is also arid and barren, giving rise to a simple diet based on pulses and grains, and a minimal amount of seasonal greens. The upper castes stick to a simple vegetarian diet, while the others cook spicy meat and fish dishes to supplement this fare. Maharashtra's Konkan Coast concentrates on fish and seafood, which can be sampled at the numerous inexpensive seafood restaurants that dot Mumbai.

Marathi Brahmin food is the epitome of minimalist cuisine. The best examples of this are found in the city of Pune, the state's culture and heritage capital. A homely meal here consists of rice, roti, **tuvar daal** (yellow lentil daal) and a vegetable. Probably nowhere else in India is daal so simple – it is just boiled with salt and turmeric and then flavoured with a hint of ghee, asafoetida and jaggery. Vegetables too are just tossed with mustard seeds, curry leaves, and grated coconut. A unique source of protein is a large

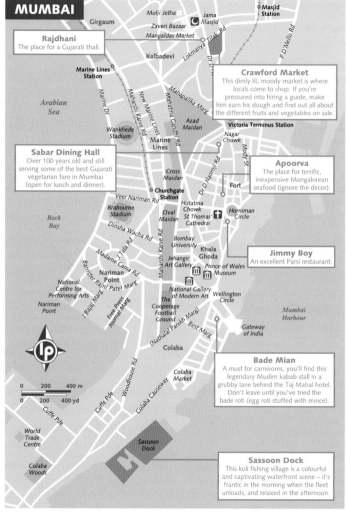

MUMBAI

Girgaum

Mulji Jetha

Jama Masjid

Masjid Station

Zaveri Bazaar

Mangaldas Market

Kalbadevi

Rajdhani
The place for a Gujarati thali.

Lokmanya Tilak Rd

Dr Dr

P D'Mello Rd

Marine Lines Station

Mahapalika Marg

Mahatma Gandhi Rd

New Marine Lines Rd

Maharshi Karve Rd

Marine Dr

Crawford Market
This dimly lit, moody market is where locals come to shop. If you're pressured into hiring a guide, make him earn his dough and find out all about the different fruits and vegetables on sale.

Azad Maidan

Victoria Terminus Station

Arabian Sea

Wankhede Stadium

Marine Lines

Nagar Chowk

Mody St

Sabar Dining Hall
Over 100 years old and still serving some of the best Gujarati vegetarian fare in Mumbai (open for lunch and dinner).

Cross Maidan

Dr D Naoroji Rd

Fort

Apoorva
The place for terrific, inexpensive Mangalorean seafood (ignore the decor).

Veer Nariman Rd

Churchgate Station

Hutatma Chowk

Brabourne Stadium

Oval Maidan

St Thomas' Cathedral

Horniman Circle

Back Bay

Dinsha Wacha Rd

Bombay University

Khala Ghoda

Madame Itala Rd

Jehangir Art Gallery

Jimmy Boy
An excellent Parsi restaurant.

Prince of Wales Museum

Barrister Rajni Patel Marg

Nariman Point

National Gallery of Modern Art

Wellington Circle

National Centre for Performing Arts

Free Press Journal Marg

J Balaji Marg

The Cooperage Football Ground

Mumbai Harbour

Nariman Point

Nathalal Parekh Marg

Best Marg

Gateway of India

Colaba

Bade Mian
A must for carnivores, you'll find this legendary Muslim kabab stall in a grubby lane behind the Taj Mahal hotel. Don't leave until you've tried the bade roti (egg roti stuffed with mince).

Woodhouse Rd

Colaba Market

Cuffe Pde

0 200 400 m
0 200 400 yd

Colaba Causeway

World Trade Centre

Sassoon Dock

Colaba Woods

Sassoon Dock
This koli fishing village is a colourful and captivating waterfront scene – it's frantic in the morning when the fleet unloads, and relaxed in the afternoon.

variety of sprouts, such as mung-bean sprouts. These are usually made into a sweet & sour curry called **birdha**, using spices, tamarind and jaggery. Apart from rice, **bhakri** (a thick roti made from a variety of grains such as millet, sorghum, rice, wheat and corn) is another staple. A farmer's working meal might be as simple as bhakri with pickle, raw onions and chillies.

A large part of the vegetarian diet is the ritualistic food prepared for religious fasts. Over the centuries a rigid list of 'fasting foods' has been laid down. From these, housewives prepare the most delicious meals, making a fast seem more like a pleasure than a penance. **Saboo dana** (sago) is a main ingredient during this time, and the most delicious **vadas** (fried salty doughnuts) and **khichdi** (a kind of risotto) is made combining this with potatoes and peanuts.

Along with a range of sweets, particularly **ladoos** (sweetmeats, usually ball-shaped), there's a vast variety of savoury items, made for festivals, special occasions or just about any time you feel like treating yourself. In fact, nowadays many festive dishes are eaten as everyday fare. Topping the list is **chuda** (a tasty low-cal munchy mixture of flattened rice, peanuts and gram, pepped up with crispy fried onions, curry leaves and other spices). Other savouries are **chakli** (crunchy spirals of gram flour), **sev** (fried besan sticks), **bakar vadi** (crunchy whorls of neem leaves layered with gram paste) or **bhajiya** (onion and potato fritters).

A serving of the popular snack bhelpuri, Mumbai, Maharashtra

However, the snack synonymous with Maharashtra, especially Mumbai, is **bhelpuri**, a riotious mix of sweet, sour, hot, soft and crunchy sensations. Tossed up in a leaf plate or newspaper is crisp-fried thin dough mixed with puffed rice, slivers of boiled potatoes, chopped onions, peanuts, fine hair-like besan sticks, sweet tamarind chatni, a piquant green coriander and chilli chatni, a generous squeeze of lime and a fresh sea breeze. Roadside vendors hawk their wares at public gardens, street corners and along the sea front at Mumbai's Chowpatty and Juhu beaches.

Fish is the staple of non-vegetarian Marathi food and features in **kaalvan** (curried fish with a thick gravy of ground coconut and red chillies, tempered with fried garlic). To make another favourite, **fried fish**, thin slices of fish are marinated in garlic paste, lemon or tamarind juice and red chilli powder, dipped into a batter and fried. At the seafood restaurants, you can order this along with rice and a free bowl of coconut-based gravy for a most satisfying lunch. Maharashtra's favourite fish is **bombil** (Bombay duck). This misnomer stands for a slimy, pike-like fish, which is had fresh or sun dried. If you go to Mumbai's seaside a strong, fishy smell will fill your nostrils even before you can see the rows and rows of Bombay ducks drying on lines in the sun. Bombay duck – or will it soon become Mumbai duck? – can be curried or fried, but is always marinated in pungent spices to take away its sharp smell.

Bombay duck (bombil) from Bandir Bazaar on Grant Road, Mumbai, Maharashtra

One of the most delicious Indian meat dishes is **Kolhapuri mutton**, named after a town in southern Maharashtra, and a fiery example of Maratha cooking. Its dark gravy comprises fried garam masala, coriander seeds, **copra** (dried coconut) and plenty of red chillies. Chicken gets the same spicy treatment in inland Vidarbha. The common ingredient in all Marathi non-veg cuisine is **kala masala** (also known as **goda masala**), a unique blend of powdered spices that, apart from the usual cinnamon, cardamom and cloves includes uncommon star anise and allspice).

Goa

Goa has a unique feel that stems from the intermingling of the highly developed Goan culture and 450 years of Portuguese rule. The Portuguese were the first colonisers to arrive in India and the last to leave. Goa was kept in an isolated cocoon from the rest of the country and a unique cuisine evolved that is as casual and vivacious as the Goans

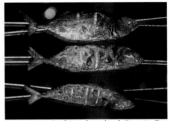

Barbequed mackerel, Panaji, Goa

themselves. It's reflected in rich curries, roasts coated in masalas and marinated in palm vinegar, cakes made of semolina, jaggery and coconut and bread that's leavened with **feni** (see Regional Spirits in the Drinks chapter). Food and drink are integral to a lifestyle that revolves around dance, music and celebration – 'to enjoy' is the Goan instinct.

This rich and fertile land has the ocean on one side and is criss-crossed by a maze of canals, streams and rivers. It is little wonder that fish is the Goan staple, with over 100 varieties of freshwater and saltwater fish and seafood, including succulent prawns as big as your fist. This is the third state, along with Kashmir and Bengal, where Brahmins eat fish without the slightest qualms about polluting their 'holy status'.

Fish aside, chicken and pork are also favoured meats, and spicy Goan sausages – pickled in vinegar and red chillies – are a meaty must-try. Goan Hindus eat a lot of vegetables but the Christian diet is dominated by non-vegetarian foods with the occasional salad tossed in. While fish is routine, Sundays and celebrations are marked with meat.

A typical Goan lunch starts with a mildly spicy side dish such as **cafreal** (pieces of fried chicken coated in a green masala paste) or **caldeen** (fish simmered in coconut milk, ginger and cumin), both of which are normally served with soft, square-shaped little loaves called **pao**. The second and main course might be **caril de peixe** or **ambot-tik** (both fiery hot fish curries) along with the compulsory crisply fried fish had with rice. The Portuguese influence shows up more prominently in the evening meal. It might start with **sopa de camarao** (prawn soup – complete with heads and shells), followed by a side dish like chicken galantine or stuffed squid, to complement a main course like **assado de bife** (roast beef). Dessert could comprise coconut-filled crepes or a **fool** (mashed fruit and cream) made with mangoes.

Goans specialise in elaborate puddings, cakes, and sweet snacks. Don't miss **bathique** (a cake made of semolina, coconut and eggs), **dodol** (a black cake made of jaggery, rice flour and coconut cream) and famous **bebinca** (the layered 40-egg sweet, rich with ghee and coconut milk).

Goans need only the flimsiest excuse to celebrate and almost every month has a festival (Hindu or Christian) or a saint's day, which are always marked by worshipping, feasting and drinking. Weddings are occasions to indulge gastronomic fantasies. Receptions begin with toasts, the cutting of an elaborate multi-tiered cake and ballroom dancing. The meal will feature roast suckling pig and other pork dishes like **sorpotel** (pork and pig liver curry, in which pig's blood was traditionally added) and **pork vindaloo** (a pickled pork curry), so fiery that it has been nicknamed 'find a loo' by tourists taken by surprise. Seafood will also be prominent with dishes like fish aspic (set in gelatine) oyster pie, stuffed and grilled **surmai** (mackerel) and curried or fried prawns. Desserts might include bebinca, creme caramel and **leitria** (an elaborate sweet made with tender coconut covered by a lacy filigree of egg yolks and sugar syrup).

Chicken Cafreal (Fried Chicken in a Green Masala Paste)

Ingredients

1.5kg (48oz)	jointed chicken
4	cloves
4	seeds of 4 cardamom pods
1	cinnamon stick
1 tbs	cumin seeds
10	peppercorns
2 tbs	malt vinegar
5	cloves garlic
2½ cm	piece ginger
4	green chillies (de-seeded if you don't want it too hot)
2 cups	fresh coriander
1 cup	fresh mint
1 tsp	salt
3 tbs	vegetable or sunflower oil

First put the cloves, cardamom, cinnamon, cumin and pepper into the food processor and grind the spices finely. Now add the vinegar, garlic, ginger, chillies, coriander and mint along and grind until you have a smooth paste. Make slits in the chicken pieces and rub with salt. Marinate the chicken in the masala mix for around 2 hours. Heat oil in a large non-stick frying pan and fry the chicken pieces on a high flame for 5 minutes. Next add ½ cup water, cover and cook until the chicken is done (about 15 minutes). Serve garnished with fried onion rings (optional).

Serves 6

South India

Though it would be a travesty to clump all South Indian food together, there are common themes that lend it cohesion. Binding features are the predominance of rice and the unfailing use of sambar (vegetable and daal stew) and rasam (daal broth) but each of these is different in each state.

You'll also find sour dishes in every South Indian meal, believed to off-set the large quantities of chillies which are used to cool the body in these warmer climes. The **curry patta** (curry leaf) is commonly used, along with mustard seeds and **hing** (asafoetida). The combination of these three ingredients creates a typical flavour, and anyone from the rest of India could taste it blindfolded and exclaim "ah, South Indian food!"

Dosas, a large family of freshly fried fermented rice-flour crepes, are a South Indian breakfast speciality that can be eaten at any time of day, either as a full meal or substantial tiffin. The dosa is an icon of Indian food, now enjoying popularity all over the country in restaurants, homes and street stalls. To make the batter for dosa, rice and lentils are soaked and ground separately; the rice into a slightly granular paste and the black lentils into a light foamy one. The two are combined and left to ferment, usually overnight. The thick batter is poured over a hot griddle, drizzled with oil around the edges, and cooked on one side for a minute or until tiny holes begin to appear on the surface. The dosa is served with a bowl of hot, orange sambar and another bowl of mild coconut chatni – Yin and Yang at its best.

Our favourite is the **masala dosa** (a large crepe stuffed with a delicious filling of potatoes cooked with onions and curry leaves), but there are many dosa varieties, each a speciality of a different region. There's also the spicy, crisp **Mysore dosa**, (like masala with more vegetables and chilli in the filling) the **pessarettu dosa** (batter made with mung-bean daal) from Andhra Pradesh, the **rava dosa** (batter made with semolina), the **paper dosa** (a two-foot long papery wonder), the **butter dosa** which is smothered in the stuff, and **addai** (made with several lentil varieties and rice, spiced with ginger, cumin and red chillies) and so on. Dosas in Tamil Nadu are preferred more thick and soft, as compared to the thin, crisp variety you'll find in Karnataka.

Idlis are another important South Indian snack, often made with the same fermented batter as dosas. These low-cal, nutritional and easily digested snacks provide a welcome alternative to oil, spice and chilli. Idlis are spongy, round, white cakes dipped in sambar and coconut chatni, and make a terrific, healthy breakfast.

Vadas are fried salty doughnuts, made with urad (black lentil) paste, crisp and brown outside and spongy and white inside. You can make spicy vada by coarsely grinding chickpeas with chillies and onions and frying it into round balls. Other popular breakfast dishes are **appams** or **uttappams** (crisp-collared rice-flour and coconut milk pancakes) and **aval** (flattened rice).

Karnataka

Karnataka has a recorded history of over two millennia and visitors flock to the state to explore the ancient Hindu temple architecture at Badami, Belur, Halebid and Hampi, each representing an important dynasty in the history of India. In contrast the capital, Bangalore, is the country's most progressive city – it was the first place to have beer on tap, for example, and as India's Silicon Valley it exports its IT expertise all over the world.

Extensive records of South Indian food exist in ancient Kannada and Tamil literature (the region's two main languages). Studying them you

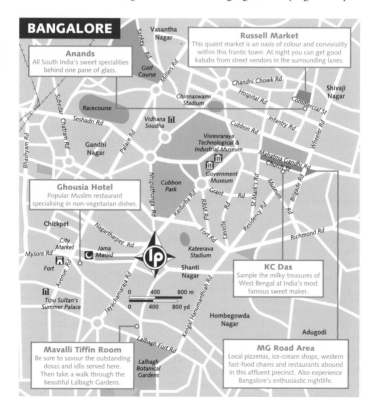

BANGALORE

Russell Market
This quaint market is an oasis of colour and conviviality within this frantic town. At night you can get good kababs from street vendors in the surrounding lanes.

Anands
All South India's sweet specialities behind one pane of glass.

Ghousia Hotel
Popular Muslim restaurant specialising in non-vegetarian dishes.

KC Das
Sample the milky treasures of West Bengal at India's most famous sweet maker.

Mavalli Tiffin Room
Be sure to savour the outstanding dosas and idlis served here. Then take a walk through the beautiful Lalbagh Gardens.

MG Road Area
Local pizzerias, ice-cream shops, western fast-food chains and restaurants abound in this affluent precinct. Also experience Bangalore's enthusiastic nightlife.

Map labels: Vasantha Nagar, Sankey Rd, Golf Course, Millers Rd, Chandni Chowk Rd, Hospital Rd, Shivaji Nagar, Commercial St, Subedar Chatram Rd, Racecourse, Chinnaswami Stadium, Seshadri Rd, Vidhana Soudha, Cubbon Rd, Infantry Rd, Wheeler Rd, Bhashyam Rd, Gandhi Nagar, Palace Rd, Visresraraya Technological & Industrial Museum, Mahatma Gandhi Rd, Church St, Brigade Rd, Nrupathunga Rd, Cubbon Park, Government Museum, Grant Rd, St Mark's Rd, Museum Rd, Chickpet, Nagarthapet Rd, Kasturba Rd, Residency Rd, Richmond Rd, City Market, Jama Masjid, Fort Rd, Lavelle Rd, Mysore Rd, Fort, Avenue Rd, Kateerava Stadium, Shanti Nagar, Tipu Sultan's Summer Palace, Jayachamaraja Rd, Kengal Hanumanthian Rd, Hombegowda Nagar, Adugodi, Lalbagh Fort Rd, Lalbagh Botanical Gardens

0   400   800 m
0   400   800 yd

realise that culinary practises here have changed little over the last millennium. The vegetarian food of Karnataka is mildly spiced and often sweetish, as compared to that in Tamil Nadu. But between the two states, you'll find a counterpart for practically every item with distinctive regional variations.

The pure vegetarian food made in Bangalore is an outstanding example of subtle finesse, perfected through centuries of tradition. As in the rest of South India, plain white rice and the liquid preparations sambar (made here with yellow lentil daal) and rasam are staples. Karnataka's sambar can be a meal in itself; it has the protein from the lentil, the vitamins and minerals from the vegetables, additional vitamin C from the tamarind used to make it sour, and it even has **hing** (asafoetida) to act as a digestive aid. In fact, every ingredient of every dish has some role to play, and South Indians are familiar with the traditional scientific principles behind each one. Curry leaves, they will tell you, keep your hair from greying.

To the basics of rice, sambar and rasam, locals add a **pallya** (dry vegetable preparation), a **kosambri** (raw salad), a raita (known here as **pachadi**), curds, pickle and pappadam. On special occasions they will serve **masala rice** (spiced rice) and a **gojju** (a hot, sweet & sour vegetable flavoured with tamarind, red chilli, sesame and coriander seeds). There are numerous masala rices including the popular **bisi bele huli anna** (an elaborate mixture of rice, lentils, potatoes, carrots, beans, capsicum and peas, cooked in ghee and powdered spices, garnished with fried peanuts and curry leaves).

A sweet ending to this elaborate meal might be **holige** (finely rolled rotis, filled with sweetened daal and scented with cardamom) or **payasam** (rice pudding). **Mysore pak** is another famous sweet, made of crumbly cubes of gram flour cooked in sugar and ghee.

The farmers of Karnataka have a unique staple called **ragi** (finger millet) that is extremely filling and high in minerals and calcium. Ragi flour is steamed to make balls called **mudde**. The balls are dipped into spicy sambar or gravy made out of farm greens called **bassar**, and popped whole into the mouth (see the boxed text Cooking Traditions & Primetime Television in the Home Cooking & Traditions chapter). They are also had with the spicy meat and fish curries enjoyed by the non-Brahmin castes. Many restaurant menus in Bangalore feature this rustic fare these days.

The cuisine of the western coast of Karnataka, the Konkan Coast, is more like Goan fare. Mangalore is the main city and even Brahmins here eat fish. Non-Brahmin Hindus eat fish, chicken and mutton, while the large Christian population add beef and pork to the fleshy diet. Coconut is a common ingredient and you'll find it grated, as milk and oil. Mangaloreans have their own rice preparations like **pundi** (rice and coconut balls cooked in starch), **bari akki** (rice dosa) and **akki roti** (rice roti) with which they have with their spicy meat and fish curries.

REGIONAL VARIATIONS

Tamil Nadu

Tamil Nadu is a cradle of traditional Indian (Dravidian) culture, has beautiful beaches, fishing villages, ancient temples and relics of the Raj – Chennai, the capital, being the first settlement of the East India Company. Tamils preserve their cultural traditions fiercely, which has led to a somewhat insular cuisine. Most Indians outside the state think that Tamils eat only idlis and dosas.

Food in Tamil homes is closely linked to ritual life and treated as pure and incorruptible. Every festival or occasion is associated with a particular dish. Modern, working women still spend hours in the kitchen to serve their families traditional meals. A Tamil meal begins with a mouthful or two of plain rice, boiled yellow lentils and ghee, which is believed to line the stomach against acidity. Next comes sambar along with a **poriyal** (dry vegetable). For variety the sambar could be replaced by **vattal kuzhambu** (a liquid preparation of sun-dried vegetables in tamarind water), or **mor kuzhambu** (a similar dish using curds instead of tamarind). The meal could also include accompaniments like a raita, **thuvaiyal** (chutney) and **kosumalli** (salad), which come in a wide variety, and may be rounded off with rice, curds and some pickle. Like all traditional cuisines, there are fixed combinations, for example sambar always goes with poriyal.

Many sweets are common to South and North India including ladoos, barfis and payasams. However, some unique sweets are made for certain festivals, such as **karchikkai** (a fried ball of sweetened coconut, covered with rice paste), which is made to celebrate the birth of Krishna, and **pongal** (sweet festive rice garnished with nuts, raisins and coconut) to celebrate New Year. Vegetarian fare predominates here, thanks largely to the cultural dominance of the Brahmins. Castes that come directly below them (like the rich landowners) mimic Brahmin behaviour and claim to be vegetari-

Deep fried vadai with onion, Tamil Nadu

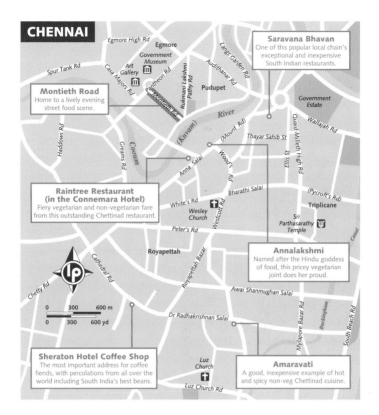

CHENNAI

Saravana Bhavan
One of this popular local chain's exceptional and inexpensive South Indian restaurants.

Montieth Road
Home to a lively evening street food scene.

Raintree Restaurant (in the Connemara Hotel)
Fiery vegetarian and non-vegetarian fare from this outstanding Chettinad restaurant.

Annalakshmi
Named after the Hindu goddess of food, this pricey vegetarian joint does her proud.

Sheraton Hotel Coffee Shop
The most important address for coffee fiends, with percolations from all over the world including South India's best beans.

Amaravati
A good, inexpensive example of hot and spicy non-veg Chettinad cuisine.

Egmore High Rd · Egmore · Government Museum · Art Gallery · Spur Tank Rd · Casa Majors Rd · Pantheon Rd · Montieth Rd · Rukmani Lakshmi Pathy Rd · Langs Garden Rd · Audithanar Rd · Pudupet · River (Kuvam) · (Mount Rd) · Government Estate · Quaid-Milleth High Rd · Wallajah Rd · Thayar Sahib St · Ellis St · Haddows Rd · Greams Rd · Anna Salai · Woods Rd · Bharathi Salai · (Pycroft's Rd) · Triplicane · White's Rd · Wesley Church · Westcott Rd · Sri Parthasarathy Temple · Peter's Rd · Royapettah · Royapettah Bazaar · Cathedral Rd · Chetty Rd · Awai Shanmugham Salai · Dr Radhakrishnan Salai · Mylapore Bazar Rd · Buckingham · South Beach Rd · Luz Church · Luz Church Rd

0 300 600 m
0 300 600 yd

an, though it is not prohibited by their religion. However, many enjoy their spicy meat and fish curries, which are generally served in small helpings, in saucer-like dishes, along with the general gamut of rice, sambar and of course fresh vegetables.

The main non-vegetarian cuisine of Tamil Nadu comes from the Chettiars, the wealthy merchant community. Heat and spice are the characteristics of this cuisine, and the most famous dishes are **kola kozhambu** (spicy meatballs in a sour gravy) and **chettinad chicken fry**, a unique stir-fried chicken with plenty of red chillies, curry leaves, onions and spices.

DON'T MISS

- Sampling South India's dosas
- A delectable dinner at Chennai's Annalakshmi restaurant
- Crunchy bread, pâté and ample cheap beer in French Pondicherry
- The exquisite vegetarian cuisines of Karnataka and Tamil Nadu
- Boating along the Keralan backwaters with nothing to do but wave at excited children and sample scrumptious regional cuisine
- Muslim specialities like kababs, biryanis and pulaos in Hyderabad
- Exploring the lanes and back streets of Jewtown in Cochin, India's spice capital
- Mysore Nuggets and Monsooned Malabar – India's finest coffee
- The unparalleled seafood of Kerala

Andhra Pradesh

This state is a fascinating melting pot of Hindu and Muslim cultures, and a rich gastronomic experience for the traveller. Ruled by Muslim emperors from the 14th century, the large community of Muslim settlers live in harmony with the indigenous Telugu-speaking Andhras, and both have adopted salient features of each other's cultures. Andhra Pradesh bears strong traces of the Nawabi culture, in which cooking was considered an art form as sophisticated as poetry. Even today in affluent homes, food is one endless chain of activity from early morning to late at night. All of India's Muslim specialities can be found here with a unique Andhra twist, often in the form of heat or spice.

Charminar is at the epicentre of Muslim Hyderabad, and tucked in between the colourful handicraft shops are food stalls that tempt you with regional treats. Hot, spicy kababs wrapped in **ulte tawe ki roti** (a thin bread cooked on an upturned convex griddle) and **achhar gosht** (pickle-like meat dish) are both Hyderabadi favourites. You can stop at the sweet shops near the Malwalla Palace to soothe your chilli-spiced palate. After a few hours shopping and sightseeing – and getting stoned by Muslim women for insensitively wearing shorts – you can stop at a biryani stall to try Hyderabad's oven-baked biryani, with layers of vegetables, meat, nuts and spices (quite different to North Indian biryanis). Top it with **boorani** (raita made with chopped tomato, cucumber and onions) and you're on your way.

REGIONAL VARIATIONS

Hyderabadi Biryani, made with chicken, Andhra Pradesh

Lamb kababs cooking over hot coals from a streetside stall, Hyderabad, Andhra Pradesh

If you're still hankering for Muslim food the next morning, visit the little restaurants outside Nampally station and buy **nihari** (a rich broth made by simmering goat's trotters over-night on low embers). Mop this up with soft and spongy **kulcha** (a bread so synonymous with Hyderabadi culture that it featured on the princely ruler's flag). Or you can buy **haleem** (a tasty wheat porridge cooked with meat and spices).

Andhra Pradesh's other major cuisine, that of the Andhras, is made up of a wide variety of lentil, vegetable, meat and fish preparations. A sour touch provided by tamarind is added to most dishes. The state's Guntoor district is famous for its red chillies and these lend a fiery touch to many dishes as well as the famous Andhra pickles.

An elaborate meal might consist of plain rice as well as **pulihora** (spicy vegetable pulao), **pappu chaar** (boiled daal seasoned with asafoetida, garlic and lime), **veppudu** (dry fried vegetable), **pulisu** (a curried vegetable in a tamarind gravy), rasam, curds and hot pickle. Non-vegetarian homes would serve most of these dishes but also add **chapa pulusu** (a flaming red fish curry), or a chicken or lamb curry in coconut sauce. The favourite Andhra sweet – eaten on special occasions – is **poornam burelu** and **araselu burelu** (fat fried dumplings with a sweet daal or rice filling). Pulla Reddy Sweets is a reliable chain found all over the state.

Pickles and chatnis are integral to Andhra cuisine. The chatnis are not sweet or fruit based, as we are used to; they can be a **podi** (dry powder) made with a combination of spices, daals and red chillies, or different wet pastes such as ginger, chillies, cucumber or raw mango.

A Muslim boy eats on Sardar Patel Road in Hyderabad

Masala Dosa
Crepe stuffed with Potatoes, Onions & Curry Leaves

Home-cooked dosas are never as thin and crisp as the ones served in shops. Even the most expert Tamil housewives, make thick, spongy dosas at home, rather than the papery, crisp ones.

Ingredients

1 cup	urad (black gram or lentils)
2 cups	rice
$\frac{1}{4}$ cup	vegetable or sunflower oil
1 tsp	salt

Batter

Soak the urad and rice separately in plenty of water for around 4-5 hours. Drain out the water from both. First put the daal into a blender and grind it with $\frac{1}{2}$ cup water. Test the paste between your fingers – it should be smooth and velvety. Put the daal paste into a large bowl. Now grind the rice with $\frac{1}{2}$ cup water, but this time the paste should be a bit coarse and grainy. Add the rice to the daal and mix well. Leave the batter to ferment overnight. The room temperature should be 30°C (85°F) or more, otherwise the batter will not ferment. In a milder climate you could keep it covered in the sun for a few hours or heat a room in the house. The next morning the dosa batter should have risen and contain tiny air bubbles.

Frying the Dosa

Add the salt to the batter and mix well with a ladle. Add water until the consistency is as thick as treacle. Use a large, clean non-stick frying pan to fry the dosas – this is essential, otherwise you and the dosas are stuck! Heat the pan to medium heat and spray or lightly smear it with oil. The surface should be just thinly coated with oil.

Pour in a ladle of batter (around ¼ cup) and spread it with the bottom of the ladle into as large and thin a circle as you can make. If the bottom of your ladle is not flat, you can use the base of a smooth, flat bowl. Cover the pan and cook the dosa for 2 minutes on low heat.

When you open the lid, the dosa should be congealed and the edges and bottom slightly brown. Now turn the flame up and drizzle a teaspoon of oil around the edges. This makes the dosa crisp and separates it from the pan. Fry for 30 seconds and gently ease it out onto a plate. The dosa should be served with the brown side down.

Ingredients for Masala Filling

This potato can also be had as a separate sabzi (vegetable) dish with pooris or roti.

500g (16oz)	potatoes
½ tsp	mustard seeds
10-15	curry leaves
2	green chillies, finely diced
1	large onion, finely sliced
½ tsp	turmeric
1 tsp	salt
2 Tbs	vegetable or sunflower oil

Peel and boil the potatoes, and crumble them into little pieces. Heat the oil in a wok or frying pan and add the mustard seeds. When they sputter, add the curry leaves, chillies and onions. Saute until the onions are light brown and add the potato mash. Stir in the turmeric and salt and then cook over a medium flame for 5 minutes.

This filling is spooned into individual dosas (around 4 Tbs per dosa) and the dosa is folded into half over it (much like an omelette).

Makes 8 dosas

Kerala

Visitors – Arabs, Chinese, Portuguese and British – have flocked to these shores since ancient times, mostly in search of Kerala's exquisite spices, which hold much the same lure for us today. As a result of this contact, Kerala is a harmonious blend of different cultures including Hindus, Muslims and Christians. Kerala has achieved 100% literacy among men and women, a unique achievement in India. Kerala is one of India's most rewarding states for food and scenery. Unparalleled fish and seafood are scooped from lush backwaters and dazzling beaches, while the dense rainforests of the mountainous Western Ghats shelter some of the globes finest spices and delicious coffee (see Coffee in the Drinks chapter). Though the two states are at opposite ends of the subcontinent, West Bengal and Kerala share three passions: fish, rum and communism.

Kerala's upper castes stick to a vegetarian diet but, due to the Christian influence, other Hindus supplement their diet with lots of meat and fish, and even eat beef without qualms. Seafood is a big favourite, and every meal will include it in a fried or curried form. Most food is cooked in coconut oil and dishes are abundantly garnished with freshly scraped coconut or coconut milk. Vegetables are never over-cooked, and are simply steamed or stir-fried to retain their natural flavours and nutrients. Similarly meats and fish are just boiled in spicy gravy, and not sautéed or browned before currying, in the typical Indian way.

A fish dish with spices steamed in banana leaves served with rice and roti bread from Mezbar Restaurant in Kozhikode, Kerala

Most of the state's vegetarian dishes can be sampled during Onam, the most important **Malayali** (Keralan) festival, which takes place in mid April. The whole community celebrates Onam and most eat vegetarian for the day. People wear new clothes and enjoy a sumptuous meal of up to 18 courses, laid out on banana leaves (see Onam in the Celebrating with Food chapter).

The Syrian Christians, one of the oldest Christian sects in India, form a large community in Kerala. Christians have no food taboos and all main meals will include beef, chicken, mutton or fish. On festive days, such as Easter Sunday, even breakfast might be chicken stew, cooked in coconut milk, and redolent with the flavour of garam masala and curry leaves. A classic combination is stew and **appam** (delicious rice pancake, that is spongy in the centre and thin and crisp around the edges, made of rice batter fermented with toddy). **Beef fry** is another standard, where beef slivers are cooked in spices then fried up with onions. Fish and prawns are relished and fiery red **meen** (fish curry) is cooked in earthenware pots and kept to mellow in flavour before it is served with rice. **Molee** (fish pieces poached in coconut milk and spices) is another favourite and many Malayali Christians consider it their speciality.

Beef fry, served with rice and mango pickle from the Mezban Restaurant, Kozhikode, Kerala

Banana chips at a roadside shop in Quilandy, near Kozhikode, Kerala

Bakeries are a legacy of the British Raj, and are dotted all over Kerala. They make excellent bread, buns and cakes. Even traditional Christmas cake is a Kerala favourite and can be bought year round.

The Kerala Muslims from the North Malabar region make a brilliant biryani that stands out for its use of coconut, poppy seed, mint and coriander and has a greenish-white tinge. The Muslims also make a unique **maida paratha** (a light, flaky fried bread) eaten with stew or meat curry. The **pathiri** (a hanky-thin roti made of rice flour) is another roti unique to the Muslim Keralites.

Lots of exotic fruits grow in Kerala's perpetually balmy conditions but bananas are a passion, and most backyards will have several varieties ripe for picking. The **nendraparram** (large orange-red banana) is a favourite. It's made into chips and cooked as a vegetable when raw, while the ripe fruit is made into halwa, fritters or candied in caramel.

shopping
& markets

The market reigns in India. It's where you'll rub shoulders with those who shape the nation's cuisine, who converge here every day in search of the freshest produce for the least rupees. Some markets are magnificent spectacles and to enter one is to be thrust, heart pumping and head reeling into the core of Indian life. Even if you don't intend to cook, you'll leave the market laden with goodies.

Wherever there's a concentration of people, there will be a **haat** (market). In a small village, there might be a collection of carts where people shop for their daily essentials, a stopgap to tide them over until the main weekend market or until they can get to the nearest town. Villagers often come to the outskirts of cities and hold regular weekend markets for suburbanites. Cities host markets for different districts, but the central one is often the oldest and most atmospheric. Some markets are planned, others grow organically. The success of one spice shop will attract other eager spice vendors and within time the street will simply become known as the spice market.

While supermarkets are springing up in middle-class suburbs throughout the country, they are still the exception and even 'so-called' modern shoppers frequently visit the traditional markets they grew up with.

A Sikh gentleman sells pickles and uncooked pappadams, Varanasi, Uttar Pradesh

A coconut seller at Howrah Station, Kolkata, West Bengal

There are different types of markets all over India, each with its own personality, reflecting the character, history and geography of the people who live in that area. Where there is a concentration of Muslims, you'll find meat. If you're near the coast, the markets will glisten with freshly caught fish. In the affluent suburbs of major cities, you'll find 'exotic' markets with edibles like mushrooms, broccoli, beetroot, kiwi fruit and grapes shipped in from mysterious lands. The grocery next door will have shelves stacked with outlandishly priced international goods like HP sauce, Bertolli Olive Oil, Campbell's soups and Pringles (often with dubious best before dates).

Wherever you wash up, head to the nearest market and gauge the mood of shoppers. Don't look at your map; follow the people walking along the streets with colourfully striped jute bags and the men pushing carts laden with fruit and vegetables, or the man with live chickens draped over his bicycle handlebars. On second thoughts, do look at the map to make sure you're going in the right general direction and not following people home.

An early morning chicken purchase in New Market, Kolkata, West Bengal

The markets are often so packed with food and people that vendors spill beyond the set boundaries into surrounding streets and labyrinthine lanes, and the market just seems to blend into the rest of the city. Approaching the 'organised' section, the thoroughfares become thick with makeshift stalls.

Some Indian markets brim with as much life as any of Asia's busiest, but compared to the mayhem of the streets they can feel like leisurely strolls. The incessant beeping recedes and there are no two-stroke vehicles threatening to take you out. There's a clear order, a sense of purpose, and they're often unusually clean.

Only the porters rush about and they are only hurrying so they can sit down again. In the morning and throughout the day, you'll see them dashing in relays delivering stock. Light on their bare feet, their lean frames glint with sweat as they wiggle under the weight of another heavy load. They hiss to clear the path and if you don't respond they'll run you over without a second thought.

Resist the temptation to reach straight for your camera, instead wander a little. You'll notice that stalls selling the same merchandise tend to clump together. Not just vegetable vendors all pitched in the vegetable section but maybe three stalls in a row selling nothing but onions and garlic. The same goes for street vendors and shops in general. You could wander around for a day looking for a spiral notebook and then find a whole street selling nothing but spiral notebooks. Indian shoppers don't buy on impulse; they know exactly where to go for each item they require, and when they get there, they want choice.

If they haven't already caught your eye, let your snout lead you to the spice stalls where you can pay homage to the stars of Indian cuisine. Vendors will be busy grinding buckets full of colourful spices, each batch filling the air with its heavenly fragrance. Sift through the different sacks, scooping handfuls to judge each bouquet. See if you can tell the difference between cinnamon and cassia. One of the vendors will take you on a virtual tour of India's spices and the more questions you ask, the happier he will be. Another will tell you the medicinal qualities of each while trying to flog you saffron, and another may ask you to sample his secret-ingredient masalas.

Walking towards the fruit and vegetable section, the smells coming from the herb stall will stop you in your tracks. The air is thick with the invigorating scent of coriander, mint and other bunches of vaguely familiar, fresh greens.

The fruit and vegetable vendors are often as bold as their displays. You'll see them perched above slopes of their produce, or their heads peeping out between a curtain of hanging gourds. Pick up an eggplant, admire its perfect shape and marvel at its vibrant colour, and suddenly he's sticking it in a bag for you and seeking payment.

Cucumber and banana leaf sellers, Bangalore City market, Karnataka

Befriending a fruit vendor can be a highlight. If you show enough interest, he'll treat you to a sample of his wares, and show you how to eat custard apples and pomegranates. He'll tell you where each fruit comes from, its season, the varieties and, of course, how much it costs.

The meat market is always quite separate to the fresh produce, hidden away to protect sensitive eyes. Us barbarians must sneak in to fill our carnivorous desires. This is an altogether different experience, and you should brace yourself if it's your first Asian market, as no effort is made to sanitise the process. You'll smell the meat market before you clap eyes on it, and the stench of blood will have you covering your nose. First you'll see cages packed beyond capacity with chickens and ducks, forlorn and resigned to the knife. A chicken chain gang is laid out along a bench, and you only realise they are still alive when one of them blinks. The air is thick with the scent of their blood and the sound of knives being sharpened. You'll see cleavers transforming poultry into dinner. Slit, pluck, chop. Slit, pluck, chop. Some people buy their chickens live, choosing to do the slaughtering themselves at home, and the chickens are handled the same whether they are alive or dead. A family of partridges hang their heads limply between the bars of another cage and you move quickly – not too quickly that you slip on the entrails – deeper into the meat market.

Time slows down, your heart beats in your mouth, your senses sharpen to take in as much as you can in the shortest length of time, usually as long as you can hold a single breath. They are always undercover and dimly lit, creating a baleful atmosphere. The noise strikes you first as the cacophony of crows squawk frantically from the rafters, pleading for a piece of the bloody action. Through the miasma, you see long, skinny goat carcasses dripping into puddles. A bucket of goats' heads sits on a nearby metal bench, one of which has fallen into your path, its eyes gaping wide. A feral cat furtively springs from one hiding place to another, trying to get dinner before being chased away. You hear a hiss and duck for cover as a blood-splattered worker passes by with a leaking carcass draped across his shoulders. The workers chat and smile as they carry out their macabre duties. One laughs at the foreigner holding his nose, and offers a handful of dripping innards to amuse his mates. You look for the natural light of the exit and head for it in a hurry, running out of oxygen. You emerge into the fish market, breathing deeply. To be so close to the kill is repulsive and repelling, fascinating and compelling.

A busy morning selling mackerel, Panaji fish market, Goa

After the grisly carnage you've just passed, the fish market looks like a picture of serenity. Silvery piles of freshly caught fish glisten on mats, some still slapping, gasping and protesting. Vendors hold them up to exhibit their freshness, and shoppers order them filleted or whole. Behind the displays, men lop off fish heads and draw out entrails with production-line efficiency. Piles of dried fish attract buzzing flies. In smaller markets, you'll see rows of women sitting behind tarpaulin mats splayed with fish fresh from their husbands' catch.

Now, go back and snap all of your photographs.

While it's almost exclusively women who cook, many men take it upon themselves to shop. Men take pride in getting the maximum bang for the family buck and consider it an affront to their manhood to pay full price. Don't think for a moment that Indian women are pushovers as they are not easily parted with their cash and are known to haggle with the best of them. But men take it as their heartfelt duty and the market provides a daily challenge, a rare opportunity to exercise the last vestiges of their primordial hunter-gatherer instinct.

But the science of haggling sometimes applies least when it comes to food, at least for foreigners. Most Indians have their preferred stalls

On the way to Chowk Bazaar, Darjeeling, West Bengal

and shops, perhaps the same places their grandparents shopped from – generations of vendors serving generations of customers, family trees blossoming in tandem. Some forge relationships with reliable vendors, and while they may have lively conversations about price and quality, it's usually more banter than haggle. Vendors tease customers with news on what's coming up, how the mango harvest is going and what annual favourites they can expect next, and shoppers store the information, looking forward to surprising their loved ones with the seasonal delights.

You're not expected to hone your haggling skills when shopping in markets. You won't be quoted outrageous prices that you are expected to halve at first bid, as with most other shopping expeditions. Nobody is going to rip you off (unless you make it too easy to resist). You're expected to pay slightly more than the locals but you should accept this with good humour and grace.

Markets keep irregular hours but most open for business by 10am and will close between 7 and 10pm. In hot climes, the market may close for lunch so the vendors can enjoy a siesta. Other markets stay open but show no signs of life but for the snoring of slumbering sellers, who you might have to rouse to make a purchase. There will always be chai stalls nearby and often places selling **tiffin** (snacks), although you won't find the profusion of eateries common to most Asian markets.

Roving Vendors

Or, you could sit on a step and wait for the market to come to you. At any time of day, market surplus is being sold on the streets; a cavalcade of fruit, vegetables, nuts, eggs and fish being pushed or dragged on rickety old carts by men happy to be out and about. Women perch baskets of fresh fruit on their heads, men hold bigger baskets packed with shining utensils that cascade over the sides. Men cycle around with fresh herbs on the carriers of their bikes and young men push ice-cream carts tempting young children and trying the patience of mothers.

You'll usually see these vendors in the afternoons – at least that's when you notice them, when things quieten down during siesta. The vendors try and coax people from their homes. Some sell vegetables by calling "sabzi, sabzi" while others sing about the virtues of the fish they've just caught or the shiny eggs that were laid that morning. The boys on the roof flying kites aren't tempted but women emerge onto balconies, squinting to appraise the produce. They beckon and the vendor stops, secure in the knowledge that he's got a sale. You don't stop the vendors to have a look. Cheerful as their whistles may be, once they've lowered their bundles, you are a buyer. Curiosity got us six wild fowls' eggs, which the vendor insisted we have with milk for "good medicine". They cost just Rs 2 each, and we did feel pretty good. If you have a door, the market will come to it.

Even if you're on a beach and dreading the idea of peeling yourself from your new sari, squint into the distance and you'll see a vendor waddling towards you with a basket of tropical fruit on their head. A peel and a chop later, the vendor has gone and the juice from the most delicious pineapple you've ever tasted is dribbling down your chin.

A seller of roasted nuts takes in the view at Chowpatty beach, Mumbai, Maharashtra

Other Shops

All of the essentials for life and leisure will be available within a short walk of an established market. Nearby there will be a whole street selling nothing but kitchen utensils, an entire boulevard draped in colourful plastic and shining kitchenware, with groups of women – men wouldn't know what to look for – haggling for the best price on a set of **dekchi** (pots).

Along the road a little further, you'll find a **mithai** (sweet) shop, with all the region's specialities tempting you behind glass. If it's a big shop and the sweets are openly displayed, you might be allowed to walk around picking until you find one you like. You pay by the piece and the weight when in bulk. Or ask the shop attendant to select the

Ladoos at a mithai, Varanasi, Uttar Pradesh

house speciality for you to sample. Sometimes there are tables, otherwise buy a piece and bring it to the nearest chai stand. If, at the back of the shop, there's a wall of colourful gift boxes you'll know that a festival is imminent. Over the next few days this shop will become the focus of every shopper's mission.

Such is the craving of the Indian sweet tooth that the mind-boggling array of Indian sweets is not enough for some, and international-style cake shops are springing up in all the major cities. Unlike most of India's culinary imitations, many Indian bakers do wonderful versions of European pastries, and you'll find these bakeries in the posh parts of most towns as well as in five-star hotels, fortunately open to non-guests.

The **gwala** (milk shop) is as much a place to eat and drink as somewhere to shop. It stocks the full gamut of Indian milk products from lassis and desserts to curds and cheese, and perhaps its own specialities (see the boxed text White Meat & Colourful Weddings in the Staples & Specialities chapter). In the north, particularly in the cities of Varanasi and Amritsar, you'll find shops and stalls specialising in magnificent lassis.

For every market there are hundreds of general provision stores, like our corner shops, selling drinks, biscuits, cigarettes and – this is when you know you're in a tourist area – toilet paper.

Things to Take Home

Many things will catch your eye and befriend your palate during your stay and, naturally, you may want to take them home. The bad news is that it can be very tricky convincing customs officers that your souvenirs are safe and they will rarely give you the benefit of the doubt. Fortunately the culinary world has shrunk to such an extent that you can find virtually any Indian ingredient at specialist Indian and Asian stores, of which every city has at least one.

But you still want to pack a portable pantry so, in your mind at least, you can stay in India for as long as you like. Spices are your best bet. Indian expats always seek out a reliable spice vendor and return with armfuls of spe-

Dried spices, Kolkata

cialist **masalas** (spice blends) to share among friends in their adopted countries. They wouldn't be welcomed back if they didn't. Spices, particularly organic ones, will provide many enchanting memories. And just as onions will make you cry, Kerala's black pepper will have you staring into space reminiscing. Make sure to pack some saffron, which comes in cute little packages ribboned with coloured thread. You'll hardly notice them in your bag, they cost a pittance, and make wonderful gifts for your friends. Resist the temptation to buy the little plastic strips of a dozen or so spices, which are strictly for show and absolutely not for cooking. It's more likely that they came from urchins who scraped them off the street than from a reliable source.

Most Indian dishes can be recreated at home but if you serve them in an Indian **thali** (plate) they'll taste better with the seasoning of authenticity. Even if they are stored beneath the sink and never used, just knowing that they are there will make Gujarat seem not so far away. Most utensils, like ingredients, can also be bought at specialist Indian shops in the west.

Don't leave Goa without a bottle of cashew **feni** (spirits) under your arm and, remember, a good homemade drop is much better than the best commercial brand so get networking.

Indian shopping bags are cute and practical, and you might like to pack a few. Get the hemp ones where possible. They are very sturdy and good for the environment. The ones made with plastic fibres also look cute but don't leave them out in the sun or they'll frazzle.

where to
eat & drink

Indians usually eat out due to necessity rather than occasion – to enjoy it would be a slight on their mother or wife's cooking – but there are still plenty of eateries to choose from. Fortunately, expense is rarely an indication of quality, and you can enjoy the finest food for a pittance in a fluoro-lit cavern as easily as in a swanky five-star hotel.

The concept of Indian restaurants, both in India and overseas, has only really taken off in the last 50 years. Traditionally, Indians ate only what was prepared in the sanctity of their own homes. Even the adventurous and affluent didn't want to pay somebody else to prepare the food that was being made to their tastes at home. Following the holocaust that took place after the partition of Punjab in 1947, millions of displaced Punjabis scattered throughout India and the world. Many established restaurants that showcased their favourite dishes and the exotic tandoor lured many Indians from their homes. Thus Punjabi food – with Mughlai touches – came to represent Indian cuisine the world over.

There are now multitudes of restaurants – or 'hotels' – and their signage will identify them as either 'veg', 'pure veg' or 'non-veg'. Pure veg indicates that no eggs are used and that there is no risk of food being contaminated with meat. Most mid-range restaurants serve one of two basic genres; South Indian (which means the vegetarian food of Tamil Nadu and Karnataka) and North Indian (which comprises Punjabi/Mughlai food). You'll also find the cuisines of neighbouring regions and states. Indians frequently migrate in search of work and these restaurants cater to the large communities seeking the familiar tastes of home, as well as locals looking for new flavours.

Except among orthodox Brahmins, the taboos on eating outside the home have been considerably loosened in recent years, although eating out remains an urban phenomenon. In rural areas you'll only find shacks and small eateries for travellers on the highway. Otherwise villagers buy food from snack stalls at fairs or outside temples. Women and children eat at shacks only if they are travelling or have come out to visit a fair or temple. Even then they will more often carry packed food. Working-class men in urban areas eat out regularly only when they live away from their family and there is no woman at home to cook for them. There is a sharp divide between eating out because of necessity and making an occasion of it. The latter only occurs among the middle and upper-middle class in cities. Fine dining in the western sense doesn't exist – Indians go for the quality of the food without much regard for the ambience and style. Only the upper elite dig fine dining and go to five-star hotels.

Likewise, you don't need to spend big to enjoy delicious and authentic food, which you'll find in many cheap restaurants. You'll recognise these because they don't rely on ambience or self promotion, they give you steel tumblers of water to avoid, are dimly lit or fluoro flashed, and the fans blow grains of rice onto your lap.

Indian hospitality is legendary but can be infuriating when offered in restaurants. Keen to accommodate the delicate foreigner, friendly waiters and kitchen staff often tone down their dishes to placate your bland palate.

The bill and some saunf, Sesh Mahal Restaurant, Bangalore, Karnataka

This is especially true of any mid-range and upper-range restaurants in well-touristed areas. It's not just a case of omitting a bit of chilli, it's really cooking to a different code and the result is often the gastronomic equivalent of having sex through an interpreter. If you think you're getting the Very Insipid Palate treatment, tell the waiter you want the dish the way it is normally cooked. But don't jump in and say "I love spicy food" because it might be taken as a challenge.

Many inexpensive and mid-range restaurants have separate 'women and family' dining areas, where the glare of grizzly men is replaced by the stares of curious children. Lone male travellers keep out.

Beside restaurants, there are lots of other places that you can duck into for a tasty, healthy snack. Look out for bakeries, sweet shops and juice stores in affluent city districts and the ubiquitous milk shop, which sells a wide range of dairy goodies.

Locals queue for chaat at the Royal Cafe, Lucknow, Uttar Pradesh

Specific Eateries
Dhabas

Literally 'wayside eateries', dhabas are actually more a way of life. These hospitable shacks are an oasis to truck drivers, bus passengers and sundry travellers going anywhere by road. A beaming chef-cum-restaurant-owner stands behind a simple counter with a row of shining brass **dekchis** (large vessels) to welcome dusty travellers. After being given a jug of cold water to drink and splash over your face, flop down on any of the **charpoys** (rope beds) that line the front of the restaurant. A plank across the charpoy serves as a table and you eat your hot food in a semi-reclining position, table manners being the last thing on your mind. This rough-and-ready but extremely tasty food has become a genre on its own known as 'dhaba food'. The original dhabas dot the North Indian landscape but you'll find lots of versions throughout the country.

Lucky Dhaba on the road to Amritsar

Coffee Houses

Each town and city has its own most famous and venerable coffee house, where students and intellectuals are said to hang out although, in truth, the clientele is just a mish-mash of people who drink coffee. Coffee houses are usually big dim halls where you can languish over filtered South Indian coffee, juices of varying quality, or a snack or two while you mull over your plans. Strangely enough, even though the South Indians drink more coffee than their northern brethren, coffee houses are more a feature of the north.

WHERE TO EAT & DRINK

Air-conditioned Family Food Halls & Restaurants

These joints are popular with families in the more affluent suburbs of major cities. Their menus are tomes and often feature South Indian, North Indian, Chinese and Continental dishes. The Indian food is always the best although the flavour is a little toned down. Some of these places – usually the ones in the cities – are models of refinement with starched linen, great food, relaxed atmosphere and waiters decked out in turbans and cummerbunds. Suburban ones can be like a laminate showroom, with gaggles of spoiled and pouty young sons running amok.

Tourist Restaurants

Wherever package tourists hang out, you'll find these places serving up bland imitations of Indian dishes and food that looks and tastes vaguely similar to the stuff you eat at home. They are overpriced because a) you can afford it and b) some tourists find high prices reassuring. Where there is stiff competition, like in parts of Goa and Kerala, some of them are actually marvellous showcases for the regional cuisines. Even the bad ones can provide some welcome cereal relief at breakfast time when you get pangs for home comforts. If you don't want hot milk on your cereal you'd better say. Not that we ever tire of Indian breakfasts, you understand.

The Bhoopathy Cafe, a popular and inexpensive vegetarian restaurant, Chennai

Udipi Restaurants

These restaurants have been set up by a particular community from Udipi in Karnataka. Udipi Restaurants bustle with life and young boys busily clear away shining stainless steel utensils before you can even finish your meal. The menu consists of the classic South Indian **tiffin** (snack) items like idlis and dosas, and the set thali meal. This food is also available in the regular restaurants or **Lunch Homes** all over the south.

Fast Food

Not to be confused with burger joints and pizzerias, restaurants in the south advertising fast food are some of India's best. They serve the whole gamut of tiffin items and often have separate sweet counters. In the north these are usually sweets and snacks shops, with Haldiram being a well-known chain. The normal procedure is to pay for your meal first and take your receipt to the serving area. Limited seating is usually available but it's called fast food because you get served quickly, eat in a hurry and skedaddle.

Western & Indian Chains

Western chains like McDonalds, Pizza Hut, KFC and TGIF started appearing in the last decade. They initially had trouble, and Bangalore's first KFC was closed down because excessive amounts of MSG were found in its food and it 'didn't come up to health standards'. The reopened outlet was again closed down by an angry coalition of farmers, vegetarians and conservationists arguing that the fast food superpowers will degrade India's culture, agriculture, economy and environment. But the virtually untapped market is too big a draw for the multinational giants and they are now settling in, largely supported by the urban money set.

McDonalds dropped its beef and introduced McAloo Tikki burgers, Maharaja Macs, McTandoori chicken burgers and the McLike. It's in the process of brainwashing a new generation of Indian children but, for the moment, seems to hold some bizarre culinary integrity with families and businessmen alike. There are also many home-grown chains particular to each city, serving much the same fare with a garnish of character, although they must be looking down the barrel with the arrival of the big boys.

Pizzas are hugely popular in cities and even home delivery has taken off in recent years – spare a thought for those poor delivery boys in this traffic! There are many indigenous pizza parlours where you can stand frantically in a queue (or semblance of one), buy a coupon and try to guess when your order comes up. If you guess right, you may be pleasantly surprised by Indian pizzas, which are about the best comfort food for those in need. Even Pizza Hut has adopted some local flavour, dishing up paneer pizza (just cheese) and Jain pizza (vegetarian without onion or garlic, or much flavour).

Military Hotels

You will find these cheap, no-frills restaurants all over the state of Tamil Nadu, and they specialise in spicy non-vegetarian food.

Five-Star Hotels

Most deluxe hotels have a number of expensive restaurants focusing on international fare, catering as they do for food-frightened foreign tourists and international Indians. You can chow Italian, Chinese, Thai, French, Continental, Japanese and Mexican, or imitations thereof (see Foreign Cuisines later in this chapter).

Such is the popularity of the foreign cuisines that if it weren't for the big business of weddings and private banquets, these hotels might not bother with Indian food at all. But thankfully there are some outstanding five-star restaurants eager to pamper you with the very best of Indian fine dining. They usually have pan-Indian menus so you can explore some of the regional treasures of this most vibrant cuisine without getting off your bum. They are outrageously expensive by Indian standards but you should pay with credit and put the expense out of your mind. When you go through your bill at home you'll laugh at your hesitant 'splurging'.

The atrium bar at the Cecil Hotel, Shimla, Himachal Pradesh

Foreign Cuisines

The Indian upper class is going gaga for international tastes lately, and ethnic cookbooks by Indian authors top the best-seller lists. Hoity-toity diners are also keen to go international but you'll find very little that hasn't been Indianised to some extent, and botched in the process.

The substantial Chinese population in Kolkata (Calcutta) is largely responsible for introducing its cuisine to India, and you'll find Chinese restaurants in most cities. Kolkata – add Bangalore and Mumbai at a stretch – has tasty and authentic Chinese food, particularly in the ethnic settlement of Tangra (see the Kolkata map). In most other places, the food is a bland hotchpotch of Chinese influences, local ingredients and Indian don't-know-how.

Continental cuisine is the next most popular alternative, which you'll regularly see on the same menus as Indian and Chinese. The genre is interpreted as 'stodge' and is best described as 'yikes!' Put the two together and you have the famed Continental cuisines of Kolkata's famous Park Street.

Up around the Himalayas, you will find lots of authentic Tibetan and Nepali restaurants that can provide a pleasant gastronomic detour. You'll find croissants and pate in the former French enclave of Pondicherry in Tamil Nadu, as well as a handful of restaurants serving great Gallic grub. But, in general, be sure to steer clear of the foreign cuisines.

Pointing the way to one of the many popular rooftop restaurants, Udaipur, Rajasthan

Guests' breakfast of bread with jam & butter and coffee at Hotel Venite, Panaji, Goa

WHERE TO EAT & DRINK

Menus

The only difficulties you will have with menus are trying to decipher the colourful Indian English terms (spaced lamb stew anyone?) and getting through the whole thing before you keel over from starvation. Some menus are like books but you should think of them more as catalogues full of possibilities rather than lists of what the kitchen can supply.

A typical Chennai menu

Outside the big hotels, most restaurants don't have menus for lunch, when there are only vegetarian and non-vegetarian thalis. Cheaper places specialising in just one or two dishes won't have any menus at all but, if he can't tell you himself, the waiter will send for the best English-speaker in the vicinity to describe each dish. Otherwise, you'll be able to see the dishes being prepared and just point to whatever takes your fancy.

Only the big hotels will serve meals in courses. All other places bring the food out as soon as it is ready, even if you think you've ordered courses.

You'll soon become familiar with the most common dishes but if you need help decoding menus, refer to the Hindi-English dictionary at the back of the book.

Tipping

As a relatively wealthy sahib or memsahib, you are expected to cough up a little of your coffers in return for any service, and the locals are rarely shy in asking for baksheesh. But because eating is a private and spiritual affair, eateries are among the few places where this applies least. However, it's always good to leave your small change. It's probably not responsible tourism but we can rarely resist tipping 'the boys' or especially friendly waiters although many places forbid tipping so don't insist. Of course, the upmarket restaurants expect the same gratuities as their counterparts around the world, a minimum of 10%.

Children

Indian children are weaned on spicy food so there are never any separate menus for them. You may ask for a child's portion but you won't get a discount. There are plenty of dishes that don't have a spice kick – roti, rice, daal, curds, soups – just ask if you're unsure.

Vegetarians & Vegans

India produces some of the best vegetarian food you'll find anywhere on the planet and eating your veggie way around the country will be more a celebration than a chore. Tamil Nadu, Karnataka and Gujarat are predominantly vegetarian as are places of pilgrimage like Varanasi and Rishikesh, and all auspicious Hindu feasts are savoured without meat. Vegetarian here means without eggs and the term 'pure vegetarian' provides reassurance for religious vegetarians that there is no contact with meat. While vegetarianism is widely understood and admired, veganism is most definitely not.

Animal products like milk, butter and curds infuse virtually every Indian dish and your first problem will be getting the cook to understand your requirements. He will usually cut you off and say, "yes, yes, pure vegetarian, I know". In cheap restaurants, give your Vegan Passport to the cashier who is usually the boss. Street food might be your best option because at least there you can see what the cook is adding and tell him what's good and not so good. There's a terrific website *(www.vegan.com)* packed full of useful advice, ideas and cautions for vegans touring India.

The Vasanta Bhavan Vegetarian Restaurant, Chennai, Tamil Nadu

All You Can Eat at the Golden Temple

Amritsar's Golden Temple is the holiest shrine of the Sikh religion. To the world's 21 million Sikhs it is what Mecca is to Muslims, the Vatican to Catholics. To the traveller, it's one of the highlights of any trip to the subcontinent.

You'll miss a heartbeat when you first catch sight of the glimmering Golden Temple. Cover your head, remove your shoes and leave your ciggies behind with a volunteer. Walk up the slippery steps leading to the marble **parkarma** (walkway) that surrounds the sacred pool called the **Amrit-sar** (pool of nectar) from where the city takes its name. The temple itself occupies a small island in the centre of the temple compound, and is connected to the parkarma by a narrow, marble causeway to the right.

Every Sikh temple has a **langar** (communal dining hall) and all visitors are requested to eat alongside one another before practising their religion. This act of communal eating is essential in **kilcha** (the removal of differences). Also for this reason, there is no 'I' at the temple, we are told. You follow the peaceful flow of squinting people walking clockwise along the dazzling parkarma. A child races gleefully from one tiled mural to another, getting on his knees and rubbing his nose against the marble in prayer just like his father showed him.

The crowd soon forks and you follow the group heading off to the left. People form orderly queues – a novelty in India – and collect a **thali** (plate) and a bowl.

It's quiet, but not at all solemn. The people seem relaxed and peaceful. You're still a curiosity but the barrage of "which country" questions give way to warm smiles. (Just as you file that mental note, you hear "which country please?" Oh well, it's different here.)

You drift into the **Guru Ka Langar**, a huge hall surrounded with arched windows admitting the stark daylight and creating silhouettes of the diners. Thin coir mats are rolled out the length of the chamber and diners sit cross-legged opposite one another. There are few words.

With practised precision, a volunteer splats a dollop of dark green **maah ki daal** (black lentil daal) into your thali and, within moments, warm rotis are falling into your cupped hands. You catch yourself before digging in because nobody else has started eating yet. A volunteer asks the question and all the Sikhs recite the name of the almighty. After **simran**, we eat.

You feel relaxed despite the discomfort of sitting cross-legged, and the feeling that the thali is a long way from your mouth when you're eating watery daal by hand for the first time. Some others are making a bit of a mess so you begin to relax into it. Rich, creamy **kheer** (rice pudding) is poured into your thali. Volunteers keep plying you with daal and roti until you make it clear that you don't want any more, by covering your thali with your right hand and avoiding any further eye contact.

Volunteers peel spuds for the free meals offered to pilgrims at the Golden Temple, Amritsar

You're pondering on the peacefulness of it all when a volunteer starts paying you special attention. Through a toothy grin he urges you to scoop up the daal and kheer with the same roti but you refuse to let his friendliness and odd eating habits spoil the moment.

Next you realise you're the last person in the hall and you're being gently shunted out. Without any crowd to follow, you're not sure of your bearings. To the left, there are maybe a hundred people washing and clanking dishes, and you go to join them. Ten turbaned helpers, who had been waiting in a chain at the bottom of the steps, rush to cut you off with a smile. One takes your dirty dishes that pass through another nine pairs of hands before being plopped in a basin of water. You linger to contemplate the scene and one of the 10 breaks from the chain, grabs your arm, and leads you on a tour of the kitchens.

You pass by groups of men in vibrant turbans – orange is an auspicious colour – peeling cloves of garlic, chipping potatoes and chopping fresh herbs. The roti room is filled with generations of women, cheerfully rolling and slapping balls of dough into, well, smaller balls of dough. On the way to the main kitchen you pass men and women hauling huge sacks of grains while others wash down the floors. A slip and a slide later, you're in the main kitchen where sweating, smiling men watch over colossal cast-iron cauldrons filled with steaming daal. You peer inside and realise that another careless slip and you could be lost in legumes.

A Sikh volunteer prepares massive cauldrons of ghee, part of the daily cooking preparation for feeding pilgrims to the Golden Temple, Amritsar

Sikh volunteers cook roti bread on a large hotplate, Golden Temple, Armritsar

These must be the happiest workers you'll ever see, and not one of them is paid. They are honoured to give **sewa** (service) at the temple, helping to feed the 50,000 people who visit each day, and the 70,000 on weekends. You can't help but be touched by the warmth and positive, peaceful energy. Even the clanking of dishes and the rhythmic slapping of dough sounds like a religious melody.

Back on the parkarma you blend in – well, not quite – to the crowd walking barefoot along the cool marble around to the temple. You're carried along by the hypnotic harmony of the singers inside the temple, whose ceaseless chanting of prayers from the Sikh's holy book, the *Granth Sahib,* is amplified throughout the grounds. Men and children bathe in the waters of the sacred pool, and the images beg to be recorded if only photography didn't seem so out of place.

The temple's dome looks like the sun's plaything, gilded with 100kg of gold. The dazzling spectacle is enhanced by the vibrantly coloured robes and turbans worn by the people on the causeway, queuing to enter the temple. Walking into the temple, you enter the space between your thoughts. You're captivated by the soothing eloquence of it all and move outside a better person.

As you leave you're given **prasad** (blessed food; eaten after being offered to the Gods), in this case sweets made from pure ghee, served by the splodge, in your hand, and not nearly as sickly sweet as most Indian sweets.

After walking past the nishan sahib tree, polished by the touch of a million hands, you reach the exit where you can get on with the rest of your life; sated for now, had after having had something to eat.

Martin Hughes

WHERE TO EAT & DRINK

Where to Drink

Indian tipplers are either working class and drink in dark, dingy drinking holes with the sole intention of getting blitzed or the urban affluent who sip spirits at home. There really isn't much of what we'd call a pub culture.

Alcoholism is a huge problem, at the root of many social evils, and prohibition was widespread not so long ago. Gujarat is now the only dry state but there are restrictive drinking laws in place all over the country, largely augmented by the ruling orthodox BJP party. Each state has regular dry days when the sale of alcohol is banned. These change between states but, wherever you are, you can forget about buying liquor on the 1st and 7th day of any month (pay-days) and all religious holidays. Anxious tipplers stock up the night before and desperate tourists can apply for Liquor Permits from Indian embassies, which will give you special imbibing privileges during prescribed dry days.

You'll find bars in all the major cities although Mumbai, Bangalore, Kolkata and Chandigarh are the only ones with thriving drinking cultures, and even these only come to life at weekends. The posh parts of these cities are peppered with western-style pubs (often of the theme variety) selling tap and bottled beer, as well as a range of spirits. There are only a few places in Delhi catering to the young yuppie set but they're about as much fun as a losing lottery ticket. Most young male drinkers – for there are few female ones – buy their booze from bottle shops and drive to their favourite restaurants, usually tandoori and kabab shops, where waiters bring their food to the car.

For the best drinking, head straight to Goa. Several good locally brewed beers complement the free flowing **feni** (coconut or cashew spirits), booze isn't subject to the exorbitant levies of other states and there are plenty of cosy bars to soak in the atmosphere of this laid-back fun-loving place. Parts of Kerala also have gregarious toddy shops but steer well clear of **arrack** (liquor distilled from coconut palm sap), the local hooch that blinds and kills hundreds of people each year (see the Drinks chapter). The former French municipality of Pondicherry in Tamil Nadu, and the tiny state of Sikkim are other drinking enclaves.

There's a thriving bootleg market in Gujarat and a friend told us he was stranded there one New Year's Eve and the hotel manager sent him a bottle of Bagpiper whisky, which he hadn't even requested. It appeared on his bill the next day as the most expensive Gujarati thali he'd ever had. Elsewhere, while boozing is legal, the typical drinking hole is filled with the feeling that you really shouldn't be drinking there unless you're a certified reprobate. These are not the kind of places thirsty female travellers should venture into alone.

Of course, there are plenty of bars along the tourist trail although a 'bar' can mean anything from a room with a pool table to a restaurant that serves drinks with food so don't get your hopes up. You'll be driven to parched distraction looking for a cold beer (see Beer in the Drinks chapter).

Go to non-vegetarian restaurants if you want to sup with your meal, as very few vegetarian places will provide for you. Stringent licensing laws discourage drinking in restaurants but some places that depend on the tourist rupee will covertly serve you beer in teapots and disguised glasses. Don't assume anything because the management might get offended and sling you out on your ear.

You are sure to get top-quality, expensive drinks if you scrub up and visit the cocktail lounges of five-star hotels although the business conference mood may make you question your motivation for going there in the first place. Was it company or booze?

Liquor stores go under different guises around the country and are known as wine shops in some states although they sell everything but wine. They keep irregular hours and it's difficult to keep track of which are dry and wet days. You can wander around the shop during the day and check out the range but in the sometimes-frantic evenings you have to order from the counter. In Delhi, you had better buy your booze during the day (see the boxed text).

A small, out-of-the-way bar, Panaji, Goa

A cold one at Leopolds Cafe & Bar, Mumbai, Maharashtra

MOTU ON A MISSION

It's 7pm and Motu (literally, chubby) is going to fetch a bottle of rum from a liquor store in South Delhi. His wife and two kids watch from the car. There's a scrum of men at the shop counter, each clamouring to get the booze wallah's attention, jostling and yelling as if they were failing brokers in a stock-market crash. Motu pauses outside the melee, and smiles back to his family.

"He's going in", say the kids, peering out the back window. "Go daddy, go!"

Motu claws his way into the booze bash and is consumed by the heaving mass. Slowly, slowly, he inches forward, guarding his wallet, his body pressed on all sides. Cash-laden hands reach out, people are shouting, imploring, screaming: "A half of whisky!" "A quarter of rum!" "The one that costs Rs 80!" "Brand or kind be damned!"

After maybe 15 minutes, Motu gets near the top and catches the eye of the booze wallah.

"Old Monk!" he says quickly.

"Don't have it!"

"Old Cask?"

"No."

In the time it takes Motu to think of his third preference, the wallah gives him a bottle of Black Negro rum. This is the first time Motu has seen this brand.

" No, give me Contessa." The man gives him a dirty look and is moving to someone else. Motu catches hold of his arm and pulls him.

"CONTESSA!" he barks.

"No" says the attendant trying to pull his arm away. But others are getting impatient and yell even more loudly.

"There it is!" implores Motu. "I can see the Contessa over there."

"No!" says the stroppy wallah, moving on.

Realising that the attendant will only sell what is within easy reach, Motu picks another bottle close by. Poking his head through the web of arms, he yells "BAGPIPER!"

The attendant pauses for a moment, and moves to the shelf. "And get me a bottle of Contessa while you're there."

"Forget the Sandpiper", Motu says when the wallah returns to the counter and harrumphs. Transaction completed, Motu emerges from the horde, beaming and bedraggled. He holds the bottle of Contessa triumphantly over his head, and the kids cheer. It's true, Daddy's clocked up another victory at the booze shop.

street food

It's on the streets where you'll find India at it vital best and revolting worst; it's most colourful and drab, joyful and depressing, meditative and unrelenting. India is laid bare in the theatre of its thoroughfares and visitors are casts in the show. These streets are a banquet for the senses. You won't like some of the courses but the tastes, smells, sights, rhythm and atmosphere of street cooking will be an experience you will never forget.

Sometimes, you feel like you could choke from the stench and the two-stroke fumes on Indian streets. And then your nostrils fill with the waft of fresh herbs and spices releasing their fragrance and you think you could eat the air. Amid the incessant beeping of horns and yelling, you hear the gentle sizzle of samosas browning, the rhythmic clanking of a wheel pressing sugarcane into juice, and the clapping of dough being shaped into various snacks. Just when you want to close your eyes to the debris and disorder, you'll be dazzled by a splay of fruit and by a disc of dough being spun into a wok and puffing up into an irresistible **poori** (deep-fried bread). When you can only move in inches through the swirling crowds, wandering livestock and traffic congestion, a chai wallah with an empty bench beckons you over. Sit and watch for a while. Pat a goat – even the livestock eat on the streets – and marvel at how life can be lived at such density.

As all human life takes place on the streets, it's only natural that it should also be sustained here. Whatever the time of day, people are boiling, frying, roasting, peeling, juicing, simmering, mixing, or baking some class of food and drink to lure passers-by. Snacking is second nature to Indians and most eat from street stalls at some time. They don't snack to tide them over between meals, they snack because they love the food and it puts the pep back in their step.

An abundance of farsan at the Crawford market, Mumbai, Maharashtra

It's a unique experience, a thrill, when you're among it and living for the moment. More than sights and photographs, this is the essence of travelling and will provide some of your fondest and most vivid memories. And, while you can make a decent stab at making samosas at home, you'll never be able to recreate the experience of Indian alfresco.

Such is the popularity of eating on the street that many establishments cook outside the front and, while there may be rows of empty tables out back, diners scramble for available space on the kerb. Other street vendors cook outside their homes, roll rickety old **thelas** (carts) to regular spots, or keep wandering looking for the prime location. Anything that can be whipped up in the open air and eaten in a jiffy is street food, and the range is staggering.

Small operations usually have one special that they serve all day while many other vendors have different dishes for breakfast, lunch and dinner. The fare varies as you venture between neighbourhoods, towns and regions but anything that can be fried in a **kadhai** (Indian wok), cooked in a pot, or fried on a griddle will be on the menu. It can be as simple as puffed rice or peanuts roasted in hot sand, as unusual as a fried egg sandwich, or as complex as the riot of different flavours known as **chaat** (any snack foods seasoned with chaat masala, see Masalas in the Staples & Specialities chapter). It will be served in biodegradable bowls made of roughly stitched sal leaves or yesterday's newspaper.

Deep-fried fare is the staple of the boulevards, and you'll find **samosas** (deep-fried pyramid-shaped pastries filled with spiced vegetables and less often meat), **aloo ki tikki** (mashed potato patties) and **bhaja** (vegetable fritters) in varying degrees of spiciness, along with **pooris** (deep-fried bread) and **kachoris** (corn or lentil savoury puff). Mouth-watering **dosas** (fermented rice-flour and lentil crepes) originated in the south but are served up by discerning vendors throughout India, along with the other southern specialities of dosas, **idlis** (spongy, round cakes made of the same batter as dosas) and **vada** (fried salty doughnuts). In the north, and most Muslim areas, you'll find kababs pounded into mouth-watering submission, doused in smooth curds and wrapped in warm bread.

In season, delicious cobs of roasted corn are hard to resist and you can't visit Mumbai without sampling **pao bhaja** (spiced vegetables with bread) and **bhelpuri** on Chowpatty beach (see Maharashtra in the Regional Variations chapter). Popular 'modern' items include omelettes, hard-boiled eggs, and even regular old sandwiches (especially tomato, cucumber and green chutney).

You'll find the best Indian cuisine in private homes but by far the most satisfying tucker is often just outside your door.

Platform Food

One of the thrills of travelling by rail is the culinary circus that greets you at every station. As the train arrives the platform springs into frenzy. Roving vendors accost the trains yelling and scampering up and down the carriages; bananas, omelettes and nuts are offered through the grills on the windows; and platform chefs try to lure you from the train with the sizzle of fresh samosas.

Roti wallahs dish out the nosh to customers from the North East Express train en route to New Delhi, Mughal Serai Station, Varanasi

Frequent rail travellers know which station is famous for which food item, and indulge their appetites accordingly. Lonavla station in Maharashtra is famous for **chikki** (nut and jaggery toffee), Agra for **petha** (crystallised gourd), and Dhaund near Delhi for **biryani** (fragrant steamed rice with meat or vegetables). In the bigger stations, platform vendors are either contracted rail staff or licensees so they have to comply to certain standards. However, with all that rushing about, food is occasionally dropped, although we've never seen any be discarded.

Directions

You had a hunch that there might be a downside to street food. There are obvious risks involved in eating on India's unsanitary streets but as long as you use your common sense and don't head straight from the airport to the kabab stand, you should be all right. We've been sick a couple of times here but have never had a bad reaction to anything we ate on the street. Remember, fortune favours the brave (and strikes down the stupid).

Give yourself a few days to adjust to the conditions and make sure you build up slowly. Ask a few well-heeled strangers (usually not hotel staff unless you're multi-starring it) about the best areas for street food. If they are Brahmin or are *too* well-heeled, they might tell you that absolutely, under no circumstances should you eat from the street. Persist and they will often confide that yes, they sometimes go to such and such a place.

You know the rule about following a crowd – if the locals are avoiding a particular vendor, it's probably not because he doesn't add enough salt. But you should also take notice of the profile or breadown of the customers. Any place frequented by women and families will be your safest bet, followed by groups of tidy men. Do not follow the rickshaw drivers to the hectic lean-to.

Chaat wallahs serve-up bhajiya & pakoras and samosas, Hyderabad, Andhra Pradesh

Have a look and remember that a clean old wooden thela is much safer than a dirty marble workbench. Most places try and take your order straight away but don't be shy about weighing up your options. Ask where you can wash your hands and buy yourself time and space. Check how and where they are cleaning the utensils, how and where the food is covered. If they are cooking in oil, check that it is clean and looks reasonably fresh. And if the pots or surfaces are dirty, there are food scraps about or a few too many buzzing flies, split and wave off the yells at your back.

Don't be put off when you order some deep-fried snack and the cook throws it back into the wok. It is common practise to par-cook the snacks first and then finish them off once they've been ordered. In fact, frying them hot again will kill the germs.

Don't eat meat from the street. Most of the snacks are vegetarian but check if it's not obvious. Sweet lemon and sugarcane juicers are ubiquitous and dubious. It is usually safe if they press the juice in front of you but never have what is stored in the jug. No matter how hot and bothered you are, don't be tempted by the pre-sliced melon and other fruit, which keeps its luscious veneer with the regular dousing of water. (See the Fit & Healthy chapter for more information.)

'The Great Pani Puri Seller', Chowpatty beach, Mumbai, Maharashtra

EATING OFF THE STREET

The huge, blackened, cast-iron pot gleams in the morning sun and sizzles with **aloo barra** (deep-fried balls of potato, onion, spices, a little chilli and a lot of fresh herbs). Men of various shapes and sizes form a semi-circle; some leaning on the handlebars of their scooters, others standing with hands on hips all staring at the wok. The cook turns down the flame and dips his slotted spoon into the vessel. The onlookers purse their lips and hold their collective breath … but it's too soon. The jhanna emerges empty and the group exhales with a gentle sigh, gazes fixed on the wok.

The cook continues to prepare the next batch; peeling dough from inside a cut-off drum, rolling it into balls, stretching it around the filling and then pinching off the doughy top to ensure an even coating. More men gather as the crispy moment approaches and the group is positively skittish by the time the cook passes 30 golden balls to his colleague who places them in bowls made from sal leaves joined together with stick-pins. He adds a dollop of sauce to each, and fills the reaching hands that threaten to engulf him.

More men arrive just as the freshly cooked aloo barra disappear. They slump in resignation and begin the wait for the next load. A woman appears and adds some feminine sparkle to the male proceedings. After surveying the pot for a few moments, she seems satisfied and reaches behind her, pulling forward a young boy before she steps back. The boy, no more than 12, is immediately transfixed. He stands, legs apart, hands on hips, staring at the pot while his guardian quietly recedes into the background. All men again. All under the spell of the sizzle.

They don't sell chai here but you order it as if they do, and it's delivered as if they do. The chai wallah hops and skips his way around the group delivering milky, sweet distraction with careless fingers. The next round of aloo barra are distributed, and the gazes are released. After the first few mouthfuls, the group relaxes into chattering huddles. The young boy jumps on the back of a scooter, one hand clutching aloo bara, the other his mother's waist as they quickly disappear into the surrounding fuss and commotion.

The **kachori** are next. These are deep-fried, daal-filled breads that fluff up like balloons (the same as pooris but for the addition of daal as a filling) and are served with a sour tamarind sauce flavoured with fenugreek seeds. More unfed arrive and eye the kachori with satisfaction. An infant holds his father's finger as they both serve their time staring at the pot. A man arrives on a scooter, bushy eyebrows first, and I think of fluffy dice in dinky cars.

The group of men beside me speak in serious, aggressive tones. An argument is about to erupt, methinks, but it's only a tease and climaxes with raucous laughter. One of the men, having had his fill of aloo barra, draws a stool up beside the cook, and helps him mould the dough for kachori, gathering cosily around the great vessel.

A turbaned man cycles up to the throng, with bunches of mint flapping on his carrier, and the arresting, clean aroma alerts the group. With a look of stern concentration, he works his way through the crowd and delivers a handful of sprigs to the cook. Without comment or payment he heads back to his bike and is gone. I feel a tap on my shoulder. A man offers me some mint that he's stolen from the seller's load – no wonder he looked so determined. The sprig is passed around the group and picked bare amid laughs and nods acknowledging the fantastic quality of the pilfered herb.

As shop doors begin to open across the narrow, busy street, the piping hot kachoris are dispatched. One middle-aged man sits on somebody else's scooter with his foot on a wheel, immodestly posed, lowering the food into his mouth. A gentleman with a toothless grin prances around the group picking up the discarded bowls and empty chai glasses. A young girl stands outside the ring of masculinity. She has rosy cheeks and gleaming white teeth. Her striking pink sari captures the brilliant morning sun as she rings her hands and swivels with embarrassment in front of all these men. Two kachori are delivered; she gives the cook half a wave, smiles broadly, turns and walks away. (Nobody seems to be paying for anything.)

Another tap on my shoulder and I'm offered a spoonful of kachori, most unusual in India where people would normally never even eat out of the same bowl, never mind with the same spoon. I try to decline, rubbing my belly and explaining "two aloo bara, two kachori already" but the smiling, urging face won't hear it. I reassure him that no, Indian food is not too hot for me. His broad, expectant smile sinks and he turns away in utter disappointment.

A tray of samosas, with twisted doughy crowns, is lowered into the sizzle. A light-skinned local with bleary eyes, red teeth, and a pot belly parting his shirt and pants, walks into the action and surveys the scene: samosas in about five minutes; a foreigner writing notes. He eyes me curiously and stands over me on the step, beside the wok. With an eye on the samosas, he rubs his belly in anticipation. He slowly scratches his bottom and slides his hand around to cup his balls, applying a delicate juggle and then a two-fingered lift for a gentle genital finale. With a deep rumble that sounds like a rickshaw rounding the corner, he clears his throat and propels a heavy spit, which arcs deftly over the hot wok of newly-made samosas.

"More chai vicar?"

The cook wallah clicks his fingers and points to me.

"Chai?"

"No, it was a joke."

"Chai yes?"

"Oh, go on then."

This could be any street and any food stall in India. The kachoris identify it as North India, the aloo barra as specifically northwest, and the effeminate daisy petal-shaped earrings of the men as unmistakably Rajasthan – Udaipur to be precise.

Despite having sat on this step stuffing my face for almost two hours, I enjoy the samosa like I'd just returned from a hearty morning stroll. I stand up now to settle my account, and the cook asks me for Rs 11.

"Rs 11!? For two aloo barra, two kachori, one samosa and two chai?! "This is daylight robbery", I say, handing over the few rupees but nobody tries to stop me as I walk away, back to dodging rickshaws.

Martin Hughes

fit & healthy

We all like to think that nothing untoward will come to us when we're travelling in India; our immune system will deal with whatever is thrown at it and exotic bugs will remain foreign. But, in actuality, most visitors – no matter how cautious or adventurous – are likely to encounter some unpleasantness, although in most cases it will only be a dose of the runs. The good news is that you don't need a medical degree to stay healthy, just an awareness of likely problems and a dose of common sense.

The first and most important consideration is acclimatisation. Arriving in India is a daunting experience, no matter how many times you've been before and you shouldn't plan on hitting the ground running. Take your first few days slowly, getting used to the heat, pollution and food. Don't head straight from the airport to the street kebab stall. For your first week, eat in clean, well-heeled establishments, and drink plenty of bottled water. Factor in regular breathers and ensure that you're getting a balanced diet.

Hygiene

Many 'tropical' diseases (dysentery, typhoid and hepatitis for example) are caused by poor hygiene. While many parts of India choke with dirt and pollution, you'll find that most Indians are meticulous about personal hygiene. What count for acceptable standards in the complacent west could leave you vulnerable to illness in India, and you should adopt Indian habits.

Wash your hands before you eat (there's always a basin or jug for this purpose in any Indian eatery, even many street stalls) and always after using the toilet. Short fingernails are easier to keep clean than long ones and if you've got the habit of biting your nails, lose it while you're here. Other local customs worth observing are not letting your mouth touch a shared drinking vessel (pour the water into your mouth). The Indian custom of using the left hand for toilet duty and the right for eating is a very important habit to adopt.

Basket beauty, Bangalore city market, Karnataka

Fluids

You'll need to drink plenty of fluids to replace the amount you're sweating out – cool bottled, boiled or purified water is best, but any not-too-sweet soft drinks, fruit juice or green coconut juice are good. Always have a supply of safe drinking water on hand and remind yourself to keep sipping from it regularly while you're out. Remember that tea, coffee and alcohol all have a diuretic effect (they make you lose fluid) so go easy on them.

Don't drink the tap water and think twice about even brushing your teeth with it. Whether you're in a home or a restaurant you'll always be given a tumbler of water before you eat. Most of this water will be filtered to some extent but if in doubt, go without. Don't be shy about asking your host about the source. If it wasn't from a bottle, just say you'd better not because of your 'very weak stomach'. Ice is obviously only as safe as the water it's made from. But where you find ice, it is usually meant for tourists and is generally safe. Fresh lassi places often use crushed ice, and we've drunk lassis all over India without any problems. However, do use caution and get used to having your drinks without it. After you have acclimatised, you may relax your restrictions – many travellers even take to drinking water of dubious quality without getting sick – but do not become complacent and use your common sense.

Drinking bottled water is the obvious option, and it's widely available throughout India. Most brands are just treated tap water but are generally safe (despite Coca-Cola's scare mongering). If you're going to drink bottled water, stick to familiar brands and absolutely do not buy a bottle with a broken seal.

Spare a thought for India's environment though, which is choking with billions of discarded plastic bottles. You'll go through a lot of water here and, even if you're only staying for a month, you'll leave around 100 plastic bottles that will remain here long after you've crumpled up and gone to the great recycling plant in the sky. Three responsible alternatives are boiling, purifying and using disinfectants (see your local camping shop, Lonely Planet's Healthy Travel Asia or any Lonely Planet guidebook for more details).

Mineral water, Chennai, Tamil Nadu

Safe Food

Of course you can get sick from food anywhere but you increase your risk when travelling, particularly in India, where sewage systems are inadequate and there is more chance that food, utensils and hands are going to be contaminated with bugs, mainly from faeces. For example, if a fly lands on your food at home, it probably hasn't had a chance to wipe its feet on a pile of faeces beforehand, but the same cannot be said for India.

Bugs like heat and humidity, and multiply gleefully in food left sitting around in these conditions. You can build up immunity to some diarrhoeal diseases, but you can't build up immunity to many of the more serious diseases (such as dysentery or food poisoning) or to parasites (such as liver flukes), so it's worth taking a few precautions to minimise your risks. However, advice on safe food can seem unrealistic at best and ludicrous at worst. It's down to common sense basically, plus a little local knowledge. These are tips that you should bear in mind but you needn't take them all on board as gospel. After you have acclimatised – and probably after your first bout of diarrhoea – you can start to be a little more adventurous (see also Directions in the Street Food chapter).

Boys from Hyderabad get together at Mir Alam Market

- Remember the old colonial adage: 'if you can't peel it, clean it or cook it, don't eat it'.
- 'How' is more important than 'where' when it comes to preparation of food – street snacks cooked in a steaming hot wok in front of you are a safer bet than food left out on display in an upmarket hotel buffet.
- Heating kills germs, so food that's served piping hot is likely to be safer than lukewarm or cold food, especially if it has been sitting around.
- Fruit and vegetables are difficult to clean, but they should be safe once peeled or cooked. Cut fruit with your own knife and make sure to keep it clean. If you're going to eat the skin of the fruit, wash it in safe water first.
- Well-cooked meat and seafood should be safe, but don't over indulge. You'll only increase your risk of becoming ill.
- Follow the well-heeled crowd.
- Dirty dishes, cutlery or utensils can contaminate good food; blenders used for fruit juices or making lassi are prime suspects.
- Food that looks and smells delicious can still be seething with bugs.
- Hot spices don't make bad food safe, just more palatable.
- Avoid salads because they are hard to clean and are often contaminated with dirt. Also, they are often washed in unsafe water. Avoid salads – it's worth repeating. One of us got complacent, ate a mouthful of salad, got food poisoning and couldn't eat for a week.
- Steer clear of unpasteurised milk in rural areas.
- Avoid anything that could be diluted with unsafe water, like fruit juices and other drinks, particularly from shonky street stalls.
- Be wary of food that has been kept frozen; power cuts are a feature and the foods may be thawed and refrozen.

Eating For Health

Eating well is all about making sure you get enough of the right nutrients to enable you to function at your best, mentally and physically. It also makes you less vulnerable to illness.

Everybody needs six basics: water, carbohydrates, protein, fat, vitamins and minerals. The best way to ensure you get enough of the right things is to eat a varied diet, which you won't find difficult in India. As a guide, you need to eat a variety of foods from each of five core groups:

- bread, cereals and potatoes
- fresh fruits and vegetables
- milk and dairy products
- nuts, daal, meat, fish
- fat and sugary foods (in moderation)

INDIGESTION

A change in diet, the stress of travel, and a sudden surge of spicy foods can lead to a touch of indigestion. Don't reach for antacids, which can weaken the power of your own stomach acid to fight off infections. Instead, look for the miraculous digestive, **hing** (asafoetida), a gum that you can find in any Indian market. You can ask to have it cooked into your meal or dissolve the powdered form in water. Also, try eating small, regular meals and go easy on the spice.

Children from a fishing village near Guwahati, situated on the banks of the river Brahmaputra

Fading Away

Losing weight in India is pretty common and, in fact, it's one of the most appealing factors for many who come here. But even if you have some padding to spare, keep an eye on how much weight you lose – stations and city streets have scales – because if you lose too much too soon, you'll be drained of energy and prone to illness.

If you're not eating meat, remember that with a vegetarian diet you generally have to eat larger quantities of plant foods to get the same amount of energy. Increase your quota of energy-giving foods, including fats, and consider taking multivitamin supplements.

Diarrhoea

'Happiness is ... a dry fart', wrote one stricken philosopher in an Indian guest book. You will all miserably turn to these pages at some stage, for as certain as warm beer, you'll get at least one episode of the trots as you travel through India, one of the world's diarrhoea hot spots.

If you understand how diarrhoea is passed from person to person, it will help you avoid it. It sounds gross, but basically you get diarrhoea by eating other people's faeces – in food (mainly), water and other drinks, and from dirty utensils. Hands used to prepare food may not have been washed thoroughly or at all, flies can transfer bugs via their feet, and a lack of general environmental cleanliness means that dust and dirt is more likely to be contaminated with faeces.

Diarrhoea usually strikes early in your trip, can be accompanied by vomiting and can last for three to five days, and may revisit you the following week. A few rushed trips to the loo without any other symptoms is not indicative of a serious problem so don't panic.

Drink lots of fluids – juice from tender coconuts, water, weak black tea (not chai), and fizzed-out drinks (not cola) are good – and make sure to keep yourself hydrated. The most useful items in your snazzy little medical kit, and probably the only

> **Food on the Runs**
>
> **Eat** plain rice, idlis, plain bread, dry biscuits, bananas
>
> **Avoid** fruit (except bananas), vegetables, spicy and greasy foods, dairy products

ones you'll use, are the little sachets of rehydration salts. These will replace the vital salts you're flushing away and give you back your zip. Avoid diuretics like alcohol and caffeine, and steer clear of India's oft-sweetened dairy produce. If you think your case calls for anti-diarrhoeal remedies, you're best off going to a doctor because these medications can cause more problems than they solve.

NEEM

The neem tree is a living legend, with its uses being heralded to the high heavens in everything from ancient Ayurvedic treatises to US courts fighting for patents over its various uses. Probably no other plant has so many benefits – medicinal, cosmetic, environmental and even culinary. The fruit, leaves, seeds, bark and oil are used to treat ailments ranging from leprosy, diabetes, jaundice, ulcers, skin disorders, chickenpox, malaria and allegedly even cancer and AIDS.

Neem goes into making soap, cream, toothpaste and shampoo. A twig of neem is the toothbrush of choice for millions of Indians. Mothers who want to cure their daughters of acne coax them into drinking a spoon of bitter neem juice everyday. People afflicted with skin rashes find relief by bathing with water in which neem leaves have been boiled. Health-conscious gourmands fry a handful of tender neem leaves and eat it with rice, secure in the knowledge that it will cleanse their liver and blood.

Neem is also one of the most effective controls for household and farm pests, and it's organic all the way. The hardy tree flourishes all over the tropics, including arid areas, and helps to combat desertification, deforestation and global warming. More than 30 patents have been granted for its uses in the US and Japan, while sleepy Indian entrepreneurs lag far behind. Environmental groups have been alarmed by the rush for patents, raising the question of who controls a country's natural resources, traditional cultures or global corporations.

If you feel like eating, go ahead (see the boxed text on previous page). Your overworked guts will appreciate small amounts of food at regular intervals rather than great big meals. Contrary to the spirit of this book, stick to a bland diet while recovering from diarrhoea. If you don't feel like eating, don't force yourself. It might make you feel a little bit wobbly but as long as you're fairly fit to begin with, a couple of days without food will do you no harm.

Finally, while the vast majority of cases are nothing but temporary inconveniences, diarrhoea can also be a symptom of serious illnesses, including malaria and hepatitis. So if you're passing blood, running a high fever, or showing any other unusual symptoms, consult a doctor.

eat your words

language guide

Guide to Transliterations
Vowels
Short Vowels
a	as the 'a' in 'bad'
ah	as the 'u' in 'nut'
e	as the 'e' in 'bet'
i	as the 'i' in 'sit'
u	as the 'u' in 'pull'

Long Vowels
aah	as the 'a' in 'father'
aw	as the 'aw' in 'saw'
ay	as the 'ay' in 'day'
ee	as the 'ee' in 'meet'
o	as the 'o' in 'go'
oo	as the 'oo' in 'food'

Nasal Vowels
Some vowels in Hindi are pronounced partly through the nose. English-speakers nasalise a vowel when it appears before an 'ng' sound as in 'fling'. In this book, nasalised vowels are indicated with a tilde (˜) above the vowel.

Short Vowels
ã	as the 'u' in 'sung'
ẽ	as the 'e' in 'bet' + the 'ng' in 'sing'
õ	as the 'o' in 'song'

Long Vowels
ãã	as the 'a' in 'father' + the 'ng' in 'sing'
ẽẽ	as the 'ee' in 'meet' + the 'ng' in 'sing'
õõ	as the 'oo' in 'food' + the 'ng' in 'sing'

Consonants
Consonants not described here are pronounced as they are in English.

ch	as the 'ch' in 'chocolate'
g	as the 'g' in 'game'
j	as the 'j' in 'join'
ky	as the 'cu' in 'cute'
ng	as the 'ng' in 'bang'
r	slightly trilled
s	as the 's' in 'sin'
y	as the 'y' in 'yellow'

Aspirated Consonants
Many Hindi words, such as Buddhist include aspirated consonants, which are pronounced with a puff of breath following the consonant. The difference between aspirated and non-aspirated consonants can be heard in the following pronunciations of the letter 't'.

tick   aspirated – with a puff of breath
stick   non-aspirated – no puff of breath

When an 'h' appears after the consonants **b**, **d**, **g**, **j**, **k**, **p** or **t**, the 'h' represents that a puff of breath follows the consonant. However, when 's' is followed by **h**, the combination is pronounced as the 'sh' in 'ship'.

Anglicised Indian Words
For ease of reference, we've included Anglicised equivalents of Indian words alongside transliterations in the Glossary and Dictionary. While many Anglicised equivalents are widely known (such as **roti**, **lassi**, **tandoori**), you may not find all forms given here written on menus and elsewhere. Anglicised forms may also vary slightly from place to place.

English	Pronunciation	Anglicised Form
papaya	pah-pee-taah	*papita*
to simmer	dee-mee äähch pahr pah-kaah-naah	*dimi anch par pakana*

Hindi
Useful Phrases
Have you eaten?	kyaah aahp-ne kaah-naah kaah-yaah?
Yes, I've eaten.	jee hääh, mä-ne kaah-naah kaah-yaah
I like sweets.	mu-je mit-aah-ee ah-chee lag-tee hä
Do you like sweets?	kyaah aahp-ko mi-taa-hee a-chee lag-tee hä?
I don't eat a lot of sweets.	mä bah-hut mit-aah-ee nah-hëë khatha /khati (m/f)

Eating Out
Do you speak English?	kyaah aahp-ko an-gre-zee aah-tee hai?
Table for ..., please.	... ke li-ye mez chaah-hi-ye
Do you accept credit cards?	kyaah aahp kre-dit kaahrd le-te hä
Do you have a highchair for the baby?	cho-te ba-che ke li-ye kaahs kur-see hai?
Can I smoke here?	ya-haah si-gret pee-naah teek hai?
Can I pay by credit card?	kyaah mä kre-dit kaahrd se paise de sak-taah/sak-tee hoõ? (m/f)
(cheap) restaurant	(sah-staah) res-traah

Just Try It!
What's that?	vo kyaah hai?
What's the speciality of this region?	is kshe-trah/i-laah-ke kaah kaahs kah-naahkyaah hai?
What's the speciality here?	ya-haah kaah kaahs kah-naah kyaah hai?
What do you recommend?	aahp ba-taah-i-ye kyaah kaah-naah chaah-hi-ye?
What are they eating?	vo kyaah kaah rah-he hä?
I'll try what s/he's having.	mu-je vo dee-ji-ye jo vo kaah rah-he hä

The Menu

Can I see the menu please?	men-yoo kaahrd dee-ji-ye
Do you have a menu in English?	men-yoo kaahrd an-gre-zee mẽ hai?
What are today's specials?	aahj kyaah bahn gah-yaah hai?
I'd like ...	mu-je ... dee-ji-ye
What does it include?	us mẽ kyaah kyaah mil-taah hai?

Throughout the Meal

What's in this dish?	is mẽ kyaah hai?
Do you have pickle/chutney?	kyaah ah-chaahr/chat-nee hai?
Not too spicy, please.	ba-hut tee-kaah mat bah-naah-i-ye
Is that dish spicy?	kyaah vo vyahn-jahn tee-kaah hai?
I like it hot and spicy.	mu-je tee-kaah kaah-naah ah-chaah lag-taah hai
It's not hot. (temperature)	ye garm nah-hẽẽ hai
I didn't order this.	mu-je ye nah-hẽẽ chaah-hi-ye taah
I'd like something to drink.	kuch pee-ne ke li-ye chaah-hi-ye
Can I have a (beer) please?	mu-je (bi-yaahr) dee-ji-ye
No ice, please.	bahrf mat daah-li-ye
I can't eat spicy food	mã tee-kaah kaah-naah nah-hẽẽ kaah sahk-taah/sahk-tee (m/f)
Is the water filtered?	kyaah paah-nee fil-tahrd hai?
I don't want the salad.	mu-je sah-laahd nah-heẽ chaah-hi-ye

Please bring me ...	... laah-i-ye
an ashtray	ash-tra
some bread	ro-tee
chutney	chaht-nee
a cup	kahp
a fork	kããh-taah
a glass	glaahs
a knife	chu-ree
mineral water	min-ah-rahl vaah-tahr
a napkin	nap-kin
some pepper	kaah-lee mirch/gol mirch
pickle	ah-chaahr
a plate	plat/thali
some salt	nah-mak
a spoon	chah-mach
a teaspoon	cho-taah chah-mach
a toothpick	toth-pik
some water	paah-nee
some wine	mah-di-raah
water to wash my hands	haaht do-ne kaah paah-nee

This food is ...   ye kaah-naah ... hai
    cold   tan-daah
    brilliant   bah-ri-yaah
    burnt   jah-laah
    spoiled   kah-raab
    stale   baah-saah
    undercooked   kach-chaah

It's taking a long time.   bah-hut der ho rah-hee hai
Please hurry up.   jal-dee laah-i-ye
Thank you, that was delicious.   shu-kri-yaah, kaah-naah bah-hut hee bah-ri-yaah hu-aah

Please pass on our compliments to the chef. bah-naah-ne vaah-le ko bah-taah-i-ye ki hahm ko kaah-naah ah-chchaah lah-gaah
The bill, please.   bil laah-i-ye

You May Hear
kuch awr chaah-hi-ye   Anything else?
aahj ... nah-heẽ ha   We have no ... today.

Family Meals
I've just had some tea.
  mã chaah-i pee kar aah-yaah/aah-yee hõõ (m/f)
I've already eaten
  mã kaah-naah kaah kahr aah-yaah/aah-yee hõõ (m/f)
You're a great cook!
  aahp bah-hut ah-chaah kaah-naah bah-naah-te hã!/aahp bah-hut ah-chaah kaah-naah bah-naah-te hã!
This is brilliant!
  ye bah-hut hee mah-ze-daahr hai
Do you have the recipe for this?
  kyaah is kee re-si-pee de dẽ-ge? *(Will you give me the recipe for this please?)*
Is this a family recipe?
  ye aahp kee hee re-si-pee hai? *(Is this your own recipe?)*
Are the ingredients local?
  is mẽ sahb staah-nee-yah chee-zẽ hã?
I have not had such a delicious meal before.
  mã-ne it-naah ah-chaah kaah-naah peh-le kahbee nah-hẽẽ kaah-yaah
If you ever come to (Australia) I'll cook you a local dish.
  ah-gahr aahp kah-bee (aah-stre-li-yaah) aah-yẽ to mã aahp ke li-ye hah-maah-raah kaah-naah bah-naah-oõ-gaah/bah-naah-õõ-gee (m/f)
Could you pass the (salt) please?
  (nah-mahk) de dee-ji-ye
The meal was very good, thank you.
  kaah-naah bah-hut ah-chaah taah, shu-kri-yaah *(The meal was delicious, thanks)*

I really appreciate it.
mu-je bah-hut ku-shee hu-ee *(It made me happy)*
Is this very spicy?
kyaah is mẽ bah-hut mir-chee hai?
I can't eat very spicy food.
mã bah-hut mir-chee nah-heẽ khaah sahk-taah/sahk-tee (m/f)
Can I eat with my hand?
kyaah mã haaht se khaah sahk-taah/sahk-tee hõõ? (m/f)
How do you eat with your hand?
haahth se ka-se khaah-te hã?
I can't eat with my right hand.
mã see-de haaht se kaah-nah-heẽ sahk-taah/sahk-tee (m/f)
Is this water filtered?
kyaah ye paah-nee fil-tahrd ha?
I can only drink boiled water.
mã sirf ub-laah hu-aah paah-nee pee sahk-taa/sahk-tee hõõ (m/f)
Can I watch you make this?
kyaah mã dek sahk-taah/sahk-tee hõõ ki aahp kai-se bah-naah-tee hã? (m/f)

Can I have some more …	kuch awr … dee-ji-ye
I'm full to the brim.	pet bahr gah-yaah gah-le tahk
Enough, thank you.	bahs, bahs, shu-kri-yaah
I eat very little.	mã bah-hut kahm kaah-taah/kaah-tee hõõ (m/f)
I don't eat a lot of sweets.	mã bah-hut mi-taah-ee nah-hẽẽ kaah-taah/ kaah-tee (m/f)
One's enough, thank you.	ek kaah-fee hai, shu-kri-yaah

Do you use … in this?	kyaah aahp is mẽ … daahl-tee hã?
Is this a vegetable?	kyaah ye sab-zee hai?
Is this a fruit?	kyaah ye pahl hai?
I really like this.	mu-je ye bah-hut pah-sahnd hai
What type of daal is this?	ye kawn-see daahl hai?
Can I wash my hands?	kyaah mã haaht do-lõõ?

Roadside Restaurant – Dhaba

What have you got today?	aahj kyaah mi-le-gaah?
Do you have …?	kyaah … hai?
Bring it hot.	gahrm gahrm laah-naah
We don't want water.	paah-nee maht laah-naah *(Don't bring water)*
Where do I pay?	pa-se kis-ko de-te hã?
How much is it?	kit-naah hu-aah?
Where's the toilet?	to-i-let kah-hããh hai?
This food is cold.	ye kaah-naah tahn-daah hai
Where can I wash my hands?	haaht kah-hããh do-te hã?

Bring ...   ... laa-o
  chutney   chaht-nee
  more daal   awr daahl
  more rice   awr chaah-vahl
  more roti   awr ro-tee
  papadams   paah-pahr
  pickles   ah-chaahr
  tea   cha-i

Is this sweet?
  kyaah ye mee-taah hai?
This plate isn't clean.
  ye plat saahf nah-heē hai
Where can I get a (bottle of whisky/beer)?
  wis-kee/bi-yaahr kah-aāh mi-le-gaah?

Vegetarian & Special Meals

I'm a vegetarian.
  mā shaah-kaah-haah-ree/sahb-zee kawr hōō (m/f)

I don't eat ...   mā ... nah-hēē kaah-taah/kaah-tee (m/f)
  beef   gaah-ee kaah gosht
  chicken   mur-gee
  fish   mahch-lee
  goat   bahk-raah
  meat   gosht
  pork   su-ahr kaah gosht
  poultry   mur-gee

Do you have any vegetarian dishes?
  kyaah shaah-kaah-haah-ree/sahb-zee kawr
  kaah-naah yahaāh mil-taah ha? (m/f)
Can you recommend a vegetarian dish, please?
  kawn-see sahb-zee ah-chee hai?

Does this dish have meat?   is mē gosht hai?
Is the sauce meat-based?   kyaah saws mē gosht hai?
Does this dish have gelatine?   is mē ge-laah-teen to nah-hēē hai?

Does it contain eggs/dairy products?
  is mē ahn-de yaah gaahy kee ko-ee cheez to nah-hēē hai?

I'm allergic to ...   mu-je ... kee a-lo-gee hai
Is there ... in this?   kyaah is mē ... ha?
  milk   dood
  salt   nah-mahk
  sugar   chee-nee
  wheat   ge-hoō

Is this halal?   kyaah ye hah-laahl hai?

At the Market

I'd like some ...	mu-je ... chaah-hi-ye
asafoetida	hing
cumin	zee-raah
eggs	ahn-de
flour	aah-taah (wholemeal)/maida (plain flour)
fruit & vegetables	pahl awr sahb-jee

Where's the nearest market?	baah-zaahr kah-hããh hai?
Where's the vegetable market?	sahb-zee kaah bah-zaahr kah-hããh hai?
Where can I find the (sugar)?	(chee-nee) kah-hããh mil-taah hai?
I don't want a plastic bag.	mu-je po-lee-theen nah-hẽẽ chaah-hi-ye

Can I have a ...	mu-je ... chaah-hi-ye
bottle	bo-tahl
box	boks
can	tin
packet	paket
sachet/bag	thai -lee
tin of ...	... kaah teen

How much?	kit-ne pai-se?
How much is (a kilo of cheese)?	(ki-lo pah-neer) kit-ne kaah hai?
Do you have anything cheaper?	is se sahs-taah nah-hẽẽ hai?
Give me (half) a kilo, please.	(aah-daah) ki-lo dee-ji-ye
I'd like (six) slices of	... ke (che) tuk-re dee-ji-ye
I'm just looking.	mã sirf dekh-ne aah-yaah/aah-yee hõõ
No!	nah-hẽẽ!
Can I taste it?	kyaah mã chahk sahk-taah hõõ?
	kyaah mã chahk sak-tee hoõ?

Is this the best you have?	aahp ke paahs is se beh-tahr nah-hẽẽ hai?
What's the local speciality?	yah-hããh log kyaah kaah-te hã?

At the Bar

Shall we go for a drink?	kuch pee-ne ke li-ye ch-lã?
I'll buy you a drink.	mã pi-laah-naah chah-taah/ chah-tee hõõ (m/f)

Thanks, but I don't feel like it.	mu-je nah-hẽẽ chaah-hi-ye
I don't drink (alcohol).	mã shah-raahb nah-hẽẽ pee-taah/ pee-tee (m/f)

Where's the wine shop?	ahn-gre-zee shah-raahb kee du-kaan kah-hããh hai?

Where can I buy alcohol here.	yah-hããh shah-raahb kah-hããh mil-tee hai?
What would you like?	aahp kyaah lē-ge?
You can get the next one.	ag-lee baahr aahp lee-ji-ye

I'll have ...	mu-je ... chah-hi-ye
It's my round.	me-ree baah-ree hai
OK.	teek hai
I'm next.	me-ree baah-ree hai
Excuse me.	maahf kee-ji-ye

I was here before this lady/gentleman.
  mã peh-le aah-yaah/aah-yee hõõ (m/f)

I'll have (a) ...	mu-je ... dee-ji-ye
beer	bi-yaahr
brandy	bran-dee
rum	rahm
whisky	wis-kee

No ice.	bahrf mat daah-li-ye
Can I have ice, please?	barf dee-ji-ye
Is food available here?	kyaah yah-hããh kaah-naah mil-taah hai?
This is hitting the spot.	ye kaah maahl ha
Where's the toilet?	to-i-let kah-haah hai?
I'm a bit tired, I'd better get home.	bah-hut tahk gah-yaah/ gah-yee, gahr jaa-naa chah-hi-ye

I'm feeling drunk.	nah-shaah chahr gah-yaah
I'm pissed.	nah-shaah chahr gah-yaah
I feel ill.	me-ree ta-bi-yaht teek nah-hẽẽ hai
I want to throw up.	ul-tee ho-ne ko hai
S/he's passed out.	be-hosh ho gah-yaah/gah-yee
I'm hung over.	sir mẽ bah-hut dahrd hai

ASSAMESE
Useful Phrases

Hello. (pol/inf)	nah-mos-kaahr/hay ree
Goodbye.	aah-hõõ day
Thank you.	dhon-yah-baahd

What's your name?	
(to elders)	aah-pah-nahr naahm kees
(inf)	to-maahr naahm kee

My name is ...	mor naahm ...
I'm a vegetarian.	mo-i nee-raah-mis khaah-ãw
I don't eat meat or fish.	mo-i maahs mahn-kho nah khah-a-õõ
Can I have that please.	mo-i hay to lo-bo pah-rõõ ne kee?
What do you recommend?	aah-po-naahr mot kee?; aah-po-nee kee kmo-i?

No ice/milk in my ...	mor saah-ot/do-hi-gho-lah-te ...
please	bo-rahf/gaah-khir ne dibo
lassi	los-si-te
tea	te
Can I have some tea please?	mo-i ek kop saah khah-bo pah-rõõ ne kee?
I want some water.	mo-i paah-ni khaah-bo khu-jõõ
Can I have a ... please?	mo-i ... lo-bo paah-rõõ ne kee?

At the Restaurant – Khoa Loathaite   kho-aah lo-aah-thai-te

ashtray	ci-ge-rayt-daah-nee
bill	bil
cup	kop
drinks	sorbaht
fork	kaah-taah
knife	kah-taah-ree/su-ree
menu	bho-jan taah-li-kaah
toilet	gaah dho-aah thah-ee
toothpick	ho-ri-ka/tooth-pik
wash area	dho-aah thah-ee

Vegetables – Hak Pasoli   haahk paah-so-li

cabbage	bahn-daah ko-bee
capsicum	sim-lah jaah-lo-ki-aah
cauliflower	phool ko-bee
eggplant	bah-ee-ge-naah
green beans	seem/u-ro-hee
lentils	dael
onion	pee-yah-j
peas	ma-tor
potatoes	aah-loo
pumpkin	ron-gaah lao
spinach	paah-leng/pah-lĕg
tomato	bi-laah-hee

Fruit – Phalmul   phahl mool

apple	aah-pel
banana	kawl
guava	mo-dhu-ri-am
jackfruit	ka-ta-hal
lime	ne-moo/le-moo
orange	kah-mo-laah
papaya	o-mi-taah
peach	pees phal
pineapple	ah-naah-rahs
sultana	kis-mis
a local sour fruit	thek-raah

Meat – **Mankho**

maahn-kho

beef	go-maahn-kho
chicken	mur-gee maahn-kho
fish	maahs
goat	saah-gu-li maahn-kho
pork	gah-o-ree maahn-kho

Spices & Condiments – **Mosola**

mo-sol-aah

basil	tu-loh-khee
cardamom	ah-ay-laah-see
chilli	jaah-lo-ki-aah
cinnamon	daahl-se-nee
coriander	dho-ni-aah
cloves	lawng
cumin	ji-raah
garlic	na-ha-rooh/ne-ha-rooh
ginger	aah-daah
mint	po-dee-naah
nutmeg	jaah-ay-phal
pepper	jaah-luk
salt	ni-mok/la-bawn
tamarind	tay-te-lee
turmeric	haah-lo-dee

Nuts – **Badam**

baah-daahm

almonds	kaahth baah-daahm
cashews	kaah-ju baah-daahm
pistachio	pis-taah baah-daahm

Dairy – **Dugha Pam**

du-ghah paahm

butter	maah-khon
cheese	senaah/po-neer
cream	kreem
curd	do-hee
ghee	ghēē (eu)
ice cream	ah-ees kreem
milk	gaah-khir
yoghurt	do-hee

Drinks

lassi	los-si-te
tea	te
water	paah-ni

BENGALI
Useful Phrases

Hello.
no-mosh-kaahr ki ko-bor kah-mon aah-chen?
(lit: hello, what news?, how are you?)

Goodbye.
no-mosh-kaahr aah-bahr de-kaah ho-be
(lit: see you again)

Peace be upon you.
shu-ke-ye, shahn-ti-ta tah-kun
(lit: live in happiness, live in peace)

Thank you.	don-no-baahd
What's your name?	aahp-nahr naahm ki?
My name is …	aah-mahr naahm …
I'm a vegetarian.	aah-mee shaah-kaah-haa-ree
Can I have that, please?	aah-mee e-tah ne-bo?
What do you recommend?	aahp-naahr mot ki?

No ice/milk in my …   aah-mahr … bo-rof/dood de-ben naah
    lassi   lahs-si-ta
    tea   chaah-ye

Will you give me something to eat?
aah-mah-ke ki-chu ke-te de-ben?

At the Restaurant

ashtray	ash-tra or chah-i daah-ni
bill	bil
cup	kahp
fork	kääh-taah
hot (taste)	jaahl
hot (temperature)	go-rom
knife	chu-ree
match box	desh-lah-ee
menu	me-nyu
small	cho-to
toilets	baht-room/lat-reen
toothpick	toot-pik
wash area	do-bahr ja-gah
water	jol

Fish – Maach   Maahchh

hilsa	elish
carp	rui pona/katla cheetol magur
climbing perch	koi banshpaata
mango fish	topshay

Meat – **Mangsho**   mahng-sho
beef   go-rur mahng-sho
chicken   mur-gi
fish   maahch
goat (billy/nanny)   paah-tah/bo-kree
mutton   be-rahr mahng-sho
pork   shu-o-rer mahng-sho

Vegetables – **Shobji**   shob-jee
cabbage   bahn-dah ko-pi
capsicum   shim-laahr/kahsh-mee-ree lon-kah
cauliflower   ful ko-pi
eggplant   be-goon
green beans   beens
lentils   daahl
onion   pe-yããj
peas   mo-tor shu-ti
potato   aah-loo
pumpkin   kum-ro
spinach   paah-lok shaahk
tomato   to-mah-to

Fruit – **Phal**   phawl
apple   aah-pel
banana   ko-laah
coconut   nahr-ko-le
  green coconut   daahb
custard apple   aah-taah
dates   ke-jur
grapes   aahn-gur
guava   pe-yah-raah
jackfruit
  green, cooked as a vegetable   en-chor
  ripe, eaten as a fruit   kahn-taahl
lemon   le-boo
mandarin   kom-lah lebu; mu-sahm-bee kom-lah
mango   aahm
orange   maw-shahm-bee
papaya   pe-pe
pineapple   ah-naah-rosh
pomegranate   be-dah-nah
watermelon   tor-mooj

Nuts – **Badam**   baah-dam
almonds   baah-dam
cashews   kaah-ju
pistachios   pes-tah

Spice & Condiments – Mashola Maw-sho-laah

basil	tul-si
cardamom	e-lahch
chilli	lon-kah
cinnamon	daahr-chee-nee
cloves	lo-bon-go
coriander	do-na
cumin	jee-ra
garlic	ro-shun
ginger	aah-dah
honey	mo-du
mint	pu-di-nah paah-tah
nutmeg	jah-i phol
pepper	go-le mo-rich
red chilli	laahl lon-kah
salt	noon
salty	non-tah
sugar	chee-nee
sweet	mish-tee
tamarind	tan-tool
turmeric	ho-lood

Dairy – Milk Products

butter	mah-kon
cream	kreem/no-ni
cheese	cheej
ghee	gee
ice cream	ah-is kreem
milk	dood
yoghurt	do-ee

Drinks – Paniyo pah-ni-yo

fruit/sugar-based drink	mri-du pah-ni-yo
ice	bo-rof
lassi	lahs-si-ta
soft drink	shor-bot
tea	chaah-ye
water	jol

GUJARATI
Useful Phrases

How are you?	kem cho
Goodbye.	aw jo
Thank you.	aah-baahr
What's your name?	tah-maah-rõõ-naahm shõõ-che?

My name's ...	maah-rõõ-naam ... che
I'm vegetarian.	hõõ-shaah-kaah-haah-ree chõõ
I don't eat meat or fish.	hõõ-pahr-maah-ti ke maah-chlee kah-to nah-ti
Can I have that, please?	mah-ne pe-lõõ-aahp-sho
Can I have a ..., please?	mah-ne .... aahp-sho
What do you recommend?	tah-maah-ro shõõ-maht che
Can I have some tea, please?	mah-ne to-ree chaah aahp-sho

Please give me a lassi without ice.
   bah-rahf vah-gahr-nee chaahs aahp-jo
Please give me tea without milk.
   dood vah-gahr-nee chaah aahp-jo

At the Restaurant

ashtray	ash-tra
bill	bil
cup	kahp
fork	kääh-to
knife	chah-ree
menu	men-yu
restaurant	res-tah-rahnt
small	naah-nũ
toilets	jaah-jah-roo
toothpick	tot-pik
wash area	haahh do-vah-nee jah-gyah

Meat – Mans; Parmati

	mããhs; pahr-mah-tee
beef	gost
chicken	mur-gee
fish	maah-chah-lee
goat	bah-kree
mutton	mah-tahn
pork	duk-kahr nu mããhs

Vegetables – Shakbhaji

	shah-bhah-jee
cabbage	ko-bee
capsicum	go-lahr mahr-chaah
cauliflower	fool-ko-bee
eggplant	rin-gah-naah
green beans	fah-nah-see
lentils	daahl
onion	dun-glee
peas	lee-laah vah-taah-naah
potato	bah-te-tah
pumpkin	paht-kaah-lu
spinach	baah-jee
tomato	tah-me-tah

Fruit – Phal

	phaahl
apple	sah-fahr-jahn
apricot	jahl-daah-roo
banana	ke-laah
guava	jahm-ruk
jackfruit	raahm-pahl
lemon	lim-bu
mango	ke-ri
orange	sahn-tah-raah
papaya	pah-pah-yah
peach	aah-roo

Nuts – Sukomevo

	soo-ko-me-vo
almonds	bah-daahm
cashews	kaah-ju
pistachio	pis-tah

Spices & Condiments – Masala & Achar

	mah-saah-lah & ah-chaahr
basil	tul-si
cardamom	el-chi
chilli	mahr-chŏŏ
cinnamon	tahj
cloves	lah-ving
coriander	daah-naah
cumin	jee-roo
fenugreek	me-tee
garlic	lah-sahn
ginger	lah-du
mint	po-di-no
mustard seed	raah-ee
nutmeg	jaah-i-pahl
pepper	mah-ree
red chillis	laahl mahr-chŭ
salt	mee-tŏŏ
tamarind	aahm-li
turmeric	hahl-dahr

Dairy – Dudhghar

	doodh-ghaahr
butter	maah-kahn
cheese	pah-neer
cream	mah-laah-ee
ghee	gee
ice cream	ah-is kreem
milk	dood
yoghurt	dah-hẽẽ

Drinks – Pihnu | pee-hnõõ
buttermilk | chaahs
coffee | ko-fee
cordial | sahr-baht
lemonsquash | lim-bu sahr-baht
rosewater | gu-laahb-jahl
tea | chaah
water | paah-nee

KANNADA
Useful Phrases

Hello. | nah-mah-skaah-rah
Goodbye. | nah-mah-skaah-rah
Thank you. | vahn-dah-ne
What is your name? | ni-nah he-sah-ru ye-nu?
My name is ... | nah-nah he-sah-ru ...

I'm a vegetarian. | nah-nu sah-syah-haah-ree
I don't eat meat or fish. | nah-nu mahm-sah-haah-ree ah-tah-vah
  | mee-nu ti-nu-di-lah

Can I have that please? | dah-yah-vi-tu nah-nah-ge ko-di?
What do you recommend? | ye-nu che-nah-gi-de he-li?
Can I have some tea, please? | nah-nah-ge dah-yah-vi-tu chaah ko-di?
Can I have a ..., please? | nah-nah-ge dah-yah-vi-tu ... ko-di?

No ice/milk in my ... please. | dah-yah-vi-tu ah-i-su/haah-lu be-dah nah-nah
  lassi | lah-si-ge
  tea | chaah-nah-li

At the Restaurant

ashtray | a-shu-tra
bill | bi-lu
cup | kah-pu
fork | for-ku
knife | chaah-ku
menu | men-yu
restaurant | res-tau-rant
toilets | to-i-let
toothpick | tut-pi-ku
wash area | to-le-u-vah jah-gah

Nuts

almonds | baah-daah-mi
cashews | go-dahm-bi
pistachios | pis-tah

Meat – **Mamasa**

	mah-mah-saah
beef	hah-su
chicken	kow-li
fish	mee-nu
goat	me-ke
mutton	ku-ri
pork	hahn-di

Vegetables – **Dharkari**

	dhar-kah-ree
cabbage	kaw-su
capsicum	dah-pah men-si-nah-kaah-ee
cauliflower	hu-ko-su
eggplant	bah-dahne-kaah-ee
green beans	hu-rah-li-kaah-ee
lentils	be-le-gah-lu
onion	ee-ru-li
peas	bah-tah-ni
potato	aah-lu-ge-de
pumpkin	kum-bah-lah-kaah-ee
spinach	so-pu
tomato	tah-mah-to

Fruit – **Hanu**

	hah-noo
apple	se-bu
banana	baah-le-hah-nu
guava	si-be
jackfruit	hah-lah-si-nah to-le
lemon	nim-be
mango	ki-tah-le
orange	maah-vi-nah hah-nu
papaya	pah-rahn-gi
pomegranate	daah-lim-be

Dairy

butter	be-ne
cheese	chee-su
cream	ke-ne
ghee	tu-pah
ice cream	ah-i-skri-mu
milk	haah-lu
yoghurt	mo-sah-ru

Drinks – **Pania**

	pah-nee-ah
coconut water	ye-la-nee-ru
lassi	majjige/lah-si-ge
tea	cha
water	nee-ru

Spices & Condiments – Masala
	mah-saah-lah
basil	tu-lah-see
cardamom	ye-lah-kee
chilli	men-si-nah-kaah-ee
cinnamon	chah-ke
cloves	lah-u-ahn-gah
coriander	ko-tahm-bah-ree
cumin	ji-ri-ge
garlic	be-lu-li
ginger	shun-ti
mint	pu-di-nah
nutmeg	jaah-kaah-ee
pepper	me-nah-su
red chilli	kem-pu men-si-nah-kaah-ee
saffron	ke-sah-ree
tamarind	hu-nah-se-hah-nu
turmeric	hah-si-si-hah

KASHMIRI
Useful Phrases
Hello./Goodbye.	waah-ray (lit: peace be upon you)
Thank you.	shu-kriya
What's your name?	chay kya chuy naahv?
My name's …	mãy chu naahv …
I'm a vegetarian.	ba chus vash-nev
I don't eat meat or fish.	ba chus ne maahz ya gaahd kha-waahn
Can I have that please.	ba hak-aahy ye nayth
What do you recommend?	che kya chuk wã-nan?
No ice/milk in my … please.	mãy-ne … trav-zeny sheen/dodh
lassi	lah-say
tea	chah-yay
Can I have a … please.	mãy hak-yeah aahkh … mee-leth

At the Restaurant
ashtray	ash-tray/soor-dy-ean
big	bod
bill	ra-kam
cup	kup/pyah-ah-lah
fork	kään-te
knife	shrak-puch
menu	khay-nekh cheez
small	lo-kut
toilets	zal-ghar/pak-kha-na
toothpick	dand touj

Vegetables

cabbage	bandh
capsicum	shim-la mar-ch-vãã-gun
cauliflower	phool
eggplant	wãã-gun
green beans	raz-ma-hym-be
lentils	hym-be
onion	gan-de
peas	matar
potato	oo-luv
pumpkin	aahl
spinach	paah-lak
tomato	ta-ma-tar

Fruit

apple	chuunth
apricot	chear
banana	ke-ayl
guava	ahm-rood
jackfruit	kahth-hahl
lemon	ny-oumb
mango	aahmbh
orange	sahng-tahr
papaya	pah-pi-tah
peach	che-aah-nahn

Meat

beef	gav-maahz
chicken	ko-kur
fish	ga-ad
goat	kath
mutton	maahz/syo-un
pork	soor-maahz

Dairy

butter	thea-ãy
cheese	chaah-mahn
cream	mah-le-ay
ghee	gy-ahv
ice cream	mah-lah-i-kulfi
milk	dodh
yoghurt	zahm-dodh

Drinks

water	trea-ahsh/aahb/py-on
tea	chah-i

Spices & Condiments

basil	tej-paht-tah
cardamom	aah-el
chilli	mahr-ch-vãã-gun
cinnamon	daahl-cheen
coriander	dãã-ewahl
cloves	rõgh
cumin	zy-ur
garlic	ro-hahn
ginger	ahd-rahkh
mint	pud-nah
nutmeg	zaah-fahl
pepper	mããrch
red chillies	waah-zul mahr-ch-vãã-gun
tamarind	tym-ber
turmeric	lay-the

Nuts

almonds	baah-dahm
cashews	kaah-ju
pistachios	pis-te

KONKANI
Useful Phrases

Hello.	nah-mah-skaahr/bah-ro aahs mu
Goodbye.	nah-mah-skaahr
Please.	kru-paah
Thank you.	up-kaahr jahl-le/ah-bhi-wah-dahn
What's your name?	tu-gahl naahv kahs-le?
My name is …	mah-gah-le naahv …

I'm a vegetarian.	hããhv shaah-kaah-haah-ree
I don't eat meat or fish.	hããhv mããhs kaah-yi-nah

Can I have that please?	mahk-kah ta dit-tah va
What do you recommend?	tu kahs-lee shi-faah-rahs?
No ice in my lassi please.	mah-gahl-lyah lahs-sin-tu bahrf nahk-kah
No milk in my tea please.	mah-gahl-lyah chaahn-tu dood
Can I have some tea, please?	kru-paah mah-kah chaah di?
Can I have a …, please?	kru-paah mahk-kah di-tah va?

Drinks

coffee	ko-fee
lassi	lahs-sin
tea	chaah
water	o-nu daahk

At the Restaurant

ashtray	ash-tra
big	hod
cup	kahp
fork	kaahn-to
knife	chaah-koo
menu	men-yu
small	saahn
toilets	sahn-daahs/paahy-kaah-naah
toothpick	tut-pik
wash area	mo-ree/naah-nee gahr

Fruit – Pha-la

phah-la

apple	sah-fahr-chahnd
apricot	jahr-daah-loo
banana	kyahn-le
guava	pe-ru
jackfruit	pah-nahs
lemon	nim-bu-vo
mango	aahm-bo
orange	mo-sahm-bee
papaya	po-pah-yee

Spices & Condiments – Masala

mah-saah-lah

basil	tu-lahs
cardamom	yaah/i-laah-yah-chee
chilli	meer-saahng
cinnamon	daahl chee-nee
cloves	lah-vahng
coriander	co-tahm-bah-ree
cumin	jee-raah
fenugreek	me-thee
garlic	lah-soon
ginger	ahl-le
mint	poo-di-naah
mustard seeds	saah-sahm
nutmeg	jah-i-pahl
pepper	mee-ree
red chilli	su-kee meer-saahng
salt	meet
tamarind	cheench
turmeric	haah-lah-dee

Nuts

almonds	bah-daahm
cashews	kaah-joo-bee
pistachios	pis-taah

Vegetables – Randayee Kaayee

rahn-dah-yee kaah-yee

cabbage	ko-bee
capsicum	bop-lee mir-chee
cauliflower	pool-wahr
eggplant	van-gahn
green beans	fah-rahs-bee
lentils	daah-lee
onion	kaah-lee
peas	vah-taah-no
potato	bah-taah-taah
pumpkin	bop-lo
spinach	paah-lahk
tomato	to-mah-to

Meat – Maanse

mããhs

beef	ga-che maahns
chicken	komb-dee peel
fish	maah-sah-lee
goat	bok-kah-dee
mutton	bok-kah-dee maahns
pork	doo-kah-raahn-chen maahns

Dairy

butter	lo-nee
cheese	chees/pah-neer
cream	saah-ee
ghee	tup
ice cream	ah-is kreem
milk	dood
yoghurt	dãh-yee

MARATHI
Useful Phrases

Hello	nah-mah-stē-nah-mah-skaahr
Goodbye	ah-chaah, pun-haah be-tu-yaah
Thank you	dahn-yah-vaahd
What is your name?	tum-che naahv kaah-ee?
My name is ...	mah-ze naahv ...

I am a vegetarian.	mee shaah-kaah-haah-ree aah-he
I don't eat meat or fish.	mee maahns mahch-chee kaaht naah-hee

Can I have that, please?	kru-pah-yaah mah-laah te mi-lel kaah?
What do you recommend?	tum-hee kah-shah-chee shi-fah-rahs ka-taah?

No ice/milk in my ... please. maahz-hi-yaah bahr-fah/dood nah-kaah gaah-loo
    lassi   lahs-sit
    tea   chah-haaht

Can I have a ..., please?
kru-pah-yaah mah-laah ... dyaahl kaah?

At the Restaurant

ashtray	ash-tre
bill	bil
cup	kahp
fork	kaah-taah
knife	su-ree
menu	men-yu
small	lah-haahn
soap	saah-bahn
spoon	chah-mahch
towel	to-wel
toilets	swahch-chaah-taah gri-hah; to-i-let
toothpick	kaah-ree
wash area	ba-sin

Meat – Mutton

	mah-tahn
beef	gaah-yi-che mããhs
chicken	komb-dee
fish	maah-saah/maah-so-lee
goat	bo-kah-dah-che mããhs
mutton	mah-tahn
pork	du-kraah-che mããhs

Vegetables

cabbage	ko-bee
cauliflower	phul ko-bee
eggplant	vaahn-ge
green beans	shrah-vahn gev-daah
lentils	daahl
onion	kaahn-daah
peas	mah-taahn
potato	bah-taah-taah
pumpkin	bo-pah-laah
spinach	paah-lahk

Dairy

butter	lo-nee
cheese	cheez/pah-neer
cream	saahy
ghee	toop
ice cream	ah-is kreem
milk	dood
yoghurt	dah-hee

Fruit

apple	sah-fahr-chahnd
banana	ke-lee
capsicum	dahb-bu min-chee
guava	pe-ru
jackfruit	pah-nahs
lemon	lim-boo
mango	aahm-baah
orange	sahn-tre
papaya	pah-pah-ee
sapodilla	chee-koo
tomato	tah-maah-taah

Nuts

almonds	bah-daahm
cashews	kaah-joo
pistachios	pis-te

Spices & Condiments – Spices & Condiments

basil	tu-ahs
cardamom	vel-do-daah
chilli	mir-chee
cinnamon	daahl chee-nee
cloves	lah-vahng
coriander	ko-tim-beer
cumin	jee-raah
garlic	lah-soon
ginger	aah-le
mint	pu-di-naah
nutmeg	jaah-i-pahl
pepper	kaah-le mi-re
red chillies	laahl mir-chyaah
sugar	saah-kahr
tamarind	chinch
turmeric	hah-lahd

Drinks – Paya

	pay-ya
coconut juice	shah-hah-laah
ice	bahr-fah
lassi	lahs-sit
lemonade	shar-bad
raw mango drink	pahn-ha
tea	chah-haaht
water	paah-nee

ORIYA
Useful Phrases

Hello./Goodbye.	nah-mahs-kaahr
Thank you.	dhah-nyah-baahd
What's your name.	aah-pah-nāh-kah naah-mah kah-nah
My name's ...	mo naah-mah ...
I'm a vegetarian	mū ni-raah-mi-shaah-shee
I don't eat meat or fish.	mū māāh-sah baah maah-chhah khaah-e naah-i
Can I have that please.	mū se-i-taah ne-i- paah-re ki
What do you recommend?	aah-pah-nāh-kah mah-tah kah-nah?
No ice/milk in my ... please.	mo ... bah-rah-fah/doo-dhah di-āh-tu naāh-i
lassi	lah-si
tea	chaah-re
Can I have a ... please.	mū go-tae ... ne-i paah-re ki

At the Restaurant

ashtray	ash-tray
big	bah-rah
bill	bil
cup	kahp
fork	kāh-taah chaah-much
knife	chhu-ri
menu	men-yoo
small	chho-tah
toilets	paah-ee-khaah-naah
toothpick	dāāh-tah-kho-laah
wash area	haah-tah dho-i-baah jaah-gaah

Dairy

butter	lah-u-nee
cheese	che-naah
cream	sah-rah
ghee	ghi-ah
ice cream	ah-is kreem
milk	doo-dhah/khee-rah
yoghurt	dah-hi

Meat – Mansa

	māāh-sah
beef	go-ru māāh-sah
chicken	ku-ku-raah māāh-sah
fish	maah-chhah
goat	chhe-lee
mutton	mē-raah māāh-sah
pork	ghu-su-ri māāh-sah

Vegetables – Pariba

	pah-ree-bah
cabbage	bã-dhaah go-bee
capsicum	sim-laah meerch
cauliflower	phu-lah go-bee
eggplant	baah-i-gah-nah
green beans	been-chh¥-i
lentils	daah-li
onions	pi-aah-jah
peas	mah-tah-rah
potato	aah-lu
pumpkin	kah-khaah-ru
spinach	shaah-gah
tomato	bi-laah-ti baah-ee-gah-nah

Spices & Condiments

basil	tul-see
cardamom	ah-le-ee-chah
chilli	lãh-kaah
cinnamon	daahl-chi-ni
coriander	dhah-ni-aah
cloves	lah-bãh-gah
cumin	jee-raah
garlic	lah-su-nah
nutmeg	jaah-ee-phah-lah
pepper	go-lah mah-ree-chah
red chillies	lãh-kaah mah-ree-chah
tamarind	tē-tu-lee
turmeric	hahl-dee

Fruit

apple	ah-pel
apricot	ah-pree-kot
banana	kah-dah-lee
guava	pi-ju-li
jackfruit	pah-nah-sah
lemon	lē-bu
mango	ããh-bah
orange	kah-mah-laah
papaya	aahm-roo-tah bhãh-daah
peach	peech

Nuts

almonds	baah-daahm
cashews	kaah-ju
pistachio	pes-taah baah-daahm

Drinks

beer	beer
butter milk	gho-lah dah-hi
coffee	ko-fee
ice	bah-rah-fah
lemonade	lē-bu paah-ni
purified water	mi-ne-ral wa-ter
tea	cha-ha
water	paah-ni

PUNJABI
Useful Phrases

Hello./Goodbye.	saht-shree-ah-kaahl
Thank you.	shu-kri-yaah
What's your name?	twaah-dah naah kee a?
My name is ...	me-raah naah he-gaah ...
I'm vegetarian.	mã sab-jiyaãh kahn-daah haãh
I don't eat meat or fish.	mã meet mah-chee nah-eē kahn-daah
Can I have that please?	kir-pyah mõ lah-e sahk-daah haãh

What do you recommend?
  tus-sı kee so-chah-de ho? twaah-daah kee kah-yaahl ha?
No milk in my tea, please.
  me-ree chaah vich dud naah paah-yo ha
No ice in my lassi, please.
  me-ree lahs-see vich bah-raf naah paah-yo ha
Can I have a ..., please?
  kir-pah kahr-ke ma-nu ... mil sah-kah-daah ha?

At the Restaurant

ashtray	sir-gaht waah-lee tahs-tah-ree
bill	bil
cup	kahp
fork	kaahn-taah
knife	chahk-ku
menu	men-yu
small	chot-taah
roadside restaurant	dhab-ba
toilets	gu-sahl-kaah-naah
toothpick	daahnd saahf kah-rahn waah-lee til-li
wash area	tyawn waah-lee jah-gaah

Nuts – Meve

	me-ve
almonds	bah-daahm
cashews	kaah-ju
pistachios	pish-te

Spices & Condiments
Mircha & Garam Masala

	meer-chah & gah-ram mah-saah-lah
basil	baahsh-naah waah-lee paht-te
cardamom	laah-chi-yãh
chilli	mir-chãah
cinnamon	daahl chee-nee
cloves	lawng
coriander	dah-ni-yaah
cumin	jee-raah
fenugreek	me-tah-re
garlic	lah-sahn
ginger	ahd-drahk
mint	pu-din-naah
nutmeg	jah-i fahll
pepper	kaah-lee mir-chãah
red chilli	laahl mir-chãah
saffron	ke-sahr
tamarind	im-lee
turmeric	hahl-dee

Meat – Maans

	mããhs
beef	gãah daah meet
chicken	chuj-jaah
fish	mah-chee
goat	bah-kah-ree
mutton	mur-ge daah meet
pork	su-aahr daah meet

Vegetables – Sabjintinya

	sahb-jin-teen-yah
cabbage	paht-tah gob-bee
capsicum	shim-laah mirch
cauliflower	ful gob-bee
eggplant	bah-tah-üü
green beans	fahl-li-yãh
lentils	daah-lãh
onion	gahn-de
peas	mah-tahr
potato	aah-loo
pumpkin	kahd-du
spinach	paah-lahk
tomato	tah-mah-tar

Drinks – Thandda

	thaand-dah
ice	bah-raf
lassi	lahs-see
tea	chaah
water	paah-nee

Fruit – Phul

	full
apple	sev
banana	kel-laah
guava	ahm-rood
jackfruit	kah-teel
lemon	nim-boo
mango	aahmb
orange	sahn-traah
papaya	pah-pit-taah
peach	aah-roo
pomegranate	ku-maah-nee
sapodilla	chee-koo

Dairy – Dudh, Diyan & Chijan

	doodh, dee-yahn & chee-jahn
butter	mah-kahnn
cheese	pah-neer
cream	mah-lah-ee
ghee	kyo
ice cream	ah-is kreem/kul-fee
milk	dudd
yoghurt	dah-i-ẽ

TAMIL
Useful Phrases

Hello.	vah-nah-kahm or he-lo
Goodbye.	paahr-kah-laahm (see you)
Thank you.	nahn ri
What's your name?	un-gah pe-yahr en-nah?
My name is …	en pe-yahr …
I am a vegetarian.	naahn saivahm
I don't eat meat or fish.	naahn kah-ri meen saah-pidu vahdi-lah-ee
Can I have that, please?	e-nahk-ku ah-du kudu-kah-rin-galah?
What do you recommend?	neen-gah en-nah sol-reen-gah?

No ice/milk in my … please.	en … isu/paahl vahn-dahm
lassi	mor il
tea	tee il
Can I have a …, please?	kon-jahm … vah-num?

Meat – Mamisam

	mah-mee-saahm
beef	maht-tu kah-ri
chicken	ko-li kah-ri
fish	meen
goat	aht-tu kah-ri
mutton	mah-tahm
pork	pahn-ni kah-ree

At the Restaurant
ashtray	ash-tray
bill	bil
cup	kahp
fork	mul-lu
knife	kaht-ti
restaurant	otel
small	chin-nah-tah
toilets	to-i-let/kahk-koo-se
toothpick	pahl-ku-chi
wash area	kah-i kah-lu-vah-rah e-dum

Vegetables – Kai
	kaah-ee
cabbage	moo-tah ko-se
capsicum	ko-dah-ee mu-lah-gah-ee
cauliflower	kah-li-flaw-vahr
eggplant	kaht-ri-kah-ee
green beans	beens
lentils	pah-rahp-pu
onion	ven-gah-i-yahm
peas	paht-tah-nee
potato	u-ru-lah-ki-langu
pumpkin	poos-ni-kah-ee
spinach	kee-raah
tomato	tahk-kah-lee

Fruit – Pallam
	paahl-lahm
apple	a-pahl
banana	vah-i-yaah pah-lahm
guava	koi-ya-kai pah-lam
jackfruit	pah-lah pah-lahm
lemon	e-lim-chee pah-lahm
mango	mahm-pah-lahm
papaya	pahp-paah-lee pah-lahm
pomegranate	maadalam pah-lahm

Nuts – Khotay
	kho-tay
almonds	baah-daahm pah-rup-pu
cashews	mund-dree
pistachios	pis-taah pah-rup-pu

Drinks – Kudi Vaghai
	koo-dee vah-ghah-i
ice	isu
lassi	mor
tea	tee; te-neer; chah-i
water	neer/thah-neer

Spices & Condiments – **Masala** mah-saah-lah
basil — tu-lah-see
cardamom — e-lahk-kah-ee
chilli — mi-laah-gah-ee
cinnamon — paht-tah-ee
cloves — ki-rahm-bu
coriander — ko-tah-mah-lee/dahr-ni-yaah
cumin — see-rah-kahm
garlic — poon-du
ginger — in-jee
mint — poo-di-naah
nutmeg — jah-tik-kaah
pepper — mi-lah-gu
red chilli — vah-raah mi-lah-gah-ee
tamarind — pu-lee
turmeric — mahn-jahl po-dee

Dairy
butter — ven-nah-ee
cheese — chees
cream — kreem
ghee — ney
ice cream — ah-i-skreem
milk — paahl
yoghurt — tai-ru

TELUGU
Useful Phrases
Hello. — nah-mah-skaah-rah-mu
Goodbye. — nah-mah-skaah-rah-mu vel-li vahs-tah-mu
Thank you. — tank yu
What's your name? — mee pe-ru e-mi-ti?
My name is … — naah pe-ru …
I'm vegetarian. — ne-nu ve-ge-ta-ri-an
I don't eat meat/fish. — ne-nu mum-sum/che-pah ti-nah-nu
Can I have that, please? — nah-ku ah-di is-tah-rah pleez?
What do you recommend? — mee-ru e-mi ahn-tah-ru?

No ice/milk in my … please. — na … lo ah-i-soo/paah-lu vah-du
    lassi — las-si
    tea — tee
Can I have a …, please? — naah-ku o-kah .. is-tah-rah pleez?

Nuts
almond — baah-dahm
cashews — jee-dee pahp-poo
pistachios — pis-tah

280

At the Restaurant

ashtray	ash-tra
bill	bil
cup	kah-poo
fork	for-koo
knife	kah-tee
menu	men-yu
small	chin-nah-dee
toilets	bat-room/to-i-let
toothpick	toot-pi-ku/pool-lah
wash area	ahsh ba-sin

Meat – Mumsum

mum-sum

beef	beef
chicken	ko-dee mum-sum
fish	che-pah
goat	mah-kah mum-sum
mutton	mat-tan
pork	pork

Dairy

butter	ven-nah poo-sah
cheese	cheez
cream	kreem
ghee	ne-yi
ice cream	ah-is kreem
milk	paah-loo
yoghurt	pe-ru-gu

Spices & Condiments

cardamom	el-lahk-kah kaah-yah
chilli	kaah-rah-mu
cinnamon	dahl-chee-nah po-di
cloves	lah-vahn-gaah-loo
coriander leaves	ko-ti mee-rah
coriander powder	dah-ni-yaah-lu po-di
cumin	jee-lah-kahr-rah
fenugreek	me-tu-loo
garlic	vel-lul-lee paah-yah
ginger	ahl-lah-moo
mint	po-di-nah
mustard seeds	aah-vah-lu
nutmeg	jah-i pahl
pepper	mi-ri-yaah-lu
salt	oop-poo
tamarind	chin-tah pahn-du
turmeric	pah-su-pu

Vegetables

cabbage	ca-be-gee
cauliflower	caw-li-faw-vahr
eggplant	vahn-kaah-yah
green beans	chik-ku-du kaah-yah
lentils	pahp-pu
onion	ul-li-pah-yah
potato	bahng-ah-lah doom-pah
pumpkin	goom-mah-dee kaah-yah
spinach	to-tah koo-rah
tomato	to-mah-to-lu

Fruit

apple	a-pahl
banana	ah-rah-tee pun-doo
guava	jah-mah kaah-yah
jackfruit	pah-nah-sah pun-doo
lemon	nim-mah kaah-yah
mango	mah-mi-dee kaah-yah
orange	naah-rin-jah pun-doo
papaya	bob-bah-sah kaah-yah
sultanas	kis-mis

Drinks

lassi	las-si
tea	tee
water	mun-chee neel-lu

A

almond	*baah-daahm*	badam
anise	*saunf*	saunf
aniseed	*saunf*	saunf
apple	*seb*	seb
apricot	*khu-baah-nee*	khubani
asafoetida	*hing*	hing

B

bacon	*su-ahr kaa gosht*	suwar ka gosht
bag	*thai-laah*	thaila
bake	*bek kahr-naah*	baik karna
banana leaf	*ke-le kaah paht-taah*	kele ka patta
banana	*ke-laah*	kela
to bargain	*mol-tol kahr-naah*	moltol karna
barley	*Jaw/jowar*	Jau/jowar
basil, sweet	*tul-see*	tulsi
basmati rice	*baahs-mah-tee chaah-vahl*	basmati chawal
bay leaf	*tej paht-taah*	tej patta
beef	*gaah-ee kaah gosht*	gayee ka gosht
beer	*bi-yaahr*	beer
beetroot	*beet/chu-kahn-dahr*	beet/chukandar
betel	*paahn*	paan
sweet and spicy	*mee-thaah*	mitha
with spices (not sweet)	*saah-daah*	sada
with tobacco	*tahm-baah-koo waah-laah/*	tambaku wala/
	zarda wah-laah	zarda wala
betel nut	*su-paah-ree*	supari
bill	*bil*	bill
bitter gourd	*kah-re-laah*	karela
black lentil	*u-rahd kee daahl*	urad ki daal
black plum	*jaah-mun*	jamun
blackberry	*kaah-lee ahn-chee*	kali anchi
black-eyed bean	*lo-bi-yaah*	lobiha
blender	*mik-see*	mixi
boar	*jahn-glee*	jangli
—wild	*su-ahr*	suar
to boil	*u-baahl-naah*	ubalna
borage	*paht-tahr chur*	patta chur
bottle	*shee shee/bo-tahl*	shi shi; bottle
bottled water	*bo-tahl kaah paah-nee*	botal ka pani
bowl	*kah-to-ree*	katori
mixing	*pahraaht*	paraat
to braise	*dam de kahr pah-kaah-naah*	dam de kar pakana
brazil nut	*chi-rāwn-jee*	chiraunji

bread		
unleavened	*naahn/ro-tee/chah-paah-pee*	naan/roti/chapati
English-style	*dah-bahl ro-tee/ pau roti*	dabal roti/pau roti
wheat flour	*pah-rāāh-thaah*	paratha
breakfast	*naahsh-taah*	nashta
broad bean	*fah-vaah*	fawa
brown lentil	*daahl*	daal
brown rice	*laahl chaah-vahl*	lal chawal
bubble	*bul-bu-laah*	bulbula
buckwheat	*ko-too*	kotu
butter	*kah-saah-ee/bu-chahr*	kasai/butcher
butter	*mahk-kahn*	makkhan
clarified	*ghee*	ghee
buttermilk	*chaahch/maht-taah*	chach/mata

C

cabbage, red	*bahnd gho-bee*	band ghobi
cake	*kek*	cake
can	*tin*	tin
can opener	*tin kol-ne vaah-lee cheez*	tin kolne vaali chiz
cantaloupe	*kahr-boo-jaah*	karbuja
capsicum	*mirch*	mirch
caramel	*ka-raah-mahl*	caramel
caraway seed	*ahj-mo-daah*	ahimoda
cardamom	*i-laah-ee-chee*	ilaychi
carrot	*gaah-jar*	gajar
cashew	*kaah-joo*	kaju
cauliflower	*phool gho-bee*	phul ghobi
cayenne	*laahl mirch*	lal mirch
cereal	*ah-naahj*	anaaj
chanterelle	*murg*	murg
cheese (milk curd)	*pah-neer*	paneer
chef	*khaahn-saah-maa*	khansama
Brahman	*mah-haah-raahj*	maharaj
cherry	*che-ree; aah-loo baah-loo*	cherry; alu balu
chestnut	*pāāh-gahr*	pagar
chicken	*mur-gee*	murgi
chickpea	*cho-le*	chole
chilli	*mirch*	mirch
green	*hah-ree mirch*	hari mirch
Chinese cabbage	*chee-nee gho-bee*	chini ghobi
chive	*jahm-boo*	jambu
chutney	*chaht-nee*	chutney
cigarette (home-made)	*bee-ree*	bidi
cinnamon	*daal-chee-nee*	dalchini
citrus	*neē-boo*	nimbu
clarified butter	*ghee*	ghee
clay oven	*tahn-door*	tandoor
clove	*lāwg*	laung

cochineal	*ge-roo*	geru
cocoa	*ko-ko*	koko
coconut	*naah-ri-yal*	nariyal
coffee	*kaah-fee*	coffee
condensed milk	*kho-yaah*	khoya
conserves	*mu-rahb-baah*	muraba
cooked	*pahk-kaah*	pakkah
coriander leaves	*paht-taah*	patta
corn	*mahk-kaah*	maka
cornflour	*baah-reek mah-kaah kee aaht-taah*	barik maka ki atta
cream	*mah-laah-ee*	malai
cress	*chahn-sur*	chansur
croquette	*kof-taah*	kofta
to crush	*pees-naah*	pisna
cucumber	*kahk-ree*	kakri
cumin seeds	*zee-raah*	zera
cup	*kahp*	cup
disposable, clay cup	*kul-hahr*	kulhar
curd	*dah-hee*	dahi
to cure	*nah-mahk lah-gaah-naah*	namak lagana
currant	*daahk/moo-nahk-kaah*	daak/munakka
curry	*kah-ree*	curry
–powder	*paw-dahr*	powder
custard apple	*shah-ree-faa/see-tha phal*	sharifa/sita phal
to cut (finely)	*(tuk-re tuk-re) kahr-naah*	(tukre tukre) katna
cutlery	*kāāh-taah chu-ree*	kanta churi
cutlets	*kaht-lets*	cutlets

D

dates	*khah-joor*	khajur
deep-fry	*tahl-naah*	talna
defiled	*jhoo-taah*	jhuta
dessert	*mee-thaah*	meetha
to dice	*mah-heen tuk-rō mē kaaht-naah*	mahin tukron me katna
diced	*mah-heen tuk-rō mē kaah-taah hu-aah*	mahin tukron me kata hua
dill	*so-aah; moo-doo-ree-kaah lah-taah*	soa; mudurika lata
dinner	*raaht kaah khaah-naah*	rat ka khana
dish (steel)	*pah-raaht*	paraat
to dissolve	*gal-naa*	galna
dried	*su-khaah hu-aah*	sukha hua
fruit	*me-vaah*	mewa
plum	*aah-loo bu-kaah-raah*	alu bukara
drinks	*pee-ne kee chee-zē*	pini ki chizen
duck	*bah-tahk*	batakh

E

egg	*ahn-de*	ande
eggplant	*bā-ēē-gahn/breen-jahl*	baingan/brinjal

F

fast (Muslim)	*rah-maah-zaahn*	Ramadan
fast food	*chaaht*	chaat
fennel	*saunf*	saunf
fenugreek	*me-thee*	methi
fig	*ahn-jeer/guu-lahr*	anjir/gular
filtered water	*fil-tahrd paah-nee*	filtered pani
fish	*mahch-lee*	machli
flavour	*svaahd/zaah-i-kaah*	swaad
flour		
corn	*baah-reek mahk-kaah kee aaht-taah*	barik makki ki atta
gram	*be-sahn*	besan
plain	*ma-daah*	maida
wholemeal	*aah-taah*	atta
food	*khaah-naah*	khana
—processor	*mik-see*	mixi
fork	*kāāh-taah*	kanta
fresh	*taah-zaah*	taza
—juice	*joos*	—juice
—water	*paah-nee*	—pani
fried		
—potato	*tah-laah aah-loo*	tala aloo
—rice	*bi-ri-yaah-nee*	biriyani
fruit	*pahl*	phal
dried	*me-vaah*	mewa
juice	*kaah ras*	ka ras
to fry	*bhoon-naah*	bhuna
deep	*tahl-naah*	talna
shallow	*kahm tel mē tahl-naa*	kam tel me talna
frying pan (large)	*kah-raah*	karhah
frying pan (small)	*kah-raah-ee*	kadhai

G

Ganges water	*gahn-gaah jahl*	Ganga jal
garlic	*leh-sun*	lehsun
ghee	*ghee*	ghee
pure	*shud de-see*	shuddh desi
gherkin	*kee-raah*	kira
giblets	*chich-re*	chichri
ginger	*ahd-rahk*	adrak
glutinous rice	*lahs-daahr chaah-vahl*	rasdar chawal
goat	*bahk-raah*	bakra

goose	*hans*	hans
gooseberry	*kaahk-bahd-ree*	kakbadri
gourd		
bitter	*kah-re-laah*	karela
green	*law-kee*	lauki
pointed	*pahr-vahl*	parval
gram (pulse)	*chah-naah*	chana
flour	*be-sahn*	besan
grapefruit	*chah-kot-raah*	chakotra
grapes	*ahn-goor*	angur
to grate	*kahs-naah*	kasna
grater	*kahd-doo kahs*	kaddu kas
gravy	*rahs/yahk-nee*	ras/yakni
green capsicum	*shim-laah mirch*	shimla mirch
green chilli	*hah-ree mirch*	hari mirch
green gourd	*law-kee*	lauki
green pulse	*moong kee daahl*	moong ki daal
green (leafy)	*(hah-raah) saahg*	(hara) saag
vegetable		
greens, wild	*jan-gli sahb-zee*	jangli sabzi
griddle, iron	*tah-vaah*	tawa
guava	*ahm-rood*	amrud

H

hand	*haaht*	hath
hare	*kahr-gosh*	khargosh
haricot bean	*sem*	sem
hazelnut	*pah-haah-ree bah-daahm*	pahhari badam
to heat	*gahrm kahr-naa*	garam karna
holy basil	*tul-see*	tulsi
hominy	*drah-li-yaah*	draliya
honey	*madhu*	madhu

I

ice	*bahrf*	barf
ice cream	*kul-fee*	kulfi
ingredient	*kaah-ne kee cheez*	khane ki chiz
iron griddle	*tah-vaah*	tawa

J

jackfruit	*kaht-hahl*	kathal
jaggery	*gur*	gur
Jain	*jain*	Jain
jelly	*je-lee*	jelly
juice	*rahs*	ras
fruit	*pahl kaah*	phal ka

K

kabab	*kah-baahb*	kabab
shami	*shaah-mee*	shami
shish	*seek*	shish
kettle	*ket-lee*	ketli
kidney	*gur-daah*	guda
kidney bean	*raahj-maah*	rajma
kitchen	*rah-so-ee; baah-var-chee*	rasoi; bavarchi kana
	kaah-naah	
knife	*chaah-koo*	chaku
knuckle	*gāāht*	ganth
kosher	*hah-laahl*	halal

L

ladle	*daah/jahn-naah/kahl-chee*	daar/jana/kalchi
lager	*bi-yaahr*	beer
lamb	*ber/mem-naah*	ber/memna
lard	*chik-naah-ee*	chiknai
leaf	*paht-taah*	patta
leek	*gahn-dah-naah/pyaahz*	gandana
left hand	*ul-taah haaht*	ulta hath
leg	*tāāhg*	tang
legumes	*daahl*	daal
black-eyed bean	*lo-bi-yaah*	lobiha
black lentil	*u-rahd kee daahl*	urad ki daal
broad bean	*fah-vaah been*	fawa been
chickpea	*cho-le*	chole
haricot bean	*sem*	sem
kidney bean	*raahj-maah*	rajma
mung bean	*moong*	moong
peas	*mah-tahr*	matar
red lentil	*mah-soor kee daahl*	masoor ki daal
split pea	*mah-tahr kee daahl*	matar ki daal
small, yellow split pea	*chah-naah*	chana daal
lemon	*nēē-boo*	nimbu
lemonade	*shahr-baht*	sherbet
lemon grass	*hah-ree chaah-ee*	hari chay
lentil		
black	*u-rahd kee daahl*	urad ki daal
brown	*daahl*	daal
red	*mah-soor kee daahl*	masoor ki daal
lime	*nēē-boo*	nimbu
liquorice	*gūg-chee*	gungchi
liver	*ji-gahr*	jigar
loaf	*dah-bahl ro-tee/pau roti*	dabal roti/pau roti
lobster	*bah-ree jēē-gaah*	badi jhingar
local	*de-see*	desi

loin	*kah-mahr*	kamar
long-grain rice	*baahs-mah-tee*	basmati
lunch	*din kaah kaah-naah*	din ka khana
lychee	*lee-chee*	lichi

M

mace	*jaah-vi-tree*	javitri
mandarin	*sahn-tah-raah*	santara
mango	*aahm*	am
marijuana	*baahng*	bhang
marinade	*ah-chaar*	achar
to marinate	*bi-gaah-naah*	bhigana
marjoram	*kut-raah*	kutra
marzipan	*baah-daahm kaah kek*	badam ka kek
mayonnaise	*ma-yo-nas*	mayonas
meal	*kaah-naah*	khana
meat	*gosht*	gosht
knuckle	*gāāht*	ganth
leg	*tāāhg*	tang
loin	*kah-mahr*	kamar
neck	*gahr-dahn*	gardan
melon	*tahr-booz*	tarbuz
menu	*men-yoo kaahrd*	menu card
milk	*dood*	dhud
condensed	*ko-yaah*	khoya
powdered	*dood paw-dahr*	dhud powder
sweet, thickened	*rahb-ree*	rabri
mineral water	*min-rahl vaah-tahr*	mineral water
mint	*pu-dee-naah*	pudina
to mix	*mi-laah-naah*	milana
mixed spices	*gahrm mah-saah-laah*	garam masala
mixing	*pahraaht*	paraat
morel	*kum-bee*	kumbi
mortar	*kah-rahl*	karal
muesli	*mus-lee*	musli
Mughlai food	*mug-laah-ee kaah-naah*	Mughlai khana
mulberry	*she-toot*	shetut
mung bean	*moong*	moong
mushroom	*kum-bee*	khumbi
chanterelles	*murg*	murg
Muslim fast	*rah-maah-zaahn*	Ramadan
mustard oil	*sar-sō kaah tel*	sarson ka tel
mustard seed		
black	*raah-ee*	rai
yellow	*sahr-sō*	sarson
mutton	*ber kaah gosht*	ber ka gosht

N

neck	*gahr-dahn*	gardan
noodles	*noo-daals*	noodles
nut		
almond	*baah-daahm*	badam
brazil	*chi-rāwn-jee*	chiraunji
cashew	*kaah-joo*	kaju
chestnut	*pāāh-gahr*	pagar
hazelnut	*pah-haah-ree bah-daahm*	pahhari badam
peanut	*moong-pah-lee*	moongphali
pecan	*gi-ree*	giri
pistachio	*pis-taah*	pista
walnut	*ahk-rot*	akhrot
nutcracker	*sah-ro-taah*	sarota
nutmeg	*jahy-pahl*	jayphal

O

oats	*ju-ee*	jui
rolled	*jah-ee*	jai
offering		
Hindi	*prah-saahd*	prasad
Sikh	*kah-raah*	kara
oil	*tel*	tel
mustard	*sar-sō kaah*	sarson ka
peanut	*moong-pah-lee kaah*	moongphali ka
sesame	*til kaah*	til ka
vegetable	*tel/vanaspathi*	tel/vanaspati
okra	*bin-dee*	bhindi
omelette	*om-let*	omelette
onion		
pickling	*ah-chaahr kaah pyaahz*	achar ka pyaz
red	*pyaahz*	pyaz
shallot	*pyaahz*	pyaz
orange	*naah-ran-gee*	narangi
oven (clay)	*tahn-door*	tandoor

P

palm	*kah-joor kaah gur*	khjur ka gur
papaya	*pah-pee-taah*	papita
paprika	*de-gee mirch*	digi mirch
parasol	*chaah-taah*	chata
Parsis	*paah-see*	Parsi
parsley	*ahj-mod*	ajmod
parsnip	*shahl-gahm*	shalgam
pasta	*paah-staah*	pasta
pastry	*pays-tree*	pastry
patties, potato	*aah-loo kee ti-ki-yāāh*	aloo ki tikiya

peach	*aahroo*	aru
peanut oil	*moong-pah-lee kaah tel*	moongphali ka tel
peanut	*moong-pah-lee*	moongphali
pears	*naahsh-paahtee*	nashpati
peas	*mah-tahr*	matar
dried split peas	*daahl*	daal
pecan	*gi-ree*	giri
peeler, vegetable	*chil-kaah ni-kaahl-ne waah-laah*	chilka nikalni wala
peppermint	*pi-pahr-mint*	peppermint
persimmon	*ten-doo/kaah-koo*	tendu/kaku
pestle	*moo-sahl*	musal
pickle	*ah-chaahr*	achar
pickling onion	*ah-chaahr kaah pyaahz*	achar ka pyaz
picnic	*pik-nik*	picnic
pigeon	*ka-boo-tahr*	kabutar
pilau	*pu-laahv*	pilaf
pine nut	*syōōt*	syut
pineapple	*ah-nahn-naahs*	ananas
pistachio	*pis-taah*	pista
plain flour	*ma-daah*	maida
plate (stainless steel)	*thaah-lee*	thali
plate	*plet*	plet
plum	*aah-loo-chaah*	alucha
black	*jaah-mun*	jamun
dried	*aah-loo bu-kaah-raah*	alu bukara
pointed gourd	*pahr-vahl*	parval
polenta	*mahk-kee kee soo-jee*	makki ki suji
pomegranate (seeds)	*ah-naahr (ke daah-naah)*	anar (ke dane)
popcorn	*pop-korn*	popcorn
poppy seeds	*kahs-kahs*	kaskas
porridge	*dah-li-yaah*	daliya
pot	*bahr-tahn*	bartan
water	*gah-raah*	ghara
lidded	*deg-chee*	degchi
pot roast	*duhm*	dum
potato	*aah-loo*	aloo
baked	*bu-naah aah-loo*	buna aloo
sweet	*shahn-kahr kahnd*	shankar kand
potato patties	*aah-loo kee ti-ki-yāāh*	aloo ki tikiya
poultry	*mur-gee*	murgi
powdered milk	*dood paw-dahr*	dhud powder
prawn	*jēē-gee mahch-lee*	jhingi machli
pressure cooker	*pre-shahr koo-kahr*	pressure cooker
prune	*ber*	ber
pulse	*dhaahl*	daal
large, yellow-brown	*ahr-hahr kee daahl*	arhar ki daal
yellow-green pulse	*moong kee daahl*	moong ki daal
black lentil	*u-rahd kee daahl*	urad ki daal

291

brown lentil	*daahl*	daal
green split pea	*kaah saahg*	ka sag
red lentil	*mah-soor kee daahl*	masoor ki daal
small, yellow split pea	*chah-naah daahl*	chana daal
split pea	*mah-tahr kee daahl*	matar ki daal
pumpkin	*kahd-doo; see-taah pahl*	kaddu; sita phal
pure	*shudd*	shuddh
to puree	*bahr-taah*	bharta

Q

quince	*shree pahl*	shri phal

R

rabbit	*kahr-gosh*	khargosh
radish		
red	*laahl moo-lee*	lal murli
white	*moo-lee*	murli
raisin	*kish-mish*	kishmish
raspberry	*rahs-bah-ree*	raspberry
receipt	*rah-seed*	rahseed
red		
–cabbage	*bahnd go-bee*	band ghobi
–capsicum	*laahl shim-laah mirch*	lal shimla mirch
–kidney bean	*raahj-maah*	rajma
–lentil	*mah-soor kee daahl*	masoor ki daal
–onion	*pyaahz*	pyaz
–radish	*laahl moo-lee*	lal murli
–wine	*laahl shah-raahb*	lal sharab
rennet	*jaah-mahn*	jaman
reservation	*bu-king*	booking
resin		
asafoetida (bitter)	*hing*	hing
black resin	*kaht-taah*	katta
restaurant (roadside)	*daah-baah*	dhaba
rhubarb	*re-vaht chee-nee*	revat chini
rice	*chaah-vahl*	chawal
basmati (long-grain)	*baahs-mah-tee*	basmati
brown	*chaah-vahl*	chawal
glutinous	*lahs-daahr caah-vahl*	rasdar chawal
short-grain	*mo-taah chaah-vahl*	motha chawal
rice pudding	*keer*	kheer
right hand	*si-daah haaht*	sidha hath
ripe	*pahk-kaah*	pukkah
to roast	*bun-naah*	bhunna
rolled oats	*jah-ee*	jai
rolling pin	*be-lahn*	belan
rosewater	*gu-laah-bee paah-nee*	gulab ka pani
rosemary	*daw-naah*	dauna
rum	*rahm*	rum

S

English	Pronunciation	Hindi
sacred cow	*pah-vi-trah gaah-ee*	pavitra gay
saffron	*ke-sahr*	kesar
sage	*tul-see ban-du*	tulsi bandu
sago	*saah-boodaah-naah*	saboo dana
salad	*sah-laahd*	salad
salt	*nah-mahk*	namak
sauce	*saws*	sauce
tomato	*tah-maah-tahr*	tomato
saucepan	*bahr-tahn*	bartan
savoury	*nahm-keen*	namkeen
scales	*tah-raah-joo*	taraju
scissors	*kā-ēē-chee*	kainchi
semolina	*soo-jee*	suji
service	*se-vaah*	sewa
sesame oil	*til kaah tel*	til ka tel
sesame seed	*til*	til
shallot onion	*pyaahz*	pyaz
shallow-fry	*kahm tel mē tahl-naa*	kam tel me talna
shami kebab	*shaah-mee kah-baahb*	shami kabab
sharpening stone	*chaah-koo tez kar-ne*	chaku tez karne
	kaah paht-tar	ka pattar
shish kebab	*seek kah-baahb*	shish kabab
short-grain rice	*mo-tah chaah-vahl*	motha chawal
sieve	*chahn-nee*	chani
sifter	*chaahl-nee*	chalni
silver foil	*vahrk*	varq
to simmer	*dee-mee āāhch pahr*	dhimi anch par pakana
	pah-kaah-naah	
skewer	*seek-chaah*	seekcha
slice	*tuk-raah*	tukra
to slice	*kaat-naah*	katna
to smoke	*du-ē se pah-kaah-naa*	dhue se pakana
smoked	*du-ē se pah-kaah hu-aah*	dhue se paka hua
snacks	*nam-keen*	namkeen (lit: salty)
soft drink (fruit)	*shahr-baht*	sherbet
soup spoon	*chah-mahch*	chamach
soya bean	*so-yaah been*	soya bean
spatula, wooden	*lahk-ree kaah chah-mahch*	lakri ka chamach
spices, mixed	*gahrm mah-saah-laah*	garam masala
spinach	*paah-lahk*	palak
spirits	*daah-roo*	daru
split pea	*mah-tahr kee daahl*	matar ki daal
small, yellow split pea	*chah-naah*	chana daal
spoon	*chah-mach*	chamach
squash	*see-taah pahl*	sita phal
steak	*gosht kee bo-tee*	gosht ka boti
to steam	*bhaahp se pah-kaah-naa*	bhap se pakana
steamer	*bhah-paah-re kaah bahr-tahn*	bhapare ka bartan

to stew	*dee-mee ahg-nee mē pah-kaah-naah*	dimi agni men pakana
stone, sharpening	*chaah-koo tez kar-ne kaah paht-tar*	chaku tez karne ka pattar
straw	*boo-saah*	bhusa
strawberry	*straah-be-ree*	strawberry
sugar	*chee-nee*	chini
palm sugar	*gur*	gur
sugarcane	*gahn-naah/eek*	ganna/ik
sugarcane juice	*gahn-ne kaah ras*	ganne ka ras
sweet (n)	*mi-taah-ee*	mithai
sweet (adj)	*mee-thaah*	mitha
sweet potato	*shahn-kahr kahnd*	shankar kand

T

table	*mez*	mez
tamarind	*im-lee*	imli
tap water	*nahl kaah paah-nee*	nal ka pani
tarragon	*prah-naahg*	pranag
tea	*chaah-ee*	chai
teaspoon	*cho-taah chah-mahch*	chota chamach
thyme	*ahj-vaah-in*	ajvain
tin	*tin*	tin
tip	*bahkh-sheesh*	bakshish
tofu	*so-yaah pah-neer*	soya paneer
tomato	*tah-maah-tahr*	tomato
sauce	*saws*	tomato sauce
tonic water	*to-nik*	tonic
treacle	*chahsh-nee*	chashni
turkey	*pe-roo pahk-shee*	piru pakshi
turmeric	*hahl-dee*	haldi
turnip	*shahl-gahm*	shalgam

U

uncooked	*kahch-chaah*	kaccha

V

vanilla	*vah-ni-laah*	vanilla
vegetable	*sahb-zee*	sabzi
vegetable (green, leafy)	*hah-raah saahg*	hara saag
vegetable oil	*vah nahs-pah-ti tel*	vanaspati tel
vegetable peeler	*chil-kaah ni-kaahl-ne waah-laah*	chilka nikalni wala
vegetables (green)	*saahg*	saag
vegetarian	*shaah-kaah-haah-ree*	shakahari
vinegar	*sir-kaah*	sirka
vodka	*vod-kaah*	vodka

W

walnut	*ahk-rot*	akhrot
water	*paah-nee*	pani
bottled	*bo-tahl kaah*	botal ka
filtered	*fil-tahrd*	filtered
fresh	*taah-zaah*	taza
Ganges	*gahn-gaah jahl*	Ganga jal
mineral	*min-rahl vaah-tahr*	mineral water
rosewater	*gu-laah-bee*	gulab ka
tap	*nahl kaah*	nal ka
tonic	*to-nik*	tonic
watermelon	*tahr-booz*	tarbuz
well done (cooked)	*ah-chee tah-raah pah-kaah*	achi taraa pakaa
wheat	*gehōō*	gehu
to whisk	*pent-naa*	phentna
white radish	*moo-lee*	murli
white wine	*sah-fed shah-raahb*	safed sharab
whole	*saah-but*	sabut
wholemeal flour	*aah-taah*	atta
wild	*jahn-glee*	jangli
–boar	*su-ahr*	suar
–greens	*sahb-zee*	sabzi
wine	*mah-di-raa*	madira
red	*laahl shah-raahb*	lal sharab
white	*sah-fed shah-raahb*	safed sharab
whisky	*vis-kee*	whisky
wooden spatula	*lahk-ree kaah chah-mahch*	lakri ka chamach

Y

yellow capsicum	*pee-lee shim-laah mirch*	pili shimla mirch
yellow split pea	*daahl*	daal
yoghurt	*dah-hee*	dahi
zucchini	*zu-kee-nee*	zucchini

A

achhar *ah-chaahr* pickle/marinade
–ka pyaz *kaah pyaahz* pickling onion
achi tara paka *ah-chee tah-raah pah-kaah* 'well done' (cooked)
ahimoda *ahj-mo-daah* caraway seed – a milder, slightly bitter cousin of cumin used in North Indian meat dishes. The sharp-pointed seeds are also valued as a body freshener: good for bad breath, wind and nausea.
akhrot *ah-khrot* walnut
Allah o akbar bismillah! *Ahl-laah-o-ahk-bahr! bis-mil-laahh* 'God is Great! In the name of God!' (*see also* **halal**)
aloo *aah-loo* potato
–dum *dum* spicy potato curry usually served with **puri**
–paratha *pah-rāāh-thaah* fried, triangular bread with a potato filling
alu balu *aah-loo baah-loo* cherry
alu bukara *aah-loo bu-kaah-raah* dried plum
alucha *aah-loo-chaah* plum
am *aahm* mango
–ka pana *kaah pah-naah* drink made from boiled, unripe mangoes, mint and cumin. Said to lessen the effects of the heat in the scorching summer.
amod *ahj-mod* parsley
amrud *ahm-rood* guava
amtee *ahm-tee* spiced lentils often served with rice.
ananas *ah-nahn-naahs* pineapple
anar *ah-naahr* pomegranate
–ke dane *ke daah-naah* pomegranate seeds, added to curds or served as an accompaniment; the dried seeds are referred to as anardana
anba kata *āāh-bah khah-taah* a seasonal dish of small green mango pieces cooked in tamarind juice along with **jaggery** and spices. Can be sour or sweet, depending on your palate and the flavour of the mango. (Orissa)
ande *ahn-de* egg

angur *ahn-goor* grapes
anjir *ahn-jeer* fig
anna/annam *ahn-nahm* cooked white rice, hence the name for the goddess of food is Annapoorna
atta *aah-taah* wholemeal flour from which most Indian breads are made

B

bada *vah-daah/bah-raah* (*see* **vada**)
badam *baah-daahm* almond (*see* **milk badam**)
badi jhingar *bah-ree jhēē-gaah* lobster
baingan *bā-ēē-gahn* eggplant/aubergine – popularly known as **brinjal**
–bhaja *bhaah-jaah* eggplant rings deep-fried in mustard oil and seasoned lightly with salt and red chilli powder (Assam, Bengal)
–bharta *bhahr-taah* spicy dish of roasted eggplant fried with onions and tomatoes. Often accompanied by cucumbers, tomatoes, onions and radishes and served with a squeeze of lime. (Punjab)
baik karna *bek kahr-naah* to bake
bajre *baahj-re* millet occasionally used in bread making but more frequently pounded with spice to make **pap-padams**.
–ki roti *kee ro-tee* bread made from millet and cooked on a **tawa**
bakra *bahk-raah* goat
balchao *bahl-chah-o* dried prawn and chilli relish
band ghobi *bahnd gho-bee* cabbage
bandha kopir dalna *baahn-dhah ko-peer daahl-nah* finely shredded and fried cabbage, potato, tomato and green peas (West Bengal)
bareloo shak *bah-re-lōō shaak* potato, onion, eggplant and zucchini pieces stuffed with **chana** flour then mixed with spices and cooked in spiced oil (Gujarat)
barf/baraf *bahrf/bah-raf* ice

barfi *bahr-fee* fudge-like sweet that can be made with different ingredients – often topped with edible silver foil (North India)

barik makki ki atta *baah-reek mahk-kaah kee aaht-taah* cornflour

bartan *bahr-tahn* pot/saucepan

basmati *baahs-mah-tee* long-grain, aromatic rice (North India)

bavarchi kana *baah-var-chee kaah-naah* kitchen

beer *bi-yaahr* beer/lager

beet *beet* beetroot (*see also* **chukandar**)

belan *be-lahn* rolling pin

ber *ber* berry; lamb; prune

ber ka gosht *ber kaah gosht* mutton

besan *be-sahn* gram or chickpea flour

bhaja *bhaah-jah* vegetables such as deep-fried eggplant, potato and okra, which are served with **daal** after **shukto** (*see* **baingan bhaja**) (West Bengal)

bhakri *bhaah-kri* thick, unleavened bread made from millet and cooked over an open flame (Maharashtra, Rajasthan)

bhang *bhaahng* marijuana leaves that can be mixed up with vegetables and fried into **pakoras** or drunk in **lassis** and other beverages. These leaves also make very strong, mind-altering, and frequently sick-inducing pot.

bhap se pakana *bhaahp se pah-kaah-naa* to steam

bhapa *bhah-pah* steamed

bhapare ka bartan *bhah-paah-re kaah bahr-tahn* steamer

bharta *bhahr-taah* roasted eggplant fried with onions and tomatoes

bhelpuri *bhel poo-ree* crisp-fried thin dough mixed with puffed rice, slivers of boiled potatoes, chopped onions, peanuts, fine hair-like **besan** sticks, sweet tamarind **chatni**, a piquant green coriander and chilli chatni, a generous squeeze of lime synonymous with Mumbai (Maharashtra)

bhigana *bhi-gaah-naah* to marinate

bhindi *bhin-dee* okra

bhujiya *bhu-ji-yaah* fried lentils with nuts and spices – eaten as a snack and a favourite when entertaining. There are as many varieties as there are regions in India.

bhuna *bhoon-naah* saute

bhunna *bhun-naah* to roast

bhusa *bhoo-saah* straw

bidi *bee-ree* thin line of tobacco wrapped in a leaf, known as the 'poor man's cigarette'

biryani *bi-ri-yaah-nee* Mughlai dish of steamed rice oven baked with meat, vegetables and spices

borar jhaal *bo-rahr jhal* fried lentil balls cooked in a sauce of mustard and tamarind (West Bengal)

bori *bo-ree* dried lentil balls

botal ka pani *bo-tahl kaah paah-nee* bottled water

brinjal *breen-jahl* eggplant/aubergine (*see also* **baingan**)

buna aloo *bu-naah aah-loo* baked potato (*see* **aloo/alu**)

C

chaat *chaaht* snack foods usually seasoned with **chaat masala** and served with **chatni** – includes **samosas**, **bhelpuri**, fried potato patties and other dishes (Mumbai)

–masala *mah-saah-laah* spice blend of black salt, amchur, cumin, sea salt, coriander powder, chilli powder, black pepper and ginger

chach *chaahch* buttermilk – a drink commonly believed to prevent sunstroke and dehydration

chai *chaah-ee* tea

–tez karne ka pattar *chaah-koo tez kar-ne kaah paht-tar* sharpening stone

chakuli pitha *cha-ku-li pi-thaah* pancakes made from rice flour and green **daal** which is fermented overnight. The mixture is cooked over a hotplate and served for breakfast. (Orissa)

chamankalyi *chaah-mahn-kahl-yee* soft cheese curry (Jammu, Kashmir)

chana/chana daal *chah-naah/chah-naah daahl* common gram or pulse, slightly sweeter version of the yellow split pea

chanar dalna *chah-nar daahl-nah* thicker, spicier version of **jhol** or curry, a Bengali favourite when cooked with home-made cottage cheese, peas and potatoes (West Bengal)

chapati *chah-paah-pee* unleavened bread cooked on a **tawa**. Also known as **roti**. (North India)

chatni *chaht-nee* chutney – can come in any number of varieties, from sweet to salty, and can be made from many different vegetables, fruits, herbs and spices. Most are made fresh and usually served in small, non-metallic bowls.

chaunkna *chāwk-naah* (see **bhaghar**)

chawal *chaah-vahl* rice

cheeku *chee-koo* sapodilla – brown fruit that originated in America but is now found in the subcontinent. It looks like a kiwi fruit on the outside but is brown inside with large black seeds

chena pora *chhe-naah po-rah* cheesecake prepared in the traditional way. Cheese is steamed overnight with **jaggery** until it develops a golden-brown tint. A favourite sweet dish available everywhere from city food stores to small, village **chai** shops. (Orissa)

chichri *chich-re* giblets

chicknai *chik-naah-ee* lard/grease

chilka nikalni wala *chil-kaah ni-kaahl-ne waah-laah* vegetable peeler

chimti *chim-tee* tongs – generally used to foment **roti** over the flame after cooking on a **tawa**. Also used to pick up and turn over deep-fried snacks such as sweets during preparation.

chini *chee-nee* sugar

chini ghobi *chee-nee gho-bee* Chinese cabbage

chiraunji *chi-rāwn-jee* brazil nut

chiriya *chi-ri-yaah* bird

chokar *cho-kahr* bran

chole *cho-le* spiced chickpea dish served with puri; also another term for chickpea (Punjab)

chom chom *chom chom* long-shaped dessert made with **chana** and cooked in sugar syrup (West Bengal)

chota chamach *chotaah chah-mahch* teaspoon

chukandar *chu-kahn-dahr* beetroot (see also **beet**)

curry *kah-ree* an anglicisation of the Tamil word kari, or black pepper

D

daak *daahk* currant

daal *daahl* the generic term for cooked and uncooked lentils or pulses

daal & bhaja *dhaahl & bhaah-jah* deep-fried eggplant, potato and okra served after **shukto** (West Bengal)

daar *daah* ladle

dabal roti *dah-bahl ro-tee* loaf; English-style bread

dahi *dah-hee* curds; served with most meals and are particularly handy for cooling down food; similar to yoghurt

–bada *dah-hee bah-raah* balls of mashed lentils fried and then topped with seasoned curds

–bhalle *dah-hee bhal-le* balls of **daal** and curds, served with tamarind chutney (Punjab)

dalchini *daahl-chee-nee* cinnamon – the word 'dalchini' comes from the Arabian term that means 'wood of China'

dalma *daahl-maah* curried **daal** and vegetables (Orissa)

dam de kar pakana *dam de kahr pah-kaah-naah* to braise

daru *daah-roo* spirits

dauna *daw-naah* rosemary

deemer dalna *dee-mer dal-nah* curried eggs and rice (West Bengal) deemer devil *dee-mer devil* devilled eggs (West Bengal)

dekchis *deg-chee* handleless aluminium or brass pot with a tight-fitting lid. Used to serve food in **dhabas**.

desi *de-see* local – refers to things that are home grown

dhaba *dhaah-bhaah* roadside restaurant – these eateries dot India's rural landscape, particularly throughout North India. Large pots of vegetables, meat dishes and lentils are served at all hours and rope beds are provided to lie or sleep on.

daal bara aroo thekra tenga *daahl bah-raah aah-roo thek-raah ten-gaah* fried lentil balls cooked in a sour curry served with plain rice *(see also **thekra**)*

dhania *dhah-ni-yaah* coriander seeds

dhokar dalna *dho-kahr daahl-nah* a popular dish made from fried lentil cubes. Yellow split peas are soaked overnight and then ground with chilli, ginger and salt. The lentil paste is heated then set on a flat surface and cut into diamond-shaped pieces which are deep-fried in oil and made into a curry with potatoes. (West Bengal)

dhokla *dhok-laah* spongy squares of steamed **besan**. Topped with fried mustard seeds, coriander leaves and grated coconut before serving. Often eaten for breakfast, tea or as a snack. (Gujarat)

dhud *dhood* milk
–dhud paudar *dhood paw-dahr* powdered milk

dhue se paka hua/ dhue se pakana *dhu-ē se pah-kaah hu-aah* smoked

digi mirch *de-gee mirch* paprika

dimi agni men pakana *dee-mee ahg-nee mē pah-kaah-naah* to stew

dimi anch par pakana *dee-mee āāhch pahr pah-kaah-naah* to simmer

din ka khana *din kaah khaah-naah* lunch

Diwali *mah-sah-lah* the festival of lights – is the most widely celebrated national festival, and takes place during October or November

do pyaz/do piaza *do pyaahz/do pia-zah* 'two onions' – meat dishes that use onions at two different stages in the cooking process – half the onions are cooked at the beginning of preparation and the other half are added once the meat becomes tender.

doi maach *doy mahch* carp cooked in a curd sauce with onion, ginger, garlic and chilli (West Bengal)

dosa *do-sah* crepe of fermented rice flour and daal. A breakfast speciality that can be eaten at any time of day, either as a full meal or substantial **tiffin**. Served with a bowl of hot, orange **sambar** and **pachadi** or a bowl of coconut **chatni**.
–butter *bah-tahr* dosa smothered in butter
–masala *mah-saah-laah do-sah* a large crepe stuffed with a delicious yellow filling of potatoes cooked with onions and curry leaves. Served with coconut chutney or **pachadi** and **sambar**.

draliya *drah-li-yaah* maize

Durga Puja *dur-gaah poo-jaah* Festival celebrated in Bengal

E

eidulfitr *eed-ul-fitr* celebration at the end of Ramadan, the Muslim month of fasting.

F

fawa bean *fah-vaah been* broad bean

ferr *fer* a seasonal fish dish usually prepared in winter. The fish is steamed and then roasted in warm coals. (Jammu/Kashmir)

filtered pani *fil-tahrd paah-nee* many people in cities have filters attached to their kitchen taps to ensure a supply of clean water. Filtered water is generally safe to drink.

G

gajar *gaah-jar* carrot

–halwa *gaah-jahr kaah hahl-vaah* sweet made with carrots, dried fruits, sugar, condensed milk and **ghee**

gandana *gahn-dah-naah/pyaahz* leek

ganga jal *gahn-gaah jahl* water from the river Ganga is considered pure and sacred. Orthodox Hindus will always keep a supply at home because it is a necessary element for the last rites.

ganna *gahn-naah/eek* sugarcane – commonly peeled and chewed for the juice or simply squeezed and drunk

ganne ka ras *gahn-ne kaah ras* sugarcane juice

ganth *gāāht* knuckle

garam karna *gahrm kahr-naa* to heat

garam masala *gahrm mah-saah-laah* an aromatic blend of up to 15 spices – black pepper, cumin seeds, cinnamon, cardamom, cloves, coriander seeds, bay leaves, nutmeg and mace. Garam means 'hot' and this masala is particularly popular in cooler areas where it is favoured over chilli.

gardan *gahr-dahn* neck

gayee ka gosht *gaah-ee kaah gosht* beef

gehu *gehōō* wheat

ghara *ghah-raah* earthenware pot, traditionally used to store and cool water

ghee *ghee* clarified butter – a popular Indian cooking medium

giri *gi-ree* pecan nut

gobar *go-bahr* cow dung – used as fuel in rural India for clay ovens

golgappa *gol-gahp-paah* deep-fried discs of dough which puff up like **pooris**

golna *gol-naa* to dissolve

gosht *gosht* meat

–aba *gosh-tah-bah* balls of pounded boneless meat, simmered in a curds gravy of milk and spices (Jammu/ Kashmir)

–ka boti *gosht kee bo-tee* steak

guda *gur-daah* kidney

gujiya *gu-jee-yaah* small pastry filled with semolina, condensed milk and sugar that's fried in **ghee**, a particular favourite in the north at the time of the Hindu festival of **Holi**

gulab jamun *gu-laahb jaah-mun* deep-fried balls of milk dough soaked in rose-flavoured syrup

–ka pani *gu-laah-bee paah-nee* rosewater extracted from rose petals, a popular ingredient which adds a sweet aroma to desserts and drinks

gular *guu-lahr* fig

gungchi *gūg-chee* liquorice

gur *gur* (*see* **jaggery**)

H

haandvo *haahnd-vo* coarsely ground rice and mixed lentils soaked overnight, then combined with finely-cut vegetables and spices. Cooked in the oven on a tray, then cut into small pieces. Eaten with curds or chutney.

halal *hah-laahl* all permitted foods as dictated by the *Quran* (the Muslim holy book)

haldi *hahl-dee* turmeric – used in cooking for both colour and flavour; as it is a natural antiseptic, it is used as medicine and cosmetic. Turmeric is also a symbol of auspiciousness and is used in rituals such as marriage.

haleem *hah-leem* a tasty wheat porridge cooked with meat and spices

halwa *hahl-vaah* sweet made with vegetables, cereals, lentils, nuts or fruit

hans *hans* goose

haram *hah-raahm* all prohibited foods as dictated by the *Quran* (the Muslim holy book)

hari chay *hah-ree chaah-ee* lemon grass

hari mirch *hah-ree mirch* green chilli

hath *haaht* hand – the conventional way to eat food in India is to use your hands. It's customary to use the right hand rather than the left, which is considered unclean.

hing *hing* fetid, ugly gum that when cooked imparts a pleasant, earthy zing and is a miraculous digestive – used in lieu of onions and garlic in **sattvic** food. Commonly called asafoetida.

Holi *Ho-lee* Hindi festival of colours celebrated in March/April

hoogadh *hoo-gadh* dried-fish curry, usually consumed in winter. Prepared from dried fish of various sizes which are cleaned with hot water and fried, either alone or with various seasonal vegetables. Depending on the type of fish, spices like chilli powder or turmeric are added. (Jammu/Kashmir)

I

idli *id-lee* fermented rice-flour and lentil cakes that are served with coconut chutney and **sambar** for breakfast or **tiffin** (South India)

ilaychi *i-laah-ee-chee* cardamom – although also available in white and black, the small, green variety abounds in savoury dishes, desserts and warming winter **chai**. The larger, black cardamom, grown in the northeast is stronger and is commonly added to meat dishes.

ilish macher jhaal *i-leesh mah-cher jhhal* **hilsa** fish cooked in mustard sauce and rice, a very hot Bengali favourite (West Bengal)

imli *im-lee* tamarind

J

jaggery *gur* a sweetening agent that is made at the first stage of sugar production. Although it's sometimes used as a substitute for sugar, it has a distinctly musky flavour of its own.

jai *jah-ee* rolled oats

Jains *jan* followers of Jainism

jal men tar karna *jahl mē tahr kahr-naah* to steep

jalebis *jah-le-bees* orange whorls of fried batter made from milk, semolina and cardamom fried in **ghee** and then dipped in syrup

jaletin *jah-le-tin* gelatin

jaman *jaah-mahn* small quantity of curd used as a starter to convert milk into curds

Janmashtami *jahn-maahsh-tah-mee jamb* the festival that commemorates the birth of Krishna (Uttar Pradesh)

jambu *jahm-boo* chive

jamun *jaah-mun* black plum also known as jambo – refers to both the tree and its fruit. Buddhists consider this tree to be sacred. Also prized for its medicinal value.

jana *jahn-naah* ladle

jangli *jahn-glee* wild
–sabzi *sahb-zee* wild greens
–suar *jahn-glee su-ahr* wild boar

jau *jaw* (see **jowar**)

javitri *jaah-vi-tree* mace

jayphal *jahy-phahl* nutmeg

jhaal *jhahl* a spicy fish dish that includes ground mustard seeds and chillies (West Bengal)

jhinga baffad *jhin-gah bahf-fahd* prawn curry in a spicy sauce made with dried chilli, cumin seed, black pepper and tomato (Goa)

–masala *jhin-ga mah-saah-laah* tasty preparation of king prawns with dried red chilli, ginger, garlic, tomato, onion, green capsicum and spices (Goa)

jhingi machli *jhēē-gee mahch-lee* prawn

jhol *jhol* Spiced vegetable soup (West Bengal)

jhoota *jhoo-taah* contaminated – many things are considered polluting especially saliva. It is unthinkable for a cook to taste a dish during preparation. Indians will not eat food that someone else has touched with their lips or use dirty plates and utensils.

jigar *ji-gahr* liver

joos *joos* freshly-squeezed fruit juice

juar *ju-aahr* millet
—roti *ju-aahr kee ro-tee* bread made from millet

jui *ju-ee* oat

K

kaafi *kaah-fee* coffee

kabab *kah-baahb* a loose term, applied to marinated chunks or ground meat, cooked on a skewer, fried on a hot plate or cooked under a grill.

kabharga *kah-bhar-gah* mutton deep-fried in **ghee** so that the bones become crisp and the meat becomes soft. Made for special occasions. (Jammu/Kashmir)

kabutar *ka-boo-tahr* pigeon

kaccha *kahch-chaah* 'uncooked' in a spiritual sense – refers to foods that are cooked in water, such as rice and **daal**. Traditionally, boiling grain or the flour produced from grain purified it when done in a prescribed pot and a ritually clean place

kachori *kah-cho-ree* corn and lentil savory puff. Served with a sour tamarind sauce flavoured with fenugreek seeds. (North India)

kadhai *kah-raah-ee* a common Indian wok deeper and thicker than the Chinese version, used for deep frying and sauteing. Balti is a northwestern name for kadhai.

kaddu *kahd-doo* pumpkin

kadhi *kah-ree* sour soup made from powdered barley dissolved in curds; also a sour **daal**-like dish made of curds and **besan** (Gujarat, Rajasthan)

kaju *kaah-joo* cashew nut
—draksh *dah-rahksh* cashew-raisin – combination used to flavour sweets and ice-cream

kakbadri *kaahk-bahd-ree* gooseberry

kakera *kaah-ke-raah* a traditional cake made from rice paste, grilled coconut, **jaggery** and **ghee**. A healthy snack

that's ideal for travelling because it stays fresh for several days. (Orissa)

kakri *kahk-ree* cucumber

kaku *kaah-koo* persimmon

kala jeera *kaah-laah jee-raah* 'black cumin'– Small, dull black seeds that despite their namesake impart a more refined flavour than cumin

kala masala *kaah-laah mah-saah-laah* blend of powdered spices (also known as goda masala) that, includes cinnamon, cardamom, cloves, star anise, allspice, black pepper, poppy seeds and coriander seeds. The common ingredient in most Marathi non-vegetarian cuisine. (Maharashtra)

kalchi *kahl-chee* ladle

kali anchi *kaah-lee ahn-chee* blackberry

kam te me talna *kahm tel mē tahl-naa* shallow-fry

kamar *kah-mahr* loin

kanta *kāāh-taah* fork
—churi *kāāh-taah chu-ree* cutlery

karal *kah-rahl* mortar

karbuja *kahr-boo-jaah* cantaloupe

karela *kah-re-laah* bitter gourd

kasai *kah-saah-ee/bu-chahr* butcher

kashi *kaah-shee* whole chicken stuffed and marinated

kasi murgi *kah-see mur-gaah* capon

kaskas *kahs-kahs* poppy seeds

kasna *kahs-naah* to grate

kathal *kaht-hahl* jackfruit

katna *kaaht-naah* to cut/slice

katori *kah-to-ree* bowl – specifically those that are placed on thalis; also the name given to the indentations on thali trays that these bowls fit into

katta *kaht-taah* black resin added to **paan** together with lime paste and betel nut

keemar dalna *kee-mahr daahl-nah* minced goat curry (West Bengal)

keemar paratha *kee-mahr pah-rāāh-thaah* fried, circular bread with a mincemeat filling (West Bengal)

kela *ke-laah* banana
–ka patta *ke-le kaah paht-taah* large leaf from the banana tree, used as a disposable plate

kesar *ke-sahr* saffron
–pista *pis-taah* saffron-pistachio – a combination used to flavour milk, sweets and ice-cream (Gujarat)

ketli *ket-lee* kettle

khaar *khaahr* the alkaline ash of dried banana used as a cooking ingredient with vegetables. It is also sprinkled on **daal** or vegetables, as part of the daily meal, also used as a digestive. (Assam)

khaaribhaat *khaah-ree-bhaaht* rice, **chana daal** and mixed vegetables cooked in oil and spices (Gujarat)

khajur *khah-joor* dates
–ka gur *khah-joor kaah gur* date palm **jaggery**

khana *kaah-naah* food/meal

khane ki chiz *khaah-ne kee cheez* ingredient

khansama *khaahn-saah-maa* chef

khare masale ka gosht *kah-re maah-saah-laah kaah gosht* mutton in **garam masala** (Delhi)

khargosh *khahr-gosh* hare/rabbit

kheer *keer* rich creamy rice pudding made by boiling milk and rice and often served in earthenware cups or bowls. It can be flavoured with cardamom, saffron, pistachios, flaked almonds, cashews or dried fruit. Muslims may eat a particular variety of this with **vermicelli** to break the fast of Ramadan on the day of Id. Also known as **payasam**.

khichdi *khich-dee* risotto-like dish of rice and lentils cooked with spices; also known as khichri

khoya *kho-yaah* milk solids produced by boiling for a long period, which are used as a base for sweets (North India)

khubani *khu-baah-nee* apricot

khumbi *khum-bee* mushroom

kira *kee-raah* gherkin

kishmish *kish-mish* raisin

kodi koora *ko-di koo-rah* chicken curry (Andhra Pradesh)

kofta *kof-taah* meatballs – often made from goat, beef or lamb

koko *ko-ko* cocoa

kolhapuri mutton/chicken *kol-hah-poo-ree mah-tahn/chi-ken* a dark gravy of fried **garam masala**, coriander seeds, copra and red chillies. Named after a town in southern Maharashtra famous for chillies (Maharashtra)

koora *koo-rah* curry (Andhra Pradesh)

korma *kor-maah* rich, thickened brown curry of chicken, mutton or vegetables. The meat is tenderised by marinating it in curds and spices before cooking. A traditional Mughlai method of cooking.

kosambri *ko-saahm-bah-ree* raw salad made with uncooked **moong–daal**, cucumber, coconut, coriander, lemon juice, vegetable oil, black mustard seeds, **urad daal**, red chilli and curry leaves (Mysore, Karnataka); known as kosumalli in Tamil Nadu.

kotu *ko-too* buckwheat

kulcha *kul-chaah* a soft, round leavened bread (Andhra Pradesh)

kulfi *kul-fee* ice cream made with reduced milk and flavoured with a variation of nuts, fruits and berries

kullarhs *kul-hahrs* biodegradable cups made of clay in which **chai** is often served. They impart a pleasantly earthy taste and, being bio-degradable can be discarded after use.

kumbi *kum-bee* morel mushroom

kutra *kut-raah* marjoram

L

ladoos *lahd-doos* sweetmeats, usually balls made with sesame seeds or nuts and often served at **Sankranti**. Offered to people while saying "eat sesame and speak sweet words".

–nariyal *naah-ri-yahl* grated coconut cooked in sugar and cardamom and formed into small balls (Assam)

lakri ka chamach *lahk-ree kaah chah-mahch* wooden spatula

lal chawal *laahl chaah-vahl* brown rice

lal maas *laahl maahs* red meat (Rajasthani)

lal mirch *laahl mirch* cayenne

lal murli *laahl moo-lee* red radish

lal sharab *laahl shah-raahb* red wine

lal shimla mirch *laahl shim-laah mirch* red capsicum

langar *lahn-gahr* community feeding hall in Sikh temples (Punjab)

langra *lahn-graah* mango variety

lassi *lahs-see* curds drink – often flavoured with salt or sugar and the essence of rosewater

lauki *law-kee* green gourd

laung *lāwg* clove

lehsun *leh-sun* garlic

lichi *lee-chee* lychee, generally eaten fresh, not from a can

lobiha *lo-bi-yaah* black-eyed beans; large white beans with a small black dot or 'eye'

luchi *lu-chee* fried flour puffs – sometimes served on the eighth day of worship during the festival of Durga Puja (West Bengal)

M

maach bhaja *maa bhaah-jaah* fried fish with rice (West Bengal)

maacher chop *maah-cher chawp* crumbed, deep-fried fish cakes made with mashed potato, chilli, onion, ginger, garlic and fish (West Bengal)

maacher kochuri *maah-cher ko-choo-ree* deep-fried **puri** with a fish filling (West Bengal)

maah ki daal *maah kee daahl* **urad daal** simmered for hours over a low fire and served with oven-fresh **roti** (Punjab)

maas *maahs* fried fish pieces cooked in a lightly spiced curry with tomato or sour spinach. The main spices include mustard seeds, anniseed and fenugreek seeds. (Assam)

–muri aru moong–daal *maahs mu-ree aah-roo moong daahl* fried head of fish cooked with lentils (Assam)

macha thukthuka *maah-chhah thuk-thu-kah* fish curry made with very small fish cooked with onion, garlic and mustard (Orissa)

machli/maachi *mach-lee* Generic name for fish in most regions

madhu *ma-dhu* honey

madira *mah-di-raah* generic Hindi and Urdu term for wine

maharaj *mah-haah-raahj* 'king' - a person of high caste; because food is treated with a kind of ritual sanctity only maharaj are permitted to cook in Hindu homes (Uttar Pradesh)

mahin tukron me kata hua *mah-heen tuk-rō mē kaah-taah hu-aah* diced

–tukron me katna *mah-heen tuk-rō mē kaaht-naah* to dice

maida *ma-daah* plain flour

maida paratha *mai-daah pah-rāāh-thaah* a light, flaky fried bread, made with **maida** eaten with stew or meat curry (Kerala)

majja *mahj-jaah* bone marrow

maka *mahk-kaah* corn

makki ki suji *mah-ke kee soo-jee* polenta

makkhan *mahk-kahn* butter

makki *mah-ke* corn meal

–ki roti *kee ro-tee* corn meal roti – it is often accompanied by **sarson ka saag** (Punjab)

–ki suji *kee soo-jee* polenta

malai *mah-laah-ee* cream added for flavour to the predominantly vegetarian food

mangshor chop *maahng-shor chawp* minced goat rissoles (West Bengal)

mangshor jhol *maahng-shor jhol* mutton curry often served with bhog at community lunches during the festival of Durga Puja (Bengal)

mangshor chop *maahng-shor chawp* minced goat rissoles (West Bengal)

mangshor polau *maahng-shor po-lah-u* fried rice cooked with eggs, meatballs, nuts, sultanas, nutmeg and other spices. An adaptation of **biryani**. (West Bengal)

mankho lusi *maahn-khoh lu-see* lightly spiced meat curry served with fine wheat bread fried in oil (Assam)

masala *mah-saah-laah* spice blends

–bhaat *bhaat* a spicy hot pilau made with vegetables and fragrant **basmati** rice. Often served with cooling cucumber salad and **ghee**. The addition of goda masala gives it a characteristic taste. (Maharashtra)

masch *mahsch* made from the same raw meat as **goshtaba** but instead of being cooked in milk, it's fried in oil and flavoured with hot spices such as chilli powder (Jammu/Kashmir)

masoor *mah-soor* red lentils, an ochre-coloured southern favourite

masoor ki daal *mah-soor kee daahl* lentil that's red in colour when raw and yellow when cooked, also known as red split lentils

matar *mah-tahr* peas

–ki daal *mah-tahr kee daahl* dried split peas

–paneer *mah-tahr pah-neer* dish of peas and fresh cheese

mathiyan *mah-thi-yā* **ghee**, salt and thymol seeds are added to plain flour, which is then kneaded with hot water. Small balls of the mixture are rolled into flat circles and then fried in oil (Punjab)

mayonas *ma-yo-nas* mayonnaise

meat palav *meet pa-lahv* meat and rice cooked with garlic, ginger, onion, tomato, cinnamon, cloves, chilli, fresh and powered coriander mint, a pinch of saffron and coconut milk. Plenty of **ghee** is added while cooking. (Karnataka)

–koimbu *meen ko-im-bu* fish curry made with a base of tamarind, tomato, onion, very hot curry powder, turmeric and salt, seasoned with mustard seeds and curry leaves. This mixture is boiled until it turns a rich golden colour. Generally smaller fish such as carp or whiting are used. Generally eaten with plain rice and **chapati**. (Tamil Nadu)

memna *mem-naah* lamb

menu card *men-yoo kaahrd* menu

methi *me-thee* fenugreek

mewa *me-vaah* dried fruits

mez *mez* table – although traditionally, Hindus sat on the floor in kitchen areas at meal times, most people in an urban setting now sit at tables

–posh *mez-posh* tablecloth

milana *mi-laah-naah* to mix

milk badam *milk baah-daahm* milk flavoured with saffron and almonds, sometimes reduced by simmering

mirch *mirch* chilli

mishti *mish-tee* sweet, eaten at the end of a meal (West Bengal)

missi roti *mis-see ro-tee* wheat, gram flour, cooked lentils and water kneaded with spices. This dough is rolled into flat circles and cooked on a hotplate. Commonly eaten with **ghee**.

misthan *mish-taahn* any sweet item (Gujarat)

mitha *mee-thaah* dessert; sweet (adj)

–paan *mee-thaah paahn* sweet and spicy mixture of betel

mithai *mi-thaah-ee* sweet (n); sweet shop

mixi *mik-see* blender; food processor

moghlai paratha *mogh-lah-ee pah-rāāh-thaah* fried, square bread filled with egg and mincemeat (West Bengal)

mol tol karna *mol-tol kahr-naah* to bargain or higgle

moong *moong* mung bean

–daal *daahl* mung bean **daal** – tiny oval lentils that are yellow in colour

moongphali *moong-phah-lee* peanut

moongphali ka tel *moong-phah-lee kaah tel* peanut oil

motha chawal *mo-thaah chaah-vahl* short-grain rice

motorshutir kochuri *mo-tor-shu-teer ko-choo-ree* deep-fried bread with a filling of ground, green-pea paste (West Bengal)

mudde *mud-de* balls of steamed **ragi** flour that are dipped into spicy **sambar** or gravy called bassar and popped into the mouth whole (Karnataka)

mudurika lata *mu-doo-ree-kaah lah-taah* dill

Mughlai khana *mugh-laah-ee kaah-naah* Mughlai food – North India food has been greatly influenced by the Mughals, who ruled the north from the 16th to the 18th centuries

munakka *mu-nahk-kaah* currant

muraba *mu-rahb-baah* conserves

murg *murg* chanterelle, a funnel-shaped mushroom

murgi *mur-gee* poultry/chicken

muri muna *mu-ri mū-aah* snack of puffed rice and **jaggery**. (Orissa)

murli *moo-lee* white radish

musal *moo-sahl* pestle

N

naan *naahn* bread – made from plain flour and cooked in a **tandoor**

nal ka pani *nahl kaah paa-nee* tap water – best avoided at all costs

namak *nah-mahk* salt

–lagana *nah-mahk lah-gaah-naah* to cure

namkeen *nam-keen* ' salty' – savoury snacks, including anything from **samosas** and **pakoras** to **bhujiya** and chips

narangi *naah-ran-gee* orange

–ka chilka *naah-rahn-gee kaah chil-kaah* zest

nariyal *naah-ri-yal* coconut

nashpati *naahsh-paah-tee* pear

nashta *naahsh-taah* breakfast

neem *neem* plant – the leaves have a variety of uses including medicinal, cosmetic, environmental and culinary

nevari *ne-vah-ri* half-moon shaped pastries filled with semolina, coconut, sugar, **jaggery**, nuts, raisins and cardamom powder (Goa)

nimbu *nēē-boo* citrus/lemon/lime

O

olo *o-lo* roasted and mashed eggplant mixed with spices and oil (Gujarat)

P

paan *paahn* mixture of betel nut, lime paste and spices, wrapped up in a betel leaf, eaten as a digestive and mouth freshener. There are two basic paan types; mitha (sweet) and sada (plain, which often includes tobacco).

–ki dukan *paahn kee dukaan* tobacconist's shop where one can purchase **paan** and cigarettes (which can be bought individually)

pachadi *pah-chah-di* a cross between a vegetable dish and chutney that often includes lentils and curds.

Pagar *pāāh-gahr* chestnut

pahhari badam *pah-haah-ree bah-daahm* hazelnut

pakkah *pahk-kaah* cooked; traditionally referred to foods that are totally cooked in **ghee**

pakora *pah-kaw-raah* **fritters** of gram flour and spinach or another vegetable

palak *paah-lahk* spinach

–paneer *–pah-neer* soft cheese in a spicy gravy of pureed spinach, served with fresh, hot **roti** (Delhi)

panch *paahnch* five; the number of ingredients in the British drink made with **arrack**, citrus juice, spices, water and sugar. However the British referred to it as 'punch'.

–gavya *gah-vya* the five products of the cow for which it was traditionally kept as a family pet: milk, urine, clarified butter, curds and dung

paneer *pah-neer* soft, unfermented cheese made from milk curd.

pani *paah-neef* water

pani puri *paah-nee poo-ree; gol gap-paah* small crisp puffs of dough filled with spicy tamarind water and spouted gram. Served as fast food or snacks.

pantua *pahn-too-ah* like **gulab jamun** but made of cheese and thickened milk instead of milk powder (West Bengal)

–bhaja *bhaah-jaah* spiced vegetables with bread (Mumbai)

papads *paah-pahr* the North Indian term for **pappadams** or wafers

papita *pah-pee-taah* papaya

pappadams *paah-pahr* **daal** wafers

paraat *pah-raaht* round, stainless steel dish with raised side, commonly used to knead wholemeal wheatflour into dough to make **chapatis**

paratha *pah-rāāh-thaah* unleavened flaky fried flat bread. More substantial versions are stuffed with **paneer** or grated vegetables.

parval *pahr-vahl* pointed gourd

pathaar jhol *pah-thaahr jhol* meat curry (usually goat) with rice; also called mangshor jhol (West Bengal)

pator maas *paah-tor maahs* small, flat fish pieces seasoned with mustard seeds and coriander leaves with a dash of mustard added before baking, or roasting on a fire. Served with banana leaves. (Assam)

pavitra gay *pah-vi-trah gaah-ee* 'sacred cow' – the cow is sacred for Hindus and beef is generally avoided. Cows were traditionally kept by Brahmans as a sign of their status (slaughtering a cow is likened to killing a Brahmin).

payasam *paah-yah-sahm* rice pudding cooked on religious and auspicious occasions such as birthdays and weddings (*see also* **kheer**) (West Bengal); known as payasam in South India

peek *peek* red spittle produced from chewing betel nut

petha *pe-taah* crystallised gourd made into a delicious sweet and covered in sugar (Agra)

phal *phahl* fruit

–ka ras *phahl kaah ras* fruit juice

pheni *phe-ni* sweet rolls made from wheat flour and rice fried in **ghee** then dipped in sugar syrup (Orissa)

phentna *phent-naa* to whisk

phul ghobi *phool gho-bee* cauliflower

phulka *phul-kaah* 'puff', small **roti** baked over an open flame or on a **tawa** so that it fills with hot air and puffs up like a balloon. Usually accompanies daal-chaval and **sabzi**. (Uttar Pradesh)

pilaf *pu-laahv* (*see* **pulao**)

pili shimla mirch *pee-lee shim-laah mirch* yellow capsicum

pili tej mirch *pee-lee tej mirch* sharp-flavoured, yellow chilli (North India)

pini ki chizen *pee-ne kee chee-zē* drinks

piniyan *pi-ni-yan* semolina fried in **ghee** with mixed dried fruits, icing sugar and milk (Punjab)

piru pakshi *pe-roo pahk-shee* turkey

pisna *pees-naah* to crush

pista *pis-taah* pistachio

plet *plet* plate

poli *po-lee* pastry made of plain flour, filled with a mixture of brown sugar or **jaggery** and fresh, grated coconut mixed with cardamom, and fried (Tamil Nadu)

poori *poo-ree* disc of dough that puffs up when deep fried – eaten with various stewed meats and vegetables, three types of which are included in a traditional wedding lunch (Uttar Pradesh)

pranag *prah-naahg* tarragon

prasad *prah-saahd* blessed food which is first offered to the gods for spiritual nourishment, and then shared among devotees

pudina *pu-dee-naah* mint

pudlaa *pood-laah* pancake-like snack made by spreading **chana** flour and spices in batter on a hotplate and cooking with oil (Gujarat)

puja *poo-jaah* 'respect'; offering or prayers; religious feast

pukkah *pahk-kaah* ripe

puliyotharai *pu-li-yo-thah-rah-ee* vegetarian rice dish of rice with a paste of black mustard seeds, **hing**, curry leaves, red chillies, tamarind juice, turmeric and chilli powder. Garnished with peanuts and coriander leaves. (Tamil Nadu)

puran poli *poo-rahn po-lee* wheat flour dough, rolled in the form of a **roti** and stuffed with a filling of boiled **chana daal**, **jaggery** and cardamom or nutmeg (Maharashtra)

puri *poo-ree* deep-fried bread made from the same dough as chapati. Served with a main meal and generally prepared for guests.

pyaz *pyaahz* shallot/red onion

R

rabri *rahb-ree* sweet, thickened milk

ragi mudde *rah-gee mud-de (see **mudde**)

rai *raah-ee* black mustard seeds

raita *rah-ee-too* plain curds combined with any number of vegetables or fruit, served chilled

raja mirch *raah-jaah mirch* exceptionally hot chilli that when mashed up with burnt dried fish makes a fiery pickle (Nagaland)

rajasic khana *raah-jasik khaah-naah* bitter, sour, salty, pungent or hot foods believed by Hindus to induce restlessness

Ramadan *rah-maah-zaahn* the month of the Muslim calendar when Muslims fast during the day and only eat between sunset and sunrise

ras *rahs* juice/gravy

rasam *rah-sahm* 'juice', tamarind-flavoured vegetable broth that's drunk from a glass or added to steamed white rice. The dish generally includes lentils, tomato, pepper and cumin. Popular in South India but made differently in each state.

rasdar chawal *lahs-daahr caah-vahl* glutinous rice

rasgolla *rahs-gul-laah* 'ball of juice', spongy white balls of **paneer** that ooze the sugar syrup in which they are boiled (West Bengal)

rat ka khana *raaht kaah khaah-naah* dinner

raza *taah-zaah* fresh fruit juice

receipt *rah-seed* receipt

revat chini *re-vaht chee-nee* rhubarb

roghan josh *ro-gahn josh* lamb or goat marinated in a rich, spicy sauce, generally flavoured with nutmeg and saffron (Jammu & Kashmir)

rosogolla *ro-so-gol-lah (see **rasgolla**)

roti *ro-tee* bread; also used interchangeably with **chapati** to describe the most common variety of bread. Although always round, roti sizes can vary dramatically.

rotli *rot-lee* wheat flour mixed with a spoon of oil and water to prepare dough, then rolled flat and cooked on a hotplate (Gujarat)

roza rakhna *ro-zaah rak-naah* Muslim fast. Muslims fast for the entire month of **Ramadan** in remembrance the Prophet's flight from Mecca to Madina

rui macher jhol *roo-ee maah-cher jhol* carp with rice (West Bengal)

rumali roti *ru-maah-lee ro-tee* 'handkerchief bread', a large superfine wholemeal bread that is thrown like a pizza base. Muslim food popularly eaten with **kababs**.

S

saag *saahg* leafy greens

saboo *saah-boot* whole – refers to spices and seed in their whole state before being crushed

–dana *daah-naah* sago

–dana vada *daah-naah vaah-dah* snack made from sago, potato and crushed peanuts. Cooked as a patty and generally eaten with curds and **chatni**. (Maharashtra)

sabzi *sahb-zee* vegetables, generally served with **daal**

sada paan *saah-daah paahn (see* **paan**)

safed sharab *sah-fed shah-raahb* white wine

sagu *sah-goo* mixed vegetable curry with ground green chilli, cumin, coriander and coconut **masala**. Generally eaten with Indian bread such as fried **puri**. (Karnataka)

sambar *saahm-bahr* spicy vegetable and lentil stew made with **tuvar daal**, tumeric, salt, sugar, eggplant, pumpkin, **hing**, tamarind paste, vegetable or sunflower oil, mustard seeds and curry leaves, often served with **dosas** and **idli** (South India)

sambharo *sahm-bhaah-ro* salad lightly cooked in oil (Gujarat)

samosa *sah-mo-saah* deep-fried pyramid-shaped pastries filled with spiced vegetables (mostly peas and potato) and less often meat. Spices such as cumin are also included. Generally served with **chatni**.

sandesh *sahn-desh* sweets made of **paneer** paste and cooked on a low heat with sugar or **jaggery**. Flavoured with palm jaggery, orange zest, mango, chocolate, rose-water or saffron, each of which will change its colour and taste. When cool it is moulded into different shapes.(West Bengal)

Sankranti *sahn-kraan-ti* northern version of Pongal.

santara *sahn-tah-raah* mandarin

sarai *sah-raah-ee* inn – a traditional drinking hole for wayfarers

sarson ka tel *sar-sõ kaah tel* mustard oil

sarota *sah-ro-taah* nutcracker

sarson *sahr-sõ* yellow mustard seed

–ka saag *kaah saahg* spiced puree of mustard greens and spinach

sattvic khana *saaht-tvik kaah-naah* foods traditionally thought to be conducive to serenity and spirituality, according to Hindu beliefs. Includes milk and its products, honey, fruit and vegetables.

saunf *saunf* refers to both aniseed and fennel because of the similarity in flavour and appearance. The smaller aniseed seeds have a fresher taste than fennel, and are often coated in sugar to make a sweet snack. A finer grade of fennel has recently been introduced and is also becoming a popular digestive and breath freshener.

seb *seb* apple

seekcha *seek-chaah* skewer

sem *sem* haricot bean

sewa *se-vaah* service

shaak *shaahk* vegetable curry (Gujarat)

shakahari *shaah-kaah-haah-ree* vegetarian

shakkar paare *shahk-kahr paah-re* dough flattened and cut into small cubes then cooked over a hotplate and covered in thick icing (Punjab)

shalgam *shahl-gahm* parsnip; turnip

shami kabab *shaah-mee kah-baahb* boiled mincemeat, ground with chickpeas and spices and shaped into cutlets (Uttar Pradesh)

shankar kand *shahn-kahr kahnd* sweet potatoes

sharab *shah-raahb* generic term for wine in Hindi and Urdu

sharbat *shahr-baht* milk, almonds and rose petal dish offered by the bride's family to the groom's family (Bangalore)

sharifa *shah-ree-faa* custard apple

sheekh *sheek* mincemeat wrapped around iron spikes. Cooked in a **tandoor** and used for **kababs** (Punjab) or laid over enormous silver platters at wazwans, or banquets (Kashmir).

sherbet *shahr-baht* soft drink made with sugar and fruit such as lemons or mangoes

shetut *she-toot* mulberry

shi shi *shee-shee* bottle

shikara *shi-kaah-raah* houseboat (Kashmir)

shimla mirch *shim-laah mirch* green capsicum

shingara *shin-gah-rah* version of **samosas** – filling is often made with cauliflower, green peas and peanuts (West Bengal)

shri phal *shree pahl* quince

shuddh *shuddh* pure

–desi ghee *de-see ghee* locally produced, pure **ghee**

–shakahari *shaah-kaah-haah-ree* pure vegetarian food – found in restaurants where meat is not handled for religious reasons

shukto *shook-to* combination of potato, eggplant, radishes, beans and

sidha hath *si-dhaah haahth* 'the straight hand', or right hand

sita pahl *see-taah pahl* squash; pumpkin

sondesh *son-desh (see sandesh)*

soya paneer *so-yaah pah-neer* tofu

srikhand *sreek-hahnd* ' ambrosia of the Gods', or a dessert made from curds, sugar and cardamom garnished with slices of almond and rose petals (Gujarat)

suar *su-ahr (see jangli suar)*

suji *soo-jee* semolina

T

tala aloo *tah-laah aah-loo* fried potato

talna *tahl-naah* deep-fry

tamasic khana *taah-mah-sik khaah-naah* cold, stale, and highly spiced foods that, according to Hindu beliefs make the eater dull and lazy. Characteristically tamasic foods include meats such as beef and pork, as well as those that are highly spiced.

tandoor *tahn-door* clay oven (Punjab)

tandoori chicken *tahn-doo-ree chi-kahn* chicken cooked in a **tandoor** after being marinated in spices. (Punjab)

–naan *tahn-doo-ri naahn* **naan** cooked in a **tandoor**

tang *tāāhg* leg

taraju *tah-raah-joo* scales

tarbuz *tahr-booz* watermelon

tawa *tah-vaah* flat, hotplate or iron griddle, used in homes to make bread

taza *taah-zaah* fresh

–pani *taah-jaah paah-nee* fresh water

tej patta *tej paht-taah* Indian bay leaves come from the cassia tree (unlike European and West Indian bay leaves)

tel *tel* oil

tendu *ten-doo* persimmon

tenga *ten-gah* sweet-and-sour fish made with **rohu**, lightly sauteed with onions and simmered in a watery gravy that's zested with lemon juice (Assam)

termos *ter-mos* thermos

thaal *taahl* common plate that a Bohris family meal is eaten off. The family generally sits down on clean white sheets on top of which this plate is placed. (Gujarat)

thaila *thah-ee-laah* bag

thali *taah-lee* metal dishes, traditionally made of gold, silver or bell metal – a mark of the owner's wealth and status but most people now use stainless steel because it's easier to clean

thalipeeth *thaah-lee-peeth* bread made from a thick mixture of millet and chickpea flour, spices and chopped, leafy vegetables. Cooked on an oiled frying pan and eaten as a light meal or heavy snack. (Maharashtra)

thela *te-laah* street vendor cart

theplaa *the-plaah* wheat flour, salt and spice mixed with a spoon of oil and water to form dough, then rolled flat into rounds and cooked on an oiled hotplate. Keeps well for a few days and is often taken on long trips or picnics.

tiffin *ti-fin* light meals or snacks eaten

throughout the day; also stainless steel carrier with three or four sealable sections in which people carry their lunch to work or meals for long journeys

til *til* sesame seed; also sesame harvest

–ka tel *til kaah tel* sesame oil

–laddus *lahd-doos* sesame balls sweetened with **jaggery**, made in winter after the **til** (Bihar)

–pitha *til pee-thaah* crisp pancake made with freshly pounded sticky rice cooked on a flat pan. The pancake is spread with a filling of sesame and **jaggery** or coconut sugar and folded. Usually cooked on festive occasions such as Bihu. (Assam)

tilkut *til-kut* thin rectangular wafers of crushed sesame and sugar (Bihar)

tin kolne vali chiz *tin kol-ne vaah-lee cheez* can opener

toddy *to-ree* a drink from the buds of palm trees (Kerala)

tukre tukre katna *tuk-re tuk-re kahr-naah* to cut finely

tulsi *tul-see* Holy basil - the most sacred plant in Hinduism and you'll find one outside the entrance of most Hindu homes. Holy basil is never used in cooking although it is sometimes made into a herbal tea that is good for relieving colds and flu.

–bandu *tul-see ban-du* sage

tuvar daal *to-vahr daahl* yellow lentils, boiled with salt and turmeric and then flavoured with **ghee**, and **jaggery**; also known as arhar (Maharashtra)

U

ubalna *u-baahl-naah* to boil

ulta hath *ul-taah haahth* 'opposite or reverse hand', or left hand

ulte tawe ki roti *ul-te tah-ve kee ro-tee* thin bread cooked on an upturned convex griddle (Andhra Pradesh)

urad *u-rahd* black gram

–ki daal *kee daahl* black lentils

usal *oo-sahl* any curry made from whole beans or peas. Dried green peas are commonly used to make this hearty dish. (Maharashtra)

uttapam *ut-tah-pahm* pancake made from rice and **urad daal**, which are ground and fermented. Finely chopped onions, green chillies, coriander leaves and freshly grated coconut are added to the dough, which is poured into a frying pan and cooked on both sides until it turns golden-brown (Tamil Nadu)

V

vanaspati tel *vah nahs-pah-ti tel* vegetable oil

vankaaya koora *van-kaah-yah koo-rah* eggplant curry (Andhra Pradesh)

vark *vahrk* flavourless, edible silver foil used to decorate sweets such as **barfi**. Thought to be a good digestive because it contains trace minerals.

vegetable chop *ve-ge-tah-bel chawp* crumbed and deep-fried mixed vegetable cake. Finely minced cauliflower, cabbage, beetroot, green peas, carrot and peanuts are fried with chilli and spices then mixed with mashed potato. (West Bengal)

vermicelli *ver-mi-chel-lee* 'little worms', the Italian pasta. It's popularly made into a milk pudding or fried in **ghee** with raisins, flaked almonds and sugar to make a sweet, dry treat.

–payasa *pah-yah-sah* dessert made with fried **vermicelli**, milk, sugar, cardamom powder, cashew nuts and raisins (Karnataka)

vindaloo *vin-dah-loo* hot and spicy pork and vinegar curry. Pork can be substituted with chicken or prawns. (Goa)

Y

yakni *yahk-nee* gravy

Recommended Reading & Useful Resources

- **Madhur Jaffrey** is the most interesting and informed expert on the culture of Indian food and drink, and her book *A Taste of India* (Pavilion, 1985) – although getting on a bit – is a wonderful culinary journey through the most important gastronomic Indian states, written in a fluent, anecdotal style. More recently she has written several excellent cookbooks aimed at the British market.

- For those with a specific interest in the cuisine of South India, particularly Kerala, look no further than **Maya Kaimal MacMillan**'s award-winning *Curried Favors* (Abbeville Press, 1996), a charming collection of photographs, authentic recipes and cultural background. **Monisha Bharadwaj**'s *The Indian Kitchen* (Kyle Cathie, 1996) is an excellent introduction to Indian staples and is packed with useful information on how they are grown, how to identify and store them, how they are used as food and medicines, as well as simple recipes with cultural background. **Pat Chapman**, founder of Britain's Curry Club, has authored a terrific collection of inexpensive books covering various themes of Indian cuisine complete with fascinating background information, including *Taste of the Raj* (Hodder & Stoughton, 1998).

- *Indian Food & Folklore* (Hamlyn, 2000), edited by **Jo Lethaby**, is light on the folklore and heavy on the recipes while **Julie Sahni**'s *Introduction to Indian Cooking* (Ten Speed Press, 1998) is a straightforward cookbook with cultural introductions to each dish that help to put them in their place. **Camellia Panjabi**'s meaty *50 Great Curries of India* (Kyle Cathie, 1994) is an exquisite collection of photographs, recipes and kitchen insight. *New Indian Home Cooking* (HP Books, 2000) by **Madhu Gadia**, puts a healthy spin on traditional Indian dishes, even when one isn't required. **Rocky Mohan**'s *Art of Indian Cuisine* (Lustre Press, 1999) is a somewhat over-stylised cookbook but the recipes are sensational.

- For anyone interesting in exploring the fascinating science of Ayurveda, there are shelfloads of books available but none better than **Robert E Svoboda**'s *Ayurveda: Life, Health and Longevity* (Penguin, 1992).